THE ART & DESIGN SERIES

For beginners, students, and professionals in both fine and commercial arts, these books offer practical how-to introductions to a variety of areas in contemporary art and design.

Each illustrated volume is written by a working artist, a specialist in his or her field, and each concentrates on an individual area—from advertising layout or printmaking to interior design, painting, and cartooning, among others. Each contains information that artists will find useful in the studio, in the classroom, and in the marketplace.

Carving Wood and Stone:
An Illustrated Manual
ARNOLD PRINCE

Chinese Painting in Four Seasons:
A Manual of
Aesthetics & Techniques
LESLIE TSENG-TSENG YU
text with Gail Schiller Tuchman

The Complete Book of Cartooning
JOHN ADKINS RICHARDSON

Creating an Interior
HELENE LEVENSON, A.S.I.D.

Drawing: The Creative Process
SEYMOUR SIMMONS III and
MARC S.A. WINER

Drawing with Pastels
RON LISTER

Graphic Illustration: Tools &
Techniques for Beginning
Illustrators
MARTA THOMA

How to Sell Your Artwork:
A Complete Guide
for Commercial and Fine Artists
MILTON K. BERLYE

Ideas for Woodturning
ANDERS THORLIN

The Language of Layout
BUD DONAHUE

Understanding Paintings:
The Elements of Composition
FREDERICK MALINS

Nature Photography: A Guide
to Better Outdoor Pictures
STAN OSOLINSKI

Printed Textiles: A Guide to
Creative Design Fundamentals
TERRY A. GENTILLE

An Introduction to Design: Basic Ideas
and Applications for Paintings or the
Printed Page
ROBIN LANDA

Package Design: An Introduction to the
Art of Packaging
LASZLO ROTH

Lithography: A Complete Guide
MARY ANN WENNIGER

Painting and Drawing: Discovering Your
Own Visual Language
ANTHONY TONEY

Photographic Lighting: Learning to See
RALPH HATTERSLEY

Photographic Printing
RALPH HATTERSLEY

Photographing Nudes
CHARLES HAMILTON

A Practical Guide for Beginning Painters
THOMAS GRIFFITH

Printmaking: A Beginning Handbook
WILLIAM C. MAXWELL
photos by Howard Unger

Silkscreening
MARIA TERMINI

Silver: An Instructional Guide to the
Silversmith's Art
RUEL O. REDINGER

Teaching Children to Draw: A Guide for
Teachers and Parents
MARJORIE WILSON and
BRENT WILSON

Transparent Watercolor: Painting
Methods and Materials
INESSA DERKATSCH

Nature Drawing: A Tool for Learning
CLARE WALKER LESLIE

Woodturning for Pleasure
GORDON STOKES
revised by Robert Lento

The Art of Painting Animals:
A Beginning Artist's Guide to the
Portrayal of Domestic Animals, Wildlife,
and Birds
FREDRIC SWENEY

Graphic Design: A Problem-Solving
Approach to Visual Communication
ELIZABETH RESNICK

Display Design: An Introduction to the Art
of Window Display, Points of Purchase,
Posters, Signs and Signages, Sales
Environments, and Exhibit Displays
LASZLO ROTH

BOOKS BY THE AUTHOR

Humorous Illustration and Cartooning
Publication Design
The Fourth Estate (with John L. Hulteng)
Editing the News (with Roy R. Copperud)
The Design of Advertising
Articles and Features
Comic Art and Caricature
Cartooning
Visits with 30 Magazine Art Directors
Fell's Guide to Commercial Art (with Byron Ferris)
Fell's Guide to the Art of Cartooning

Roy Paul Nelson, a professor of journalism at the University of Oregon, has been freelancing cartoons to magazines and newspapers for many years. In addition to serving as a graphic design consultant to various publications, corporations, and governmental agencies, he writes a monthly column on design for *Communication World*. He is the author of more than a dozen books on design, art, writing, and the mass media.

ROY PAUL NELSON

humorous illustration and cartooning

a guide for editors, advertisers, and artists

A SPECTRUM BOOK

Prentice-Hall, Inc., Englewood Cliffs, New Jersey 07632

Library of Congress Cataloging in Publication Data

Nelson, Roy Paul.
   Humorous illustration and cartooning.
   (Art & Design Series)

   "A Spectrum Book"
   Bibliography: p.
   Includes index.
   1. Cartooning.   I. Title.
NC1320.N415   1984   741.6   83-26951
ISBN 0-13-447921-1
ISBN 0-13-447913-0 (pbk.)

THE ART & DESIGN SERIES

Humorous Illustration and Cartooning
by Roy Paul Nelson

ISBN 0-13-447921-1

ISBN 0-13-447913-0 {PBK.}

10 9 8 7 6 5 4 3 2 1

Editorial/production supervision
   by Alberta Boddy
Interior design by Maria Carella
Page layout by Debra Watson
Manufacturing buyer: Edward J. Ellis

PRENTICE-HALL INTERNATIONAL, INC., *London*
PRENTICE-HALL OF AUSTRALIA PTY LIMITED, *Sydney*
PRENTICE-HALL OF CANADA, LTD., *Toronto*
PRENTICE-HALL OF INDIA PRIVATE LIMITED, *New Delhi*
PRENTICE-HALL OF JAPAN, INC., *Tokyo*
PRENTICE-HALL OF SOUTHEAST ASIA PTE. LTD., *Singapore*
WHITEHALL BOOKS LIMITED, *Wellington, New Zealand*
EDITORA PRENTICE-HALL DO BRASIL LTDA., *Rio de Janeiro*

**To Joe Wasson,
cartoonist without portfolio**

contents

preface

Most of the books analyzing cartoons, offering advice on how to draw them, or bringing a collection together to admire deal with forms that stand on their own: editorial cartoons, comic strips, cartoon panels, and gag cartoons. Although this book devotes attention to such cartoons, it emphasizes a less appreciated but far more prevalent form: humorous illustration.

America's mass media in the aggregate publish the work of fewer than 200 editorial (or political) cartoonists, a few hundred comic-strip artists and creators of cartoon panels, and maybe a thousand gag cartoonists. The media devote much more space to cartoonists who do illustrations. You find those cartoonists everywhere. The work they do appears in every conceivable publication, including publications that dismiss comic strips, gag cartoons, and even editorial cartoons as being beneath or beyond them. The *New York Times,* for instance, runs no comic strips and employs no editorial cartoonist, but it enlivens its pages, especially those in its

Sunday sections, with all kinds of applaudable humorous illustrations.

Nor do humorous illustrations confine themselves to news and feature stories in newspapers, stories and articles in magazines, and novels and nonfiction books. They creep into advertisements, too. And when you consider all the humorous art used for direct-mail pieces (a form of advertising that includes leaflets, folders, booklets, and broadsides) you begin to appreciate the ubiquity of this branch of the art.

Nobody earns a big name creating humorous illustrations, but most people in the field make better—or at least more consistent—livings than those who go the more familiar cartoon route. Most humorous illustrators freelance, but many work as staff members of newspapers, magazines, advertising agencies, public relations departments or firms, and printers. If they don't turn out humorous illustrations exclusively, they at least turn them out as the occasion for them arises. Drawing a

humorous illustration becomes a pleasant change-of-page activity from, say, designing a magazine, roughing out an ad, or writing a press release.

This book differs in still another way from earlier books on cartooning. It directs itself not only to artists who produce cartoons but also to editors and advertisers who order them. It builds a case for humorous art and shows how, through wise use, it can better serve the reader. And the book helps erase the misunderstandings that often arise between artist and editor.

Collecting the variety of examples and anecdotes that it does, the book looks for an audience of real people, too—people who read and view instead of write or draw—to help them better appreciate humorous art in all its printed forms.

In short, the book welcomes aboard just about everyone, except maybe the people who put curled fingers into the air to draw quote marks when they talk.

1
the visual oasis

ASHLEY WOLFF 82

Some of the writing in magazines, newspapers, books, and advertisements flows so smoothly or deals with subjects so compelling it doesn't need any graphic relief. Or it gets the display it needs at the hands of skilled typographers, who choose just the right typeface, and in the right size, and put the right amount of leading between the lines. Added interest comes from well-placed titles or headlines, from large initial letters to start off occasional paragraphs, from ruled lines or boxes to set off certain sections, and from subheads or extra white space to indicate changes in subject and to break the columns of copy into more convenient takes.

But the typical published piece in this visual age needs more than good writing and typographic excellence. It needs art. Art acts not only as an oasis for the reader grown weary of all the words but also as a supplement to them, explaining them, dramatizing them, elaborating upon them.

Art for editors and advertisers consists of photographs, paintings, and drawings. When used to accompany the text matter in a publication or in an ad, a painting or a drawing is an "illustration." The term ordinarily does not apply to a photograph, even when the photograph is used for illustrative purposes. A photograph is a photograph.

Unlike, say, a painting to be hung in a gallery, an illustration does not have a life of its own. It is content to play a servile role. Consequently in some quarters illustrations do not get the respect they deserve.

For that matter, *all* art designed for publication—even self-contained art—tends to suffer by comparison to what has come to be called the "fine arts." Art for publication is written off as "commercial art."

in defense of commercial art

People first encounter art not at museums or galleries but on the pages of newspapers, in the form of comic strips, or on the pages of magazines and books, in the form of illustrations. John Ashbery, writing in *New York,* calls the encounter "a first love . . . never entirely equaled afterward." When later in life people learn that this kind of art is somehow inferior, they are puzzled, but, fortunately, they are not put off.

What is it about illustrations that annoys the critics? For one thing, critics suspect that people create illustrations for the money, not to find themselves or to change the world. Illustrations also get low marks because they stoop to telling a story, or, worse, they decorate. Illustrations are created to be reproduced, not to hang in galleries or museums. Illustrations are for just anybody, not the discriminating few. So the arguments go.

Yet, a study of the best magazines and books by any open-minded observer shows that much of the best art today comes from illustrators. And much of what's seen in these publications gets there through a lot of agonizing and deep thinking and trial and error. Unlike the fine-arts painters, the illustrators cannot often take advantage of the accidents of painting and allow their work to go in some direction other than what was intended. The illustrator starts out with restrictions and lives with them.

James McMullan, one of the great illustrators in America, discusses twenty assignments in his *Revealing Illustrations* (New York: Watson-Guptill, 1981) and shows photographs taken for reference, preliminary sketches, and final illustrations. McMullan reports that "my progression on many assignments is like a long road covered with the fragments of false starts and different approaches."

the fine arts-commercial art connection

Many of the people who produce illustrations could just as well produce fine-arts paintings or drawings. David Seavey, who first gained prominence as an illustrator and cartoonist for the *National Observer*, a sprightly national weekly newspaper no longer published, and who now is editorial cartoonist for *USA Today*, the national newspaper launched by Gannett in 1982, shows his fine-arts leanings with this lithographic drawing of John J. McGraw and other early twentieth century baseball figures (Figure 1.1). Seavey made his drawing on a flat stone surface and, after applying liquid and ink, pulled proofs, in the manner of the master lithographers of an earlier era. (The original, in a fourteen-inch-by-twelve-inch size, much better displays Seavey's graceful crayon lines and strong tones than this reproduction can.)

It is not easy always to distinguish between illustration and the fine arts. Many fine-arts painters have themselves turned to illustration, or what they paint carries many of the qualities we associate with illustration, even humorous illustration. Consider the work of Andre Derain, Henri Matisse, Pablo Picasso, and Amedeo Modigliani. Or consider Milton Avery, the American modernist

Figure 1.1
Courtesy of David Seavey.

3

painter who was rediscovered in the 1980s. Hilton Kramer, the art critic, says of the work of Avery that it has "a marked and gentle humor" and that its spirit is "good-humored." Robert Hughes, another art critic, says that sometimes in an Avery painting "his lumpish ladies on the beach suggest Thurber." Avery, greatly influenced by Matisse, is an artist difficult to categorize because he was too realistic for the abstract–expressionists and too abstract for the realists. (He understood the value of illustration in that, for a good part of the time he painted, his wife supported him through illustrations she did for the *New York Times Magazine*.)

Painters like Francisco Goya, Paul Klee, and Henri de Toulouse-Lautrec belong in the fine-arts ranks, of course; yet Werner Hofmann rightly includes examples of their works in his *Caricature: From Leonardo to Picasso* (New York: Crown Publishers, Inc., 1957), along with examples by people more generally thought of as caricaturists: Honore Daumier, Gustave Dore, James Gillray, George Grosz, William Hogarth, Charles Philipon, Thomas Rowlandson, and Saul Steinberg. (Caricature, one of the most interesting branches of illustration, will be discussed in Chapter 2.)

Another tie between the commercial arts and the fine arts comes from the frequent attempts by illustrators to parody well-known paintings or artists' styles. Grant Wood's "American Gothic" often

shows up on magazine pages or in ads, with new characters taking the place of the old woman and the old man with his pitchfork. John Brainard used the "American Gothic" idea in an illustration he did for a *Harper's* article, "The Farmer on the Dole," an article that questioned subsidies. Brainard's version had dollar bills impaled on the teeth of the pitchfork and a pattern of dollar bills on the farmwife's smock. In a "Keep Cool This Summer" ad, illustrator Bernie Lettick imitated Salvador Dali's drooping-watch surrealistic style with a painting of a phone, clock, pen, and other desk artifacts (including a Rubik's cube) melting away in the heat of a room not equipped with Carrier Air Conditioning.

photography versus illustration

With the advent of photography in the nineteenth century and especially with the coming of photomechanical means of reproducing halftones (1885), illustrators, by then well established with the media, faced something of a crisis. Editors liked the realism of photography and appreciated its quickness. Advertisers thought photography was more believable. Some people predicted that the day of the illustrator was over. But interest in photography among editors and advertising people rises and falls, and illustration every few years makes a comeback if for no other reason than that it represents a change of pace from photography. In the New York City area, where so much publishing takes place, an estimated 15,000 persons in the early 1980s were making their living as illustrators. (You can see some of their best efforts, plus work by illustrators elsewhere in

the country, in the *Illustrators Annual*, which goes to about 20,000 book buyers each year.)

Both photographers and illustrators can point to advantages they offer editors and advertisers. Photographers, for instance, can provide scores of pictures in a matter of a few hours, giving editors a wealth of material to choose from. With the availability of versatile 35 mm cameras, almost anyone, including editors and writers themselves, can turn out pictures that, although not artistic triumphs, are at least publishable. Amateurism in photography is less offensive than amateurism in illustration.

Illustrators can claim as an advantage an ability to create an Everyman or an Everywoman to make an editorial point or to sell a product. No model's release or model's fee is required. We generally associate model's releases to advertisers, who clearly need them to stay on the good side of the law, but an editor is not entirely free of them, either. Even when used for news/editorial purposes (as opposed to advertising purposes) a photograph of a person can present a problem. Without a properly signed release, an editor wouldn't dare use a photograph of a girl standing beside her locker in high school to illustrate a feature on venereal disease, for instance, even if the photograph were used symbolically with the girl unidentified. The girl—or her parents—could probably prove in a libel suit that people recognized her and that her reputation was damaged as a result. Even randomly shot pictures of crowds could involve a newspaper or magazine in a suit, if only a nuisance suit.

So some stories and articles call for painted or drawn illustrations instead of photographs, where real people, even though the artist used them as models, are lost in the ambiguity of pencil, paint, or ink. An illustrator working from reference photos (or "scrap," as it is called) combines features of several people, often, to construct a single character.

Illustrators offer another advantage in that they are not bound by location, season, or lighting conditions. A photographer fails to get there in time to shoot the demonstration, let's say. No problem. An illustrator steps in to reconstruct the scene or perhaps to create an abstraction of the kind seen in Figure 1.2.

As photographers and illustrators have competed for the attention of editors and advertisers, they have imitated each other. You find photographs now—impressive ones—that are grainy, out of focus, textured, even abstract;

and you find illustrations that are super realistic. Sometimes you can tell an illustration from a photograph only by spotting a signature at the lower right edge of the reproduction.

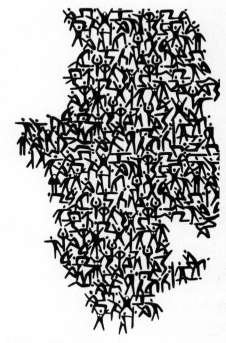

Figure 1.2
From *Gebrauchgraphik International* magazine.

what illustration can do

Illustration can serve a purpose by merely decorating a page, offering the reader a bit of graphic relief without being intrusive. Ashley Wolff's contribution (Figure 1.3) to *Pacific Sun,* a Mill Valley, California alternative weekly, serves as a good example of decorative art used as an illustration. It went with a travel piece by Pru Elliott. It is an excellent study in texture and pattern. Although it carries no caption, the drawing, the only art for the feature, is based on this sentence: "Black, silent Caribbean women dressed in bright frocks were selling fruit artistically arranged in straw baskets."

Decorative art can occupy a generous amount of space at the start

of a feature, as Ashley's art did, or it can show itself in smaller doses at intervals within the feature. It can also appear out in the margins, where margins happen to be generous. For a low-budget publication, in-the-margin art can help atone for the modesty of dry-transfer letters, strike-on composition, and copies produced by a duplicator instead of a printing press. I drew the three illustrations in Figure 1.4 for one issue of an all-typed newsletter directed to scholastic journalists and advisers.

The first went with a speech report that quoted someone as say-

Figure 1.3
Courtesy of Ashley Wolff and *Pacific Sun*.

ing humor is like a cold because a person who has it spreads it around. The second went with a reprint of a feature in a high school paper that talked about people who hate Christmas. The third illustrated a feature about mistakes made in school yearbooks. The pictured adviser has just discovered that his editor left off the name of the school—the publisher—on the title page. One of journalism's unpardonable sins. The ideas here are not elaborate, but there is a hint of a story in each of them and enough intrigue to get the reader into the copy.

Decorative art can serve as large initial letters, as Ed Cameron demonstrates in his initial "I" (Figure 1.5) used to start off his final column in a weekly newspaper he edited. That's Cameron you see "winding down" his column.

Decorative art can be humorous, realistic, or abstract. The style of the art should be consistent with the style of the writing. Unlike most other art for publication, decorative art does need explanatory captions.

Illustrative art, of course, is often more than decorative. It may do a recruiting job, for instance, using visual intrigue to stop readers and lure them into the articles. It may also further explain what an article says or add a note of its own. Under no circumstances, though, should the art take issue with the article. The two must work in tandem.

Figure 1.4

6

Figure 1.5
Courtesy of Ed Cameron and *The Lincoln Log*, Newport, Oregon.

An illustration should carry all kinds of hints about where an article is heading, but probably it should not give away the main point. Nor should it give away the author's surprise ending, when there is one. David Brenner tells a story of being locked out of his car and trying to get back in with a coat hanger. Someone comes by to say Brenner should be using a wire hanger, not a wooden one. So he uses a wire one for awhile, still without any luck. Fortunately, it is a convertible with its top down, so, finally, Brenner gets in—by reaching over the window and pulling up the nob.

Showing the car as a convertible with its top down would not do, if this story were to be illustrated. The drawing would have to be a closeup, cropped to show only part of the window with Brenner manipulating the wooden hanger.

the thin line between serious and humorous illustration

The line between serious and humorous illustration runs thin, like the line between tragedy and comedy in writing. For instance, both serious illustration and humorous illustration can move away from realism into pure fantasy. The two drawings of Figure 1.6 suggest that there are flying horses and there are flying horses. The realistic drawing on the left is from the original *Life* magazine (artist unknown). The one on the right shows what a cartoonist, W. Heath Robinson, can do with the same creature.

Figure 1.7 represents a middle ground between realistic and humorous illustration. The painfully careful pen drawing, with all its cross hatching, moves toward the comic with its exaggerated action, helped along by the shadow under the man. The shadow tells us he is up off the ground, almost flying.

Among modern artists, Norman Rockwell probably best represents the dichotomy between serious and humorous illustration. Rockwell started his career selling cartoons. *The World Encyclopedia of Cartoons* includes his biography with the biographies of all the other cartoonists it recognizes. ". . . it is not stretching definitions to say that Rockwell remained as much a cartoonist as an illustrator throughout his career." Rockwell's appeal as an illustrator stemmed not only from the down-home realism of his paintings but also from their gentle humor. His 317 *Saturday Evening Post* covers were middle-class slices of life of the kind that made readers nudge one another and smile. Slice-of-life realism is an ingredient of humor.

Figure 1.6

Figure 1.7
From *Stand Magazine*, 1898.

Figure 1.8
Reprinted courtesy of Newspaper Enterprise Association, Inc.

In the comic-strip world, it was Roy Crane who first bridged the gap between serious and humorous drawing, combining a comic style with an exotic story line in *Wash Tubbs*. The strip started out funny in 1924, then turned adventurish in 1928. Figure 1.8 shows a panel from an early strip.

Crane exaggerated action and placed things into beautifully designed panels. At first he used an almost crude pen-and-ink technique; then he experimented with grease crayon and later Craftint doubletone (paper with a built-in pattern brought out by the application of a chemical).

Nearly every comic-strip artist in the 1930s and later was influenced by Crane. Charles Schulz in the Foreword to a book Gordon Campbell and Jim Ivey compiled as a tribute to Crane (*Wash Tubbs by Roy Crane*, New York: Luna Press, 1974) wrote that when he was young he tried drawing an adventure strip like *Wash Tubbs*. "The similarity has carried over, as we all build upon the work of our predecessors. My own drawing had been influenced by that of Mr. Crane even though I am certain no one these days would ever be aware of it."

Having made the decision to create humorous rather than serious illustration, the artist nevertheless holds onto many of the affectations of realism, the better to display the distortion. The gag cartoonist, for instance, often works in wash (black and gray watercolors) in order to give photographic realism to the bulbous noses, jutting breasts, bird-like legs, and rolling desert sands. Or with pen alone, crisscrossing strokes, a cartoonist carefully rounds and molds limbs, bodies, and props to give them a third dimension you'd think they wouldn't need. See how solid, how

Figure 1.9

rounded the limbs are on Grandville's ballet dancer (Figure 1.9), how familiar he is with real anatomy. (Grandville is the pseudonym of Jean Ignace Isidore Gérard [1803–1847], a French caricaturist and illustrator said to have inspired Sir John Tenniel's illustration for Lewis Carroll's *Alice in Wonderland*.)

why make it funny?

Why should the illustration be humorous rather than serious?

The answer is that the times cry out for humor. "Humanity takes itself too seriously," Oscar Wilde observed. "It is the world's original sin. If the caveman had known how to laugh, History would have been different." An anonymous New York sportswriter told writer Roger Kahn that "Very little matters, and nothing matters much."

Most of the listings in the annual *Writer's Market,* where editors parade their needs in front of writers and would-be writers, carry the notation that humor is welcome. Editors at writers' conferences complain that they see little humor among items contributed for publication. These editors say that humor need not be confined to pieces that are meant obviously to be funny. It belongs in serious writing, too, to make reading a more delightful experience even when a message is paramount.

when humorous art is appropriate

Probably the easiest writings to illustrate with humorous art are first-person or third-person accounts of adventures or, better, misadventures. The adventures can be fiction or nonfiction. In either case, only selected pieces of action can be shown, but they will help the reader into and through the story.

Humorous art also nicely adapts itself to light-hearted essays. Often it is the writer who becomes the chief character in art drawn for essays. In such a case, the

illustrator draws the character roughly to the writer's known measurements, something Gluyas Williams did so nicely for Robert Benchley.

Humorous art works best in advertising uses when copy moves briskly and makes comparisons. Because of limited space, a single piece of art, run next to the headline to amplify it, does the job. In the creative process, the ad may

Or buy a Volkswagen.

Figure 1.10
Courtesy of Volkswagen and Doyle Dane Bernbach.

start with the art rather than with the copy, in which case the copy merely elaborates on the art or takes off from it. A classic example is the "Or Buy a Volkswagen" ad showing Charles Piccirillo's powerful, sweeping-brush closeup of a depressed man about to shoot himself in the forehead with what appears at first to be a gun but, on closer inspection, turns out to be a gas-pump handle (Figure 1.10). The ad, almost a poster, ran during one of the gas shortages. It could have been an editorial cartoon. There was no copy except for the headline.

when humorous art doesn't work

Editors sometimes turn to humorous art as a last resort, having failed to come up with a workable idea for a photograph. Often a humorous drawing can rescue a dull article. But editors should not expect too much of a humorous illustration. Except to dress it up with some charts or graphs, not much can be done to a newspaper feature on an upcoming sewer-bond issue, for instance. In Oregon, state officials are decorating annual tax forms now with cute cartoons, but you don't hear very many chuckles coming from beleaguered taxpayers.

Humorous art is inappropriate in any number of cases. It doesn't work, for instance, for articles on adoption rackets or for features on abortion or rape. If these are to be illustrated, they should be illustrated with photographs or with grease crayon sketches or abstract drawings.

Most novels would lose their impact if laced with humorous illustrations.

Nor does all advertising benefit from humorous illustration. Chiropractors (to name one group) seem given to the practice in their ads of showing cartoon drawings of sufferers, slightly bent, clutching their lower backs, with zigzag lines spreading out from that area to indicate pain. People really in need of chiropractic or medical attention see nothing funny about their condition. Advertisements taking back pain lightly are not likely to get sufferers into the sponsors' offices.

Much written humor is best left unillustrated. What it says can't be reduced to illustration, or what it says is vivid enough that readers form their own pictures.

"Women are best at room temperature," wrote A. J. Liebling. It doesn't need—couldn't use—an illustration. Nor does Dayton Allen's advice merit any art: "Always answer your telephone when it rings. It may be someone calling." Some humor is purely verbal. "I was gratified to be able to answer promptly, and I did," wrote Mark Twain. "I said I didn't know." "Drawing on my fine command of the language," wrote Robert Benchley, "I said nothing."

Art would only spoil Stephen Leacock's "He jumped on his horse and rode off in all directions" or James Thurber's "He fell down a great deal . . . because of a trick he had of walking into himself."

When used as captions for sophisticated gag cartoons, some witticisms and one-liners could work

very well. At a play rehearsal Sir Arthur Tree shouted at his cast: "Ladies, just a little more virginity, if you don't mind!" It is the kind of a line that would fit perfectly under a drawing by a *New Yorker* cartoonist.

the role of the art director

Some editors, including editors of company magazines (or house organs) and some business publications (or trade journals), do their own art buying and page designing. But on most publications, the art director makes the art and design decisions.

J. B. Handelsman, an American-born cartoonist operating out of England, captures the nature of the art director in a gag cartoon showing St. Peter standing at the gates of heaven talking to a worried-looking man on the outside. In back of St. Peter is an art director (you can tell by the hair and arty dress). St. Peter tells the worried man: "I'm terribly sorry. The art director thinks your ears are too big."

Art directors are like that. They feel strongly about how things look. Their influence on magazines, books, advertising, and now on newspapers (the last medium to give in to the visual age) has been notable. The acceptance of an article may rest as much with the art director as with the editor. In the decision process, the key question might be: how well does

the article lend itself to striking illustrations? At an advertising agency, it may be the art director rather than the copywriter who decides on the ad's copy approach or theme.

Some gag cartoonists blame art directors for killing off a large portion of their magazine market, pointing out that art directors, in their desire to unify and coordinate pages, veto gag cartoons for being intrusive. But the lack of enthusiasm for gag cartoons does not extend to *illustrative* cartoons. Most art directors, like most editors, see the value of humorous illustrations in brightening the pages of a publication.

Art directors typically do more than direct. They do the actual designing and laying out and even pasting up of their publications. On some publications they are known as *designers* or *design directors*. Buying art and dealing with artists are only part of their duties.

stock art

Nothing beats custom art, drawn to an art director's specifications. But sometimes editors and art directors work with no budget for custom art. Sometimes an unreasonable deadline beckons. Stock art may be the answer.

The various stock-art services, such as Volk Art, Inc., and Dynamic Graphics, Inc., bring professional drawings to the editor for a few pennies each, provided full books are bought or monthly services contracted. The art is slick and tight and, alas, a bit predictable, with a quality that immediately marks it, at least to the trained observer, as stock art. Art like this, understandably, must take a middle road to appeal to a wide variety of buyers.

Editor & Publisher International Year Book lists most of the stock-art services, including what used to be known as the mat services.

An editor can also get cheap art from books of public-domain art published by, among others, Dover Publications, Inc. Often this art has more character than art found in the stock-art clip-books, but it has a dated look. Editors doing historical features are best served by public-domain art.

Stock art is best used when someone who can draw modifies it, localizes it, combines several pieces to make one new piece, even redraws the art. Stock-art services probably better serve advertising than editorial people. Somehow it has an advertising look about it.

Editors can also go to photo-houses for illustrations. Rates for the photographs vary according to use and circulation. The current issue of *Literary Market Place* (*LMP*), found in most libraries, lists the various houses.

reproducing the art

To be published, any piece of art—any photograph, any illustration—goes through a process resulting in the manufacture of a printing plate. In the days when printing was done in letterpress (from a raised surface), the printer photographed the art to make a negative, used the negative to make an impression on a plate, then gave the plate a chemical bath to eat away the parts not meant to show in the reproduction. Offset lithography is the most common printing process now. The preliminary steps remain essentially the same as in letterpress, but the plate is thinner than a letterpress plate and flexible enough to wrap around a drum, has no raised surface, and on the plate is all the copy that goes on the page as well. How the actual transfer of the image occurs in offset lithography need not concern us here, but the process is based on the physical principle that grease (the ink) and water do not mix. (Both ink and a liquid solution are applied to the plate.) In offset lithography the inked image transfers itself—offsets itself—to a rubber-covered roller before it goes onto the paper. The image comes finally from a flexible surface which makes possible high fidelity on rough-textured paper, something editors couldn't get before.

The big advantage of offset lithography is that editors can reproduce art more economically than through letterpress or through the other major printing process: gravure. Most newspapers, magazines, and books are now printed by offset lithography, which means that virtually every editor can afford to show some art.

From a printing standpoint, art breaks down into either halftone art or line art. Halftone art when printed shows as a series of fine dots. Areas seen as light gray (actually, the ink is black; there is no true gray in the printing) consist of dots so fine they are barely visible. The dots are more fully developed in darker areas.

The dots get there through the intervention of a screen—a piece of glass with crosshatched lines—placed between the lens and the film when the art is photographed to make the plate. The finer the screen, the more detail the halftone can hold. Letterpress requires that the screen be rather coarse; offset lithography makes room for finer-screen halftones, even when the printing is on rough-textured paper.

To hold onto their subtle tones, photographs, paintings, and blurred or blended pencil drawings require halftone reproduction. We call such art, before it is converted into halftones, *continuous-tone art*.

Line reproduction, used to reproduce *line art*, requires no screen and shows only solid black areas and lines and clear patterns on a pure white background (or as pure white as the paper allows). Pen-and-ink or brush-and-ink drawings, drawings with Zipatone overlays or similar mechanical tones, and drawings with strong grease-crayon shading on a textured surface can take line production.

Merritt Cutler's soldiers crossing through a swamp (Figure 1.11), done in bold brush strokes with grease-crayon shading, is a line drawing requiring line reproduction. At first glance it appears to be an area of mere texture. Closer study reveals the detail Cutler has

Figure 1.11
Courtesy of Merritt Cutler.

13

skillfully put into it. It was one of several drawings he did to illustrate the text for his "*I Was Over There*," a privately published recent book about his experiences in World War I.

Editors ask for line reproduction from their printers whenever possible because line reproduction gives clean, crisp images. An editor can't be sure exactly how the art will turn out with a halftone reproduction. When an illustration requires halftone reproduction, an editor can ask for a *highlight* or *dropout* version. This will create some pure white areas within the "gray" areas. A regular photograph, though, almost always requires regular halftone treatment.

Whether ordering line or halftone reproduction, an editor can ask that it be held to actual size, reduced, or enlarged, depending on the requirements of the layout.

appreciating the original

No matter how well it's reproduced, through whatever printing process on whatever paper, the cartoon you see in print is only a copy of the original. In some cases—you can find a number of examples in this book—the printer has had to work not from the original but from a copy or print of the original. So what the reader sees often is art *third* hand. Such art is bound to lose some of its fidelity.

To really appreciate a cartoon you have to see it in its original form, with an occasional penciled-in line still showing, along with splotches of white paint or paper patches where errors have been corrected. Maybe you will see rough spots where errors have been scratched away with a razor blade. This is art with all natural ingredients.

By looking at an original, before it has been reduced to fit some stingy space, you can better appreciate the true character of the pen lines or brush strokes.

Collecting originals can be a pleasant if now a somewhat costly hobby. Years ago you could simply write to a syndicate for an original Schulz or Crane comic strip and you'd get it. Now syndicates and artists realize that these original drawings are more than pieces to be photographed for plates or prints and then tossed aside. Some galleries offer original cartoons to their patrons at prices that are higher than what the artists got from editors when the cartoons were published.

The Museum of Cartoon Art, Port Chester, N.Y., is the most popular repository for original comic strips and cartoons as well as for books and cartooning artifacts. It also conducts cartooning workshops. You can find similar—but smaller—cartoon museums in Florida, Southern California, and other parts of the country. Even universities maintain cartoon collections. Ohio State University has collections of originals by James Thurber and Milton Caniff. The University of Oregon houses a large collection of originals by editorial cartoonists Homer Davenport and Quincy Scott and comic-strip artist Clare Victor (Dwig) Dwiggins. Other collections of original cartoons can be found at the New York Public Library and the Smithsonian Institution.

Almost as good as seeing cartoons in their original form is seeing them well printed in sizes large enough to hold onto all the detail. Seeing them on microfilms is a poor substitute. Bill Blackbeard felt strongly about this when libraries all over the country, to save space, began photographing old newspapers and then getting rid of them. Blackbeard made arrangements to pick up the papers and clip and file the comic strips and cartoons in complete runs. This led to the establishment of the Academy of Comic Art in San Francisco, which has become a Mecca for cartoon and comics scholars.

2
what makes it funny?

"BOB'S SO MELLOW."

When watching TV commercials you get the impression people are ready to laugh at anything. A couple of ladies talking about coffee put "rim" and "Brim" into the same sentence and it nearly breaks them up. In another commercial, Arnold Palmer, a motor-oil freak, says people "get a kick out of it" when he tells them "Quality comes in a yellow can." Over there in a field of wheat walks Sandy Duncan confessing to orgies of Nabisco crackers eating when she was younger and telling us its "sorta funny" that she should now be selling Wheat Thins on TV.

Meanwhile, aging jocks divide evenly between those who think the beer "tastes great" and those who think it is not filling. Freshly scrubbed youths can't settle an argument over whether what they're putting in their mouths is candy or a "breath freshener." Families nearly come to blows over which toothpaste to use until one wise member finds a brand that does double duty.

Beautifully ordinary and ethnically correct people in slice-of-life commercials sing off key.

A certain lightheartedness comes through in these commercials, and the copywriters, no doubt,

believe they are in league with Peter DeVries.

Is there a local newscast around where happy talk at the end of the long hour does not blame the "weatherperson," someone given to using the terms "weatherwise" and "shower activity" for the bad weather? Kill the messenger, ha ha.

When people laugh at almost anything it is a sign that humor is about done in. Fortunately, in real life people are not so easily amused.

humor: what it is

Nobody has succeeded in adequately defining humor, and the studies analyzing it are laughable. Perhaps Robert Benchley's definition is as good as any: "We must understand that all sentences which begin with 'W' are funny."

Humor on a basic level—humor content merely to entertain—is known as comedy; humor more cerebral is known as wit. Nearly everyone who has studied humor agrees that surprise is its most important ingredient. Jackie Vernon demonstrates with an abrupt end to what starts out to be a familiar quotation. "It is better to have loved and lost—much better." *Scanlan's*, an unconventional, short-lived opinion magazine of the early 1970s, surprised its leftist readers with an announcement that it would charge to run letters to the editor, and the dumber the letter, the more the writer would have to pay.

Bill Brewer (more on him later) demonstrates how surprise can work in a comic strip in Figure 2.1. The clean, crisp, decorative look of this previously unpublished strip and its subtlety

won first prize for Brewer in a cartoon contest held in California and put the strip on display at the International Salon of Humor in Montreal and at the World Cartoon Festival in Knokke-heist, Belgium.

In most humor the reader is led to expect one thing only to get something else. Something turns out to be more than the reader expects (exaggeration) or less (understatement).

Exaggeration helps a writer or artist make a point quickly and vividly. Ezra Pound used exaggeration to describe the sloppiness of Ford Madox Ford when he said that if Ford "were placed naked and alone in a room without furniture, I would come back in an hour and find total confusion." Calvin Trillin claims that for one of his contributions to *Monocle*, a defunct magazine of satire, he received not a check but a bill, along with a note explaining that the expenses for producing the piece came to more than what the editors were planning to pay for it.

Figure 2.1
Courtesy of Bill Brewer.

Much of American humor depends upon exaggeration. Understatement, in the view of many students of humor, belongs more to the British. It also fits more closely the needs of the intellectual. John Kenneth Galbraith, the economist, employed understatement when he said that "Wealth is not without its advantages, and the case to the contrary, although it has often been made, has never proved widely persuasive." Part of the joy in this bit of understatement comes from its elaborate presentation. A tongue-in-cheek invitation to take part in a world cruise employs understatement when it warns: "Don't forget to bring a sack lunch."

A humorist often takes an ordinary phenomenon and puts it into an improper context. For instance: nicknames. What if the concept of nick*names* were applied to *numbers*? T. E. Lawrence (Lawrence of Arabia) served in the Royal Air Force with the serial number 338171. Noel Coward, the playwright and actor, once wrote to him with this salutation: "Dear 338171, /May I call you 338?" Another numbers story has a bunch of prisoners telling jokes. Having put together a big collection, the prisoners, to save time, gave each joke a number. A prisoner had only to say "seventeen" or "twenty-three" to set off gales

of laughter. A new prisoner was puzzled by the activity, but when it was explained to him he decided to enter into it. "Fourteen," he said, but nobody laughed. What was wrong? he wanted to know. Somebody explained: "You didn't tell it right."

Any embarrassment, any scene that causes the reader to wonder, "How could it possibly have happened?" would be regarded by most people as humorous, whether the scene involves human beings or animals. Harold Montiel demonstrates this in Figure 2.2.

We are amused, too, when we see someone playing a wrong role. Animals acting as though they were human can be part of it. In Figure 2.3, Montiel has some fun with a literary lion.

There is another branch of humor that allows people to behave exactly as you would expect them to. Such behavior becomes amusing because people can identify with it and feel its embarrassments. Ain't-it-the-truth! humor can be as effective as it-couldn't-possibly-happen humor. Andy Rooney deals with the former kind of humor in his tail-end segments on "Sixty Minutes."

Humor often involves people who pretend to misunderstand. Publisher William Randolph Hearst asked the owner of a competing paper: "How much will you take for the *Tribune*?" The answer he got: "Three cents on weekdays. Five cents on Sundays."

Humor also makes questionable assumptions from elusive facts. Mae West, who didn't like to fly, went by car from Hollywood to San Francisco to appear at the opening of her last movie, *Sextette*. Herb Caen, the *Chronicle* columnist, speculated about her age,

Figure 2.2
Harold Montiel.

Figure 2.3
Harold Montiel.

which was variously recorded at between 87 and 92. "I can't imagine anyone being afraid of flying at 92," he wrote, "so she must be 87."

Some of the most effective humor is sequential, which accounts for the popularity of comic strips. The early radio comedians developed feuds so that each week they could return to a theme. Sequential humor even develops on restroom walls. Someone scribbles out "I love grils." Somebody later corrects the "grils" to read "girls." Somebody else comes along and writes: "What's wrong with us grils?"

There is gentle humor, of course, and humor that goes on the attack. But most humor represents a kind of aggression, a getting it off one's chest, an expression of disillusion, a form of revenge. Mark Twain concluded that the source of humor is not joy but sorrow.

forms of humor

Whether meant to merely titillate people or arouse them to anger, humor takes many forms.

Puns lie there near the bottom, for they are not known to bring tears to the eyes of the beholders or cause listeners to clutch their sides to contain their merriment. They are more the evidence of word awareness and cleverness than of real humor. When Gyles Brandreth calls a typewriter used to type political speeches a "tripewriter," you are not so much likely to laugh as to kick yourself for not having thought of it first.

In an article on health food restaurants, Jessica Maxwell in *California* discusses the plain bad taste of some of the offerings, the "hell in health foods." She talks about "fast buckwheat artists" who "jump on the bran wagon" to establish restaurants. But there are other owners, she notes, who "have their artichoke hearts in the right place," like a woman who started a place called The Prophet in East San Diego. "I pray to the Avocado Goddess that others will follow her," writes Maxwell. "I wait for that moment with beeted breath."

More deserving of the humor label than puns are non sequiturs. Non sequiturs—bits of humor that bring two thoughts together that don't really go together—had writer Ring Lardner as their champion. " 'Shut up,' he explained" was a typical Lardner line. Lardner wrote hilarious and touching stories involving illiterate baseball players, among other characters. Long after Lardner's death a basketball coach in true Lardner style said of his team: "We're short but we're slow." The *New Yorker* resorted to a non sequitur when it said of the movie *Endless Love* that it was "a predictable fiasco—still, it's considerably worse than you might have expected."

I engaged in a non sequitur when, as a sort of experiment, I wrote the required note to the teacher to explain my son's not showing up for school the day before. "Please excuse Bryan's absence from school yesterday, because he didn't go to the beach two weekends ago." The note did its job. We live in an age of the readily accepted excuse. I have been known to continue lying on the sofa when a guest arrives. If I say, "Excuse me for not getting up, but I'm lying down," that's good enough for most folks.

Malapropisms, another form of humor, are most often unconsciously manufactured by people who don't understand the language very well and who are given to the cliché. But their clichés turn out to be all wrong. Bel Kaufman's *Up the Down Staircase,* a collection of fictitious memos by inept school officials and teachers and pathetic students, gave us countless malapropisms. Edwin O'Connor's novel *The Last Hurrah* developed a character, Ditto, who peppered his conversation with malapropisms. Archie Bunker in "All in the Family" used them often.

The "up and coming election," "a post-humorous award," "doing it in a half-hazard way," "cutting off your nose despite your face"— these are malapropisms.

Closely related to the malapropism is the spoonerism, a mistaken interchange of initial sounds in words. Spoonerisms can be traced to the Rev. William A. Spooner, who is said to have remarked in a sermon that "The Lord is a shoving leopard." H. Allen Smith in one of his books recorded a reference to a jar of "odorarm deunderant."

The highest, most demanding form of humor is irony, in which a person seems to say one thing while really saying something else or when what happens is the opposite of what you'd expect. Mark Twain's humor is generally considered as ironic.

It is ironic when a confirmed nonsmoker gets lung cancer or when a fire station burns down.

The state university president appearing before a legislative committee engages in irony when he begs for funds to make his university one "of which the football team can be proud." When Fernando Valenzuela, the 1981 rookie pitching sensation, held out for a bigger salary in 1982, Los Angeles Dodger manager Tommy Lasorda said sadly and

somewhat ironically: "All last year we tried to teach him English, and the only word he learned was 'million.'"

Irony too obvious becomes mere sarcasm, as when a passenger crawls out of a wrecked car and says to the driver: "You really know how to drive!"

Another easily recognizable form of humor is satire. Satire reaches for a human or political failing or vice and holds it up for all to see, ridiculing it in the process. It ranges from the gentle to the vitriolic. To protest what he considered Britain's exploitation of Ireland, Jonathan Swift, acknowledged as one of the world's greatest satirists, in 1729 wrote *A Modest Proposal,* suggesting that his fellow Irishmen raise their children as a crop to be eaten by the British. His *Gulliver's Travels,* written three years earlier, satirized human nature in general. It was written at two levels, one level simple enough to be enjoyed by children.

Joseph Heller's *Catch-22* stands as a more modern example of satire, dealing as it does with the military and World War II.

In "Shy Rights: Why Not Pretty Soon?" in *Happy to Be Here* (New York: Atheneum, 1982) Garrison Keillor satirizes minority-rights groups. He pretends to have been inspired by news of a fat-people's rights group. According to Keillor, the group feels that the term "overweight" is oppressive in itself "because it implies a 'right' weight the fatso has failed to make. Only weightists use such terms. . . ." But he notices that fat people refer to thin people "as being 'not all there.'"

Making his case for "shy rights," he cites history books as being prejudiced against shy people when they mention only the famous and ignore people who re-

mained in the background and had little to say.

The title of the essay tells you that Keillor affects an appropriate hesitant touch in advocating "shy rights." In his essay he offers this as one of his several slogans: "Shy is beautiful, for the most part."

Radio comedians Bob and Ray in one of their skits satirize advertising and the products that make more and more ads necessary. The deadpan duo talk about Grit, which makes a person's hands look dirty, giving an "honest workingman's appearance." Then it's Smurge, the only product that can remove Grit. And then there's Whiff, which removes the odor of Smurge.

Another example of satire: Back in the 1950s, when the phone company began to move away from easy-to-remember phone numbers like WAlnut 5-6844 to all-digit numbers and when other organizations, including the Post Office, became numbers-happy, Martin Solow and Dan Gillmor, not with much seriousness, formed an organization called the Society for the Abolition of All-Digit Dialing, Zip Codes and Acronyms (SAADDZCA). They also formed the Northern Committee for Southern Democracy Only (NCSDO), beautifully satirizing the tendency of northern liberals to point to racial problems in the South when there were plenty in the North to work on. NCSDO's slogan was: "Don't bother us about conditions up here; we're only worried about them down there." There was a sort of subslogan, too: "Something should be done about everyone else."

At the time, Solow was working for *The Nation,* which gave him plenty of opportunity to witness hypocrisy in liberal ranks. (It would have been just as easy to witness hypocrisy in conservative ranks, of course, but conservatives did not congregate at *The Nation*.)

Parody, another form of humor, differs from satire in that it makes no moral judgments. Nor does it offer a new course to follow. It does not resort to anger as satire often does. Parody merely mimics; satire would like to make some changes.

Mad, the *Harvard Lampoon*, and the *National Lampoon* have produced parody issues of the nation's leading newspapers and magazines that were vicious enough and telling enough to qualify as satires. Other groups have published parody issues of the *New York Times* (*Not the New York Times*), the *Wall Street Journal* (*Off the Wall Street Journal*), and

the *National Inquirer* (*Irrational Inquirer*).

Parodies of publications include parodies of the work of familiar artists and cartoonists as well as the work of writers.

Whether setting out to create satire or parody—or any kind of humor, for that matter—a writer or artist must first study the subject upon which the humor is based. Humor rests on facts if not on truth itself.

Nor is humor immune from the legal restrictions placed on any published works. Humor, like serious writing and drawing, can run afoul of the state laws of libel and can violate federal copyright and trademark regulations.

Even parody has its legal hazards. When *Handling and Shipping Management* magazine on one of its covers ran parody art taking off on Pac-Man—"Stac-Man: Computers in the Warehouse"—the editors received a letter from a law office representing the video-game manufacturer. The letter threatened legal action for trademark violation. *Folio* magazine, in reporting the episode, speculated that letters like this are sent out routinely by companies to establish files to prove that they have defended their trademarks, in case litigation comes up later. If not defended, trademarks can pass into the public domain. Still, an editor who doesn't want to become involved in litigation needs to proceed cautiously when publishing parody.

humor in names

Johnny Hart, who does *B.C.* and is involved in *The Wizard of Id*, and Don Martin, who draws for *Mad*, like Roy Crane before them, invent strange words for sounds. In a Martin drawing, for example, you are likely to come onto a "splabadap" or a "spwap" for someone hitting the pavement and never anything so trite as a "thud." Martin takes all of this very seriously, waving off any proffered sounds from readers wishing to be helpful. Other people don't have the feel for the art, he argues. Someone once suggested "groink" as the sound for a person being hit over the head with a crowbar. That sound, of course, would have to be "pwang" or "spwang." "Groink," Martin points out, "is when you put two fingers in someone's nose and pull it about six inches from the front of their face."

Mort Walker, creator of *Beetle Bailey* and other strips, has in-

vented a series of names for the props and effects found in cartoons. For instance, puffs of smoke caused by someone moving fast are "briffits." Parallel swish lines moving from puff to puff are "hites."

The real names of cartoonists deserve some mention in passing. Note how Mell Lazarus and Bil Keane spell their first names. A European cartoonist whose first name is Harry signs his cartoons with a backwards version: "Yr-rah." And consider Paul Szep, editorial cartoonist of the Boston *Globe*. Keane, who does *Family Circus*, says he once saw the name at the top of an eye chart.

A name to delight the cartoonists was the one carried by a U.S. Senator: Hoar. Along with his wife, the Senator was a bit sensitive about his name. The story is told that a house guest, overly conscious of the problem, came down to breakfast one morning, saying "Good morning, Senator," and, pause, "How are you, Mrs. 'W.'"

Coming up with fictitious names is a routine matter for people dealing with humor. When Laurence Welk at an advanced age announced in 1982 that he would be retiring from TV, Johnny Carson, commenting on the bandleader's longevity, said that when Welk first went on the air his program was sponsored by Preparation G and Absorbine Sr.

The *National Lampoon* has come up with some interesting possibilities for new magazines, among them *Guns and Sandwiches* and *Negligent Mother*. David Z. Orlow in a satire in *Folio* suggested *Death,* a picture magazine for an audience brought up on media violence. Hawkeye on M*A*S*H mentioned *Toilet & Garden.*

Hank Grant, who writes the "Rambling Reporter" gossip column in *The Hollywood Reporter,* calls his studio spy Onda Lotalot, his Beverley Hills spy Austin Tayshus, and his London spy Lord Halpus.

Putting two words together that don't ordinarily go together can be a nice touch. The good and the bad, working against each other. For instance, the *New Yorker* called Oscar winner *On Golden Pond* "uplifting twaddle." "Twaddle" by itself is funny enough, like "Conrad Twitty" and "nerd."

visual applications

Ordinary illustration becomes humorous illustration when it carries a visual surprise. At first glance, the picture might look ordinary; but very soon the viewer sees that something is amiss. An illustration also becomes humorous when it shows some quirk, some irony that we all can identify with, or if it reinforces some stereotype. A drawing is humorous, too, when it engages in exaggeration. Charlie Brown in Charles Schulz's *Peanuts* pitches from a mound almost as high as he is.

Some humorous illustrators take a note from Jonathan Swift, coming up with innocent looking cartoons that carry, buried somewhere within, cruel, out-of-context actions or props. But understatement in humorous art in most cases gives way to exaggeration which more readily gets the point across.

A British artist, Harry Furniss, back in 1898, put exaggeration to work to present his impression of how American interviewers do their job (Figure 2.4). So intense are the interviewers that they climb over each other, look into the interviewee's mouth, examine him with a magnifying glass, and even measure his shoe. One interviewer appears to be pushing on the interviewee's chest.

An anonymous artist puts exaggeration to work in Figure 2.5, a drawing for a book published in Germany. The speaker is so nervous that he wraps one leg around the other, but the artist is too sophisticated to use sweat marks and wiggly lines to indicate that he is shaking.

Bill Merkens, who signs his work "Crow," "a carryover from playing lead in too many Shakespeare plays," according to his editor Ed Cameron, uses exaggeration in Figure 2.6 to show that someone at a gathering is "so mellow." That the skeletonized figure sits there in so advanced a state of decay is testimony to the talent of this young artist. The authentic setting works well here, too. The somewhat spotty, cluttered style is highly appropriate to the subject. The drawing, which qualifies as a

Figure 2.4
Harry Furniss *The Confessions of a Caricaturist*
Unwin, London, 1898.

Figure 2.5
From *Deutsches Lachen*, Leipsig.

Figure 2.6
Bill Merkens
© by Crow.

"BOB'S SO MELLOW."

gag cartoon (see Chapter 10), appeared in the *Gilmore Gazette & Bayfront Funnies.*

Wayne Stayskal engages in parody in a *Chicago Tribune* editorial cartoon when he shows, around tax-filing time, a disgruntled taxpayer stopped at a sign in an Internal Revenue Service building. The sign reads: "Enter Elevator 'A.' If Floor 6 and your age are more than 42, use Elevator 'B.' To determine floor, subtract number of dependents from total of Elevator 'A.' If answer is lower than 22 percent of Elevator 'A,' add 3."

Chapter 1 pointed out that illustrators sometimes parody fine-arts paintings. They also parody famous photographs. Joe Rosenthal's AP photo of the flag raising on Iwo Jima has proved especially inspirational to cartoonists, who like to take off from it because so many people remember it and it lends itself so well to new interpretations. For instance, David Granlund, editorial cartoonist for the *Middlesex News*, Framingham,

Mass., skillfully uses the scene to show Department of Public Works workers raising a traffic sign at an intersection where many people had been killed in traffic accidents (Figure 2.7). Granlund's hill consists of broken and bent car parts.

Dick Codor employs irony in a delightful 16-panel "Overseas Letter" (Figure 2.8) that helped him win the first Charles M. Schulz Award (1981) sponsored by the Scripps-Howard Foundation. Codor, a New York illustrator and animator, did the letter while living in Jerusalem and working for Israel TV. (A sample of his work appears in Bill Novak's and Moshe Waldoks's *Big Book of Jewish Humor,* published by Harper & Row in 1981.)

Heinrich Kley provides an example of sarcasm in art in Figure 2.9, although the art needs a caption to make its point. The caption is: "Blessed with children." The tyranny here is typical of the work of this artist/misfit. Dover Publications, which brought out two collections of his haunting works (*The Drawings of Heinrich Kley,* 1961, and *More Drawings by*

Heinrich Kley, 1962), called Kley "one of the most diabolically talented cartoonists of our century." Kley was obsessed by "the ungodly absurdity of the human condition."

In real life people have long necks, they are short waisted, they have tiny heads; but no matter what the condition it is only slightly removed from the norm. In a cartoon, these characteristics, if they are part of the story, or even if they're not, grow completely out of control (Figure 2.10). And why not?

Even Picasso was not above placing both eyes on the same side of a face. In Figure 2.11, an anonymous artist, inspired by Egyptian art, puts a front-view eye into a side view.

In a gag cartoon Mischa Richter once showed a man with two heads in a tobacco shop. He was ordering: "Corona Corona." Editorial cartoonists have been

Figure 2.7
Courtesy of David Granlund and *Middlesex News.*

Figure 2.8
Courtesy of Dick Codor.

Figure 2.9
Heinrich Kley

Figure 2.10

Figure 2.11

known to put two mouths on political candidates, one mouth labeled "Tax Cut," the other "Spend." When Estes Kefauver ran for the Democratic nomination for President, Bruce Russell of the Los Angeles *Times* showed him always with a hole in his head.

Even buildings take distortion. In Figure 2.12, they turn to rubber.

To create their humor, cartoonists often resort to the cliché—the fa-

Figure 2.12
From an old *St. Nicholas* magazine.

miliar allusion. The idea is to take it literally. When it "rains cats and dogs" in the cartoonist's world, those are real cats and dogs falling out of the sky. "Raking in the money," to cite another cliché, might end up looking like Figure 2.13, involving, as it does, a farmer who has developed some new way of operating the back forty.

In a humorous illustration, people whose eyes pop out are people whose eyes really do pop out. People who lose their heads really

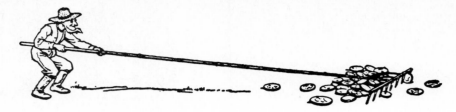

Figure 2.13
From an old *Century* magazine.

do lose their heads. People who need to pull themselves together lie scattered on the pavement; they really do need to pull themselves together. All of this can become gross, depending upon the publication running the work, but cartoonists are not known for their good taste or even their sense of fairness.

Some of the work of cartoonists has itself become a cliché and is probably best avoided. A cliché that has evolved among the editorial cartoonists is the little character in the lower left or right

corner who makes an additional comment. Pat Oliphant didn't invent the idea, but he did revitalize it, and his penguin has become the prototype for many other young editorial cartoonists. Editorial cartoonists should leave the idea to Oliphant, who brings it off superbly.

caricature

Exaggeration applied to the face of a celebrity results in caricature, an ancient and deliciously dishonorable art that made something of a comeback in the 1960s in the crosshatch art of David Levine and his imitators. Caricature becomes a chief tool of the editorial cartoonist, who uses it to put politicians in the bad light they deserve, but it has a life of its own, as well. A caricature may take the place of a photograph—a mug shot—on the cover of a magazine, as an inset in some copy about someone prominent in the news, or in a layout for a biographical piece.

A caricature isn't worth much unless it depicts someone whose features are familiar to us. Nor is it worth much if it merely depicts the victim realistically. Then all you have is a portrait. A caricature takes indecent liberties. Big becomes huge and small becomes tiny in caricature. Kathy Riethmeier, an art student, demonstrates with her crosshatch drawing of Henry Kissinger, former Secretary of State (Figure 2.14). The big nose and chin become even bigger at Riethmeier's direction, with the inclusion of a tiny hand for contrast.

Figure 2.14
Courtesy of Kathy Riethmeier.

The caricaturist needs a good, representative photograph or halftone to work from. Several photographs taken from different angles would be even better. The purpose of a caricature is not to make the viewer recognize a photograph but a person. Some photographs don't look enough like the person being drawn to be worth much. Caricaturists for some assignments have found it necessary to draw from life. But having the subject pose could hinder the caricaturist's freedom to do the subject a necessary injustice.

Often the caricaturist needs to step back to show the whole figure. Maybe the face is not unusual or expressive enough, but a body mannerism is. How better to depict Napoleon than to show his hand tucked into his front, as an anonymous artist did in Figure 2.15.

Figure 2.15
From *Bizarre Magazine*, Paris.

Jack Barrett, staff artist for the *St. Petersburg Times*, makes Woody Allen's thin face (Figure 2.16) big enough to record the wispy hair and oversize glasses, but he provides a miniature body for the head to firmly establish Allen as a movie director.

Like many of Barrett's drawings, this one should be studied, section by section, for its loving attention to detail and its careful construction. Even the various areas of shading—parallel lines as well as crosshatching—deserve scrutiny. Notice especially how Barrett's varying crosshatch and line patterns give thickness to the shirt and roundness to the bullhorn.

Figure 2.16
Courtesy of Jack Barett and *St. Petersburg Times*.

Dave Granlund, the editorial cartoonist, makes use of caricature in Figure 2.17 to show a confrontation between President Ronald Reagan and House Speaker Tip O'Neill. O'Neill's enormity, helped along by the Grafix shad-

ing, contrasts nicely with the less imposing build of Reagan. The two hair styles nicely separate the two men, too. To draw Reagan, Granlund uses just enough wrinkles and bags under the eyes and gives him the long upper lip that readily identifies his face.

One of the best caricaturist of an earlier era was, perhaps surprisingly, the well-known Italian tenor, Enrico Caruso. Figure 2.18 shows Caruso's drawing of Oscar Hammerstein, lost in thought, at the left and, next to him, an abstract, closeup caricature: Alfonso XII of Spain.

From time to time a cartoonist is called upon to produce a self-caricature. When Karl Hubenthal retired as editorial cartoonist/sports cartoonist for the *Los Angeles Herald Examiner* in 1982, the paper gave over its op-ed page to a celebration of his three decades on the paper. A number of his best cartoons were re-

Figure 2.17
Courtesy of Dave Granlund and *Middlesex News*.

Figure 2.18
Enrico Caruso

produced. Hubenthal drew a self-caricature (Figure 2.19) to go with the heading for the feature.

Occasionally in our history a state legislature has attempted to pass a law to thwart the caricaturists, but without success. Nor do caricaturists very often become involved in libel suits. The consensus seems to be that politicians, the usual victims of the caricaturists, are fair game. A problem does arise, however, when the artist captures a likeness to make money from it.

When an Indiana company, LSC Corporation, issued a poster portraying country-and-western singer Kenny Rogers, he sued, claiming that only he had the right to profit from his famous face.

Figure 2.19
Courtesy of Karl Hubenthal and the *Los Angeles Herald Examiner.*

humor
in
photography

Bill Stiles, director of public relations for a hospital, decided that, with no Norman Rockwell around, the best avenue to exaggerated realism on a booklet cover was through full-color photography. So he took his idea to photographer Bob Copeland. Stiles' art direction made of the cover and art (Figure 2.20) something reminiscent of the old *Saturday Evening Post*.

Sometimes the easiest route to humor is through photography.

The photographer has all kinds of trick lenses to use, including wide-angle, telescopic, and fisheye. Not so well known is the anamorphic—or squeeze—lens that allows the photographer to compress one dimension, width or depth, without affecting the other. You can get enormously tall, skinny people, for instance, or fat skyscrapers.

When would you want to use a distortion lens in making a print for publication? One use might involve the showing of an automobile in an ad for an auto parts store, tire store, or garage. You would want an Everybody's car to be seen, not a particular make or model. By taking a sleek nondescript model and compressing it a bit by using the right lens, you'd create a model not easily recognized. The photographer can do this at the time the picture is taken, or the printer's cameraman

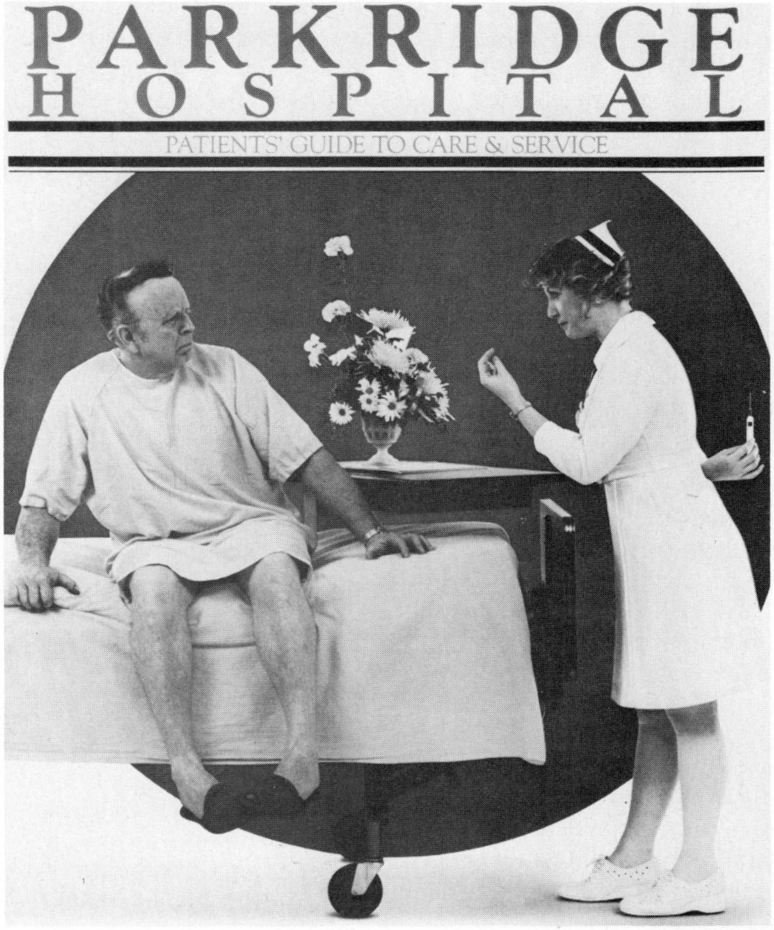

Figure 2.20
Courtesy of Bill Stiles and Parkridge Hospital, Chattanooga, Tennessee.

can take an ordinary photograph and distort it with the right lens when making the negative for the plate.

Fancy lenses are only one way to bring humor or surprise to photography. Keeping a sharp eye out for the right subject is another and probably better way. A subject's inventiveness presents one possibility. A clerk conducting store inventories in the paint section got tired of looking for a stool all the time. Because he needed only a little height, he used two paint cans as lifts, with the handles crossing his ankles to keep the cans steady. Photographer Paul Petersen's full-color shot appeared on the front page of the *Eugene* (Oreg.) *Register-Guard* as an amusing visual break.

Another photographer spotted two horses behind a partial fence. The rear of one horse showed at the left edge of the partial fence. The head of another horse showed at the right edge. The AP circulated the resulting photograph as a Laserphoto, and a newspaper caption writer titled it "A Long Shot." The caption started out like this: "Odds aren't long enough at all that such a horse would be a favorite in the stretch at any race track in the country. . . ." And later: ". . . things aren't always what they seem to be. . . ."

Sometimes the humor in photography comes from the angle chosen. Let's say you want to show a hand reaching out from a rural mailbox to accept mail from a surprised mail carrier. That you can't stuff a real person in a mail box is no problem. You can arrange things so that an early part of the arm could simply stay hidden on the other side of the box, and the photograph could be a two-dimensional rather than a

three-dimensional view. The picture would be cropped so that the back of the mailbox would be eliminated. If a three-quarters view is desirable, the photographer could break off the back of the box so that the arm could actually go through.

The angle can make a big difference. *The Province*, a daily published at Vancouver, B.C., ran an across-the-page photo by Wayne Leidenfrost showing a closeup of an open umbrella that, because of the angle it was taken from, appeared to cover all downtown-area buildings. The skyline was fuzzy because of heavy rain. For this photo, the cutlines were all-important:

"Vancouver doesn't need a domed stadium . . . the city needs a dome, or at least an umbrella big enough to do the job. The soggy weather kept work crews busy Monday unclogging . . . storm drains on several streets. . . ."

You can get an eerie effect sometimes by running a photograph upside down. For one of his photographs, Chris Lombardo lined up five young models on cement and chalked in funny faces on their shadows. The picture was run upside down, so the shadows were figures that cast real-people shadows. The photograph was cropped so that only a small part of the real-people shadows showed.

The subject itself can be turned upside down before the picture is taken. Sanka, in an ad in medical journals directed to doctors, used the headline, "Patients Bothered by Too Much Caffeine Can Still Enjoy Coffee" with a full-color photograph of a cup turned upside down on a saucer. Only the indentation on the underside of the cup was filled with coffee. A strange picture, but one that dra-

matized the idea of too little regular coffee.

Showing people or props out of correct scale can bring humor—surprise—to a photograph. By using a lens with a good depth of field, shooting with an f stop putting both front and background items in clear focus, and carefully lining up things, you can show, for instance, a hand holding a real automobile between thumb and fingers.

Another trick is to combine real people with a life-size realistic mural. Or you can combine people with a larger-than-life mural, creating even more of a surprise.

You can also patch parts of two photographs together as when you put a far-away view of a silhouetted man leaning against a silhouetted closeup of a pair of shoes. The difference in scale makes a giant of the man. To go with the advertising headline "It's a Whole New Ball Game," *Automotive News* showed a closeup of a baseball pitcher tossing a football to the batter, who swings awkwardly. Above their heads is a basketball net. Obviously some patching went on. Using a realistic medium for an unrealistic scene adds to its impact.

Many of the photographs we see are staged. They are not the result of accident. For an article on "Conservation Chic," dealing with the energy crisis, *Sohio*, a magazine published by Standard Oil of Ohio, showed a chauffeur, with cap and white gloves, pedaling a two-seat bicycle, with a well-dressed, briefcase-carrying gentleman sitting on the back seat reading a newspaper (and also pedaling). The implication was that even the rich were feeling the pinch. The subtitle for the article was: "Like

Designer Jeans, Saving Energy Will Someday Be 'In'."

A photograph was used to illustrate an article in *McCall's* on "Why Don't I *Feel* Grown-Up?" The picture showed a well-tailored businesswoman at her desk, briefcase open and papers lying all around. She was adjusting her glasses (the glasses, of course, suggest she's smart) and—surprise!—one arm dangled below the desk top to clutch a doll.

Often the photographer puts two unlikely props together and photographs them. For a cover on an issue dealing largely with word processors, *IABC News* showed a *food* processor with proofs and strips of headlines stuffed into the top, ready to be "processed." In place of the food processor name on the machine was "Word Processor."

For a photo to go with a newspaper ad celebrating a 136th birthday, the agency for Lees Carpets rolled up some rugs, stood them on end, stuffed large candles into the ends, and lit the candles. The viewer first saw the rugs as candlesticks.

In an ad for Xerox with the headline, "Every Day the Average Businessman Commutes to the Nineteenth Century," a photo showed a well-dressed modern businessman, carrying a briefcase, in the doorway of an old-fashioned office. People were in period costume; one woman was working at what might have been the first-model typewriter, with a classic wall phone and wall clock

nearby. The juxtaposition of new with old gave this photo its element of surprise.

One of America's longest running advertising campaigns had a woman in each ad standing around in her Maidenform underwear while other people went about their business fully dressed. The campaign's success rested on the photo surprise that put someone in out-of-context uniform.

The humor in photography often comes from the photograph's heading or caption. A diaper service in an ad shows a diapered baby, with focus on the baby's rear. "Diapering Costs Bottom Out . . ." reads the headline. A duo of photographs that show a cop before being ordered to shorten his hair and sideburns and afterward carries the heading: "Hair Today, Gone Tomorrow." Newspaper people and even advertising people, nice enough otherwise, seem given to such puns.

A light touch can come from the way you reproduce the photography. To show that a student on federal aid was a member of "a vanishing breed," *Bucknell World,* alumni publication of Bucknell University, showed a series of four same-pose photographs in a row, the photographs growing more faded moving from left to right.

Another way of getting humor into photography is to retouch it, as *The Oregonian* did for a feature on removing facial hair on women's faces. The photograph at the top of the feature showed a pretty, but sad, woman with a mus-

tache drawn boldly on her face in the manner of a subway artist defacing a car card. The mustache extended out into the margins where it spelled out "Fuzzy Face" in a sort of script. That was the feature's main headline. The credit line called the piece of doctored art a "photo illustration."

Like illustrations, photographs quickly become trite. The editor and photographer should keep constantly on the alert for some new presentation. Nowhere do photos become more trite than on the backs of book jackets, where serious-looking authors, pipes in hand (if male), sit next to their typewriters or perhaps stand on a patio, eyes squinting from the sun and deep thinking, the wind causing hair disarray. A photo of the late P. G. Wodehouse, about 90, bending over and touching his toes, was a welcome change for *Jeeves and the Tie That Binds,* one of his 96 comic novels.

It is easy to lie through photography, even if what is shown is factual. That famous photograph of Adlai Stevenson sitting on stage, shot shoes-first to reveal a hole in the sole, delighted the Democrats because it made Stevenson out to be a regular fellow, one who, like the rest of us, needed to have his shoes repaired. In fact, the Democrats later used the hole-in-the-shoe symbol as a lapel pin to further Stevenson's fortunes. But the symbol was hardly apt for their aristocratic and admirable candidate.

humor
in signs

A restaurant puts up this sign: "We have made a deal with the bank. They bake no pies. We cash no checks." A bank puts up a sign: "No Deposit—No return."

An optometrist's office shows this one: "Eyes Examined While You Wait." After a long period of alterations and repairs at the *New*

Yorker, James Thurber put up a sign that said, "Alterations going on as usual during business."

Posted signs often provide the humor in photography. What's said on the sign often conflicts with what's going on around it. Or maybe someone within range of the sign takes it too literally.

Harvey Weber, who conducts a monthly "Light Touch" feature for *News Photographer,* often shows humorous photographs involving signs.

The AP once sent out a photo showing a road with a sign that said, "Caution. Grandparents Playing." The caption explained that down the road was a mobile home park occupied by "old-sters." In this case the photographer didn't do much more than make a photographic copy of what was there, as one would copy a painting in a museum. Of course, the photographer had to recognize the turnabout humor of the sign when coming onto it and be the first to get it on the wires.

Bill Monroe, a photographer for *The Oregonian,* spotted adjacent signs, one for The Peep Hole, an "adult" bookstore and movie arcade, the other for an optical center conducting eye exams and dispensing glasses. His shot, with an appropriate caption, took up several columns in the paper on an otherwise dismal day.

Signs can be the vehicle for cartoonists as well as photographers. Many gag cartoons revolve around a sign in a scene, and a caption often is not needed. The sign can dominate the art. Comic-strip artists and editorial cartoonists turn to signs occasionally to make their point. Jeff MacNelly gave a *Shoe* episode over to a bumper sticker: "Honk If You Hate Noise Pollution."

Humorous illustrators resort to signs, too. A newspaper editor runs a story about a woman who advertises herself to bear the child of a childless couple. The sign in the art submitted by an illustrator reads: "Womb for Rent."

the idea behind the illustration

Ed Sullivan, who did the *Priscilla's Pop* comic strip, says that ideas are everywhere, then corrects himself: "Beginnings of ideas are everywhere." Ideas for him—and for most cartoonists—don't come as complete units, ready to use. They have to be "smacked, whacked, pushed, or pulled into place," to use Sullivan's words.

Coming up with a good, solid idea is vital to a cartoonist.

It is a mistake to think that cartoon ideas reside only in comic strips, gag cartoons, and editorial cartoons. A humorous illustration has an idea behind it, too, although the idea may not be as obvious.

In doing a gag cartoon, an artist can aimlessly sketch out some scenes and allow ideas to happen along the way or even at the end. In doing an illustration, the artist cannot indulge in such a luxury. The idea almost always comes first in an illustration. As in a self-contained cartoon, the idea for an illustration is more important than the technique or style of the drawing. It takes a special skill to be able to read through copy and capture its theme and its moments of comedy.

A humorous illustration can move in on the central theme of the article or it can deal with details.

Let's say you have a humor column by Russell Baker to illustrate. The *New York Times Magazine,* where it appears, runs a different horizontal drawing at the top each week. This week Baker writes about President Ronald Reagan's New Federalism, a plan under which "the fifty governors will be almost as important as Presidents." In the column Baker imagines a situation in which each governor takes occupancy of the White House for a week, with the two weeks left over each year going to the President. What kind of an illustration would work? Patrick McDonnell came up with this idea: a lineup of governor-types, as in a theater line where people are waiting to buy tickets. One governor is leaving the room. On the other side, another is getting up from behind the desk (which is flanked with an American flag and the Presidential flag and which has the Presidential seal in front), and another, smiling, is about to sit down.

What kind of an idea would you come up with if you were to illustrate an article on the demise of the Fuller brush man, once so visible in door-to-door sales? Pat McLelland for *Northwest Magazine,* a section of the Portland *Oregonian,* showed a businessman with a suitcase on display next to the Neanderthal man at a museum. A bemused visitor, holding a printed guide to museum exhibits, is staring.

To accompany a *Dollar Sense* article giving advice on preparing wills, John Dearstyne wrestled with the idea of a family tree. Why not show a real tree, he decided, with funny faces buried in the leaves and branches. He came up with a motley collection of people, none of course mentioned in the article. The art provided a pleasant break between a previous article and the one at hand. Readers could see such people as "Pim" with no facial features ("no known records"), Bernard with a bird on his nose ("loved animals"), and a hippie-looking Francis ("black sheep").

To illustrate a cover blurb, "Home Is Where the Computer Is," *Newsweek* showed, as art, a painting of Whistler's mother, but the old woman, still facing to the left, was sitting at a computer keyboard and terminal.

Often the best idea for an illustration turns out to be more symbolic than realistic. An article about a cry-baby public official, for instance, could call for a caricature with running faucets for eyes. For a *Time* essay on burnout, a condition stemming from job fatigue, Cathy Hull drew and painted a businessman in a vest and rolled up sleeves with a candle and smoldering wick for the neck and head. It was obvious that the candle had just gone out.

For an article in *New York* on "Wounded City," an article examining deterioration there, Eugene Mihaesco showed in a full-page, full-color pastel drawing a big apple, New York's symbol, patched and breaking apart, a mattress-like spring poking out here, a puff of air coming out there, as though the apple were deflating, a hole near the bottom with cogs and bolts pouring out, a puddle of water under the apple, with one side propped up by boards. It was cartoon-like in a fine-arts Paul Klee way.

Optical illusions or visual surprises often work as humorous illustrations. J. C. Suares for a *Time* essay on daydreams shows a short-haired, middle-aged man looking into the mirror to do a self-portrait. The mirror reflects his ordinariness, but the painting he's working on shows him as a sinister and presumably adventurous gunman.

It often helps to show a person or object completely out of scale. For instance: the artist can place a tiny businessman in a giant desk seat, making him look a little like Lilly Tomlin's girl in a rocking chair. The artist is saying, of course, that the businessman is not up to his job, or, if he symbolizes a course of action, that the action is not adequate.

Another approach is to take a familiar pose or landmark and adjust it to make it fit a new situation or benefit a client. To illustrate an article on the tightening of rules allowing foreign doctors to immigrate to the United States, *MD* showed the Statue of Liberty using an arm not to hold high her burning lamp but instead to push back the words of the article's title: "The Medical Immigrants: End of an Era." A deodorant manufacturer in one of its campaigns used the statue as a symbol of people sure enough of their protection that they could lift their arms without fear of showing any damp spots.

An imaginative illustrator often works some comment on human nature into a drawing, even though the comment may not be absolutely necessary to the purpose of the illustration. Gil Eisner for a salary survey section in *Adweek* did a cover drawing showing four ad people holding their paychecks. Each person was trying to steal a glance at the check held by the person just ahead in the line. The person up front—a top executive—was looking back (without turning his head), obviously worried. Perhaps he felt that some junior executive was creeping up on him in salary.

putting
humor
to work

Because it works so effectively to make a point, humor wrongly used or humor gone bad can be a disaster in a publication. What's funny to some readers may offend others or not work at all for them. So, people who create humor often try it out on others before releasing it. Editors let humor cool for awhile and then reassess it before going to press.

Mere cleverness should not be mistaken for humor. Cleverness shows off. Humor digs in and does a job for the reader.

3
a matter of style

Sometimes style alone can carry a drawing from the ordinary to the humorous. A clever idea may not be necessary.

Most memorable styles evolve from an artist's studying the work of others, then abandoning those studies to develop independently. B. Kliban (*Whack Your Porcupine and Other Drawings* and other books) developed his unique style not merely by *copying* the work of other cartoonists but by actually *tracing* it. "You trace . . [a drawing by Ronald Searle] and it makes your hand move differently and you get sort of an understanding of other possibilities," Kliban observes.

Coming up with a unique style is an artist's most satisfying accomplishment, but it has a built-in problem. Scores of less imaginative artists will step in to copy it; and some editors and advertisers won't see that the imitations, however ingenious, never quite measure up to the original. The imitators will get many of the assignments.

Some styles can't be copied. Such a style belongs to the *New Yorker*'s Edward Koren, he of the hairy line, the creator of people-like animals (or are they animal-like people?). An earlier style never successfully copied belonged to

Basil Wolverton, who made his name in the comic-book field. Wolverton's fiercely ugly people looked as though they were made out of worms and bubbles.

Some styles are broad enough to allow for all kinds of variations by many artists, and they are important enough to take on names. Styles like art nouveau and art deco attach themselves to certain periods in history, then die, then come back again as they are rediscovered by young artists. Today all styles from all periods have their adherents, and a single issue of a publication is likely to serve as a showcase for several of them.

looseness versus tightness

Despite the great variety, drawing styles tend to fall into two broad categories: loose and tight.

The turtles of Figure 3.1 help define the styles. Wilhelm Butch drew the turtle on the left, using a pen to make relaxed and slightly irregular strokes. He didn't worry much about the pattern on the shell; he drew it rapidly with a few hastily drawn crossing lines. That's looseness. An anonymous artist drew the turtle on the right, also using a pen but with the line more firmly controlled. The pattern on the shell is a studied one. The second turtle is done in a tight style. Each turtle is delightful to behold; it would be difficult to pick one and call it better than the other.

You can find more obvious examples of the two styles, of course,

with tightness carried to precision sharpness and with looseness put almost out of control. What style an artist uses, loose or tight, and what degree of looseness and tightness the artist picks depend upon the mood of the material being illustrated and perhaps the nature of the publication's audience. Some artists can produce only loose, relaxed drawings while others seem always to draw with some rigidity.

A brush seems best suited to loose drawing while a firm pen point works well for tight drawings. An artist given to looseness gains admiration for spontaneity in the drawings, and there may be a feeling among editors that not much time goes into the execu-

Figure 3.1

tion. This feeling may be a mistake. The drawing might well be the result of countless quick tries, and what's turned in may have a number of patches where the artist had changes of opinion.

J. J. Sempé, a French artist whose sketch of Duke Ellington in *The Musicians by Sempé* appears to be quickly done, made about 100 tries before settling on the one that was used. Which is to say that

so far as humorous illustration is concerned, there should be no distinction between fees paid for one style or the other.

The celebrated Gluyas Williams had a pleasantly tight style. His fine lines set themselves down exactly where they should be. Each drawing was lovingly and carefully designed, with spots of black strategically placed to provide emphasis and balance. The humor in his drawings was gentle, wistful; his characters seemed a bit timid and confused.

Roy Doty is another humorous illustrator with a polished, tight style. His work appears everywhere—in books, in magazines, in ads, in corporate publications. For a time he produced a comic strip based on the popular *Laugh In* TV show.

Illustrators with loose styles include Robert Osborn and Charles Saxon, both of whom rely on sweeping brush strokes.

consistency

Good style asks for consistency. Marty Garrity gives us that in Figure 3.2. The weights on the bar are not perfectly round, as they would be in real life. Instead they are bulging and angular, like the figure. Garrity executes this drawing with bold brush strokes, to emphasize the strength of the

man, and uses two different Zipatone patterns to give the drawing additional character.

In Figure 3.3 another illustrator achieves style consistency by relying on circles and partial circles. Just about everything in the draw-

Figure 3.2
Courtesy of Martin E. Garrity and the Air Force Representative Office of Aerojet-General Corporation.

Figure 3.3
From Lawton Mackall's *Bizarre and Other Stories,*
Lieber & Lewis, New York, 1922.

ing is curved: the pillow, the pattern in the pillow, the chair arms and rocker legs, the man's arms and legs, the heads, the woman's curls, the pattern in her skirt. The drawing could be considered as an early example of art deco.

Another example (Figure 3.4) emphasizes the flat, design quality of the style. Curved lines contrast with straight or near-straight

Figure 3.4
From Lawton Mackall's *Bizarre and Other Stories,*
Lieber & Lewis, New York, 1922.

lines, and a set of small black triangles adds to the geometric look. Even the small, detailed dessert dish, put there as an item of contrast to the sweeping lines of the drawing, fits the art deco mold.

Art deco ("deco" stands for decoration) was something of a reaction against the earlier art nouveau style with its billowy, flowing lines that came not from science but from nature.

simplicity

Some drawings get by with all kinds of detail and asides, especially in satirical magazines for young adults. But the trend today, with readers facing so many distractions from TV and other media, is to simplify. Illustrators keep their cast of characters and their props to a minimum.

Simplicity is more important to a humorous drawing than masterful control of line and form. Cyril

Orlington's beach rescue scene (Figure 3.5), which I have doctored slightly for this book, proves that. No one would mistake the scene as great art, but it makes its visual point quickly with just a few crude curved lines for ocean and two detail-less figures silhouetted against a plain background and overlapped at the horizon line

Figure 3.5
From *Cautionary Catches*, Basil Blacknell, London, 1931.

sketch (Figure 3.6) for a dance program shows that on a pretty girl or woman, a nose can be dropped. The breasts, a bit modest for a Mindolovich-drawn female, suggest he had in mind here a specimen of tender years. That her forearms are Popeye-like is partly the result of haste, but it is also testimony to Mindolovich's mastery of the principles of foreshortening and perspective. Those arms are reaching out to the audience as well as up.

Beginning cartoonists make the mistake sometimes of working on drawings past quitting time, filling every blank area with fussy shading and other redundancy. This results not only in visual clutter but also in art that may not reproduce as well as simpler art. You could call such artists inferior decorators.

Figure 3.6
Courtesy of Dan Mindolovich.

and tide's edge. The woman's arms form a visual funnel that helps create the effect that she is being pulled under.

A cartoonist leaves out not only unnecessary lines but also facial features if they serve no apparent purpose. Dan Mindolovich's quick

vagueness versus clarity

An illustration doesn't always have to communicate clearly or all at once. Some illustrations, especially for books, can serve more as decorative elements, worth studying for their detail and their excellence of design. A little vagueness can be an asset.

Figure 3.7 by an anonymous artist shows a goat and a bent tree trunk and foliage; what exactly is going on here is not so important as the combination of lines and their decorative quality. The entire area seems to be filled in; yet the viewer senses good design at work. This is a piece of art that can be seen over a period of time without becoming tiresome.

Vagueness can enter into an illustration when the artist moves away from realism toward abstraction. Abstraction can eliminate specific details so that what is pictured has a more universal application. For instance, a figure

Figure 3.7
From *Gebrauchgraphik International* Magazine.

Figure 3.8

reduced to its simplest shape can represent just about anyone.

The black cat by an anonymous artist (Figure 3.8) shows what is meant by an abstract drawing. It is a cat greatly simplified, flattened, smoothed out. Two features—the ears and the slanted eyes—help identify the cat for what it is. Without these features, the drawing could represent sev-

eral animals. A less-confident artist might add whiskers to the drawing, but the whiskers might be too fine, too precise a detail, moving the drawing away from the abstract.

Actually, abstraction can work two ways. It can make things vague, especially if it is misinterpreted; or it can make things clear. Too far from a realistic base, it may merely suggest a mood or a major category. Carefully planned, it can actually be more legible than realism, as with some of our road-signs and building and park markings.

Figure 3.9
From Rudolf Modley's *Handbook of Pictorial Symbols*, Dover Publications, Inc., New York, 1976.

Figure 3.9 shows a couple of public signs relying on abstraction to make their points quickly. The woman at the left marks a beauty shop at the Seattle-Tacoma Airport. The group of heads at the right is one of many Swedish recreation symbols. It marks places where there are gatherings of spectators.

all in line

The nature of the outlines can help immeasurably to define a style. Some artists use thick strokes, some thin, some a combination of both, allowing their lines to swell and then to contract in the manner of a calligrapher doing Chancery Cursive. The thickness can be controlled by pressure, as when using a flexible penpoint or a brush, or by the shape of the point. A chisel point makes a thick line when pulled one way, a thin line when pulled another.

In the hands of artists with experimental styles, the lines can turn into start-and-stops, overlaps, and other segments. R. O. Blechman, who does mostly advertising illustrations and TV commercials, uses weak, squiggly lines that barely outline his near-formless characters. Don't be misled by the simplicity, the almost child-like quality of his work. The man spends hours composing his pictures and getting the lines just right.

Some drawings use only lines, of whatever quality, with no shading or black areas for emphasis or for bulk or a third dimension. In Figure 3.10, an anonymous artist uses mostly straight lines in broad sweeps to suggest a boat-dock scene. He sets the scene without

Figure 3.10

resorting to solid blacks or texture, although he does blacken his lines in the foreground to focus on the first boat and sea captain and to give his picture some depth.

Often an all-in-line drawing such as Figure 3.10 looks more professional, suggests more sophistication than a tediously shaded drawing, and it's easier—quicker—to execute. Nor does the artist have to worry about correctly indicating a light source.

in the shadows

Another approach to drawing is to use areas of black or tone instead of lines to identify shapes.

Although the ship and boat drawing (Figure 3.11) by an anonymous artist requires line reproduction and hence would be considered a line drawing, it is mostly in solid black or fine-line tone. There is little outlining. What you see is only part of the original, but enough to help you appreciate the strength of a drawing that goes beyond mere outlines.

You can do drawings like this as scratchboard drawings, as woodcuts or linoleum-block cuts, as paper cuttings, or as brush-and-ink drawings. You can get similar effects by asking the printer to reproduce a regular photograph in line rather than in the usual halftone. Such reproductions are called "line conversions."

Using black alone, with no intermediate tones, an artist creates a

Figure 3.11

true silhouette. Such a drawing makes for good change of pace in a comic strip; for example, a couple of detailed panels, then a panel with figures done in solid black. The device is as useful as, say, the change of camera angle or distance in a movie. Used by itself, a silhouette drawing stands out from more conventional drawings in a publication.

Paul Donelan, a freelance illustrator, provides an example of a silhouette drawing in Figure 3.12.

Figure 3.12
Courtesy of Paul Donelan.

41

Figure 3.13
From *LaVie Parisenne*.

Figure 3.14

Figure 3.15
From *Gebrauchgraphik International* Magazine.

Figure 3.16

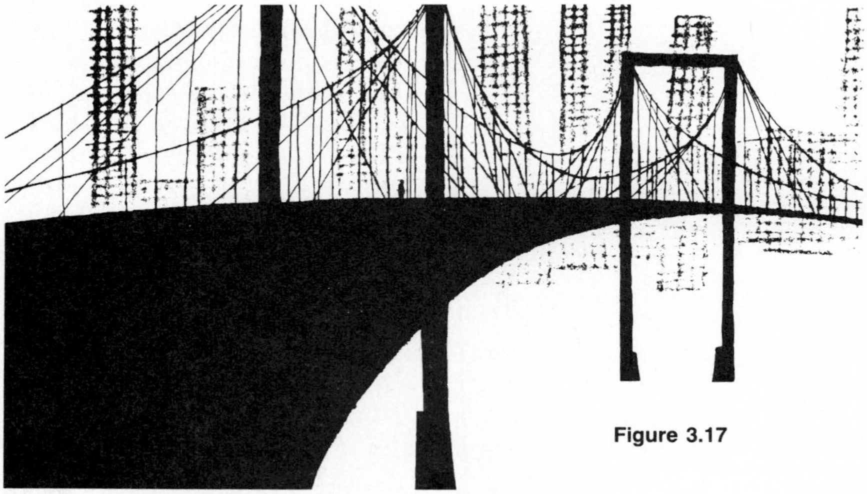

Figure 3.17

Silhouetting works best when what is shown is a side view or at least a three-quarters view. Head-on art usually doesn't lend itself to silhouetting.

Look at the character and feeling one anonymous nineteenth-cen-

tury artist got in the silhouette of a man on stage entertaining or appealing to an audience (Figure 3.13). A rough-textured edge adds to the effectiveness of this one.

An anonymous artist of the 1970s offers three black sheep, overlapping, as another example of the

silhouette technique (Figure 3.14). It is a nicely designed drawing because it so strongly holds together as a single unit. It also carries pleasing proportions, in that the distance from the top sheep's head to the middle sheep's head is different from the distance of the middle sheep's head to the lower sheep's head.

Another anonymous artist uses silhouetting to create the chickens shown in Figure 3.15, but in reverse.

Even in a shadow or silhouette drawing a few lines may come in handy to define edges in the light. The dancer in Figure 3.16, drawn anonymously, demonstrates a concern with where the light is coming from, in this case from the left and above. Logic tells the artist where, then, to brush in the black. It is not necessary, as this drawing shows, to put a shadow under the figure. Such a shadow would complicate the drawing.

Yet another anonymous artist in Figure 3.17 adds tone and some lines to a silhouette to make it more interesting. This is another drawing to study for its pleasing proportions. Note the varying distances set up by careful placement of the bridge uprights.

tools to do the job

When I was blissfully young I decided to become a baseball pitcher, because I felt I had the windup for the job in addition to other necessary mannerisms. Hours on end one spring I practiced throwing a tennis ball against the side of the garage where my grandparents lived. The secret, I was quite sure, lay in the grip on the ball, specifically where I placed my fingers. I tried throwing with one finger extended, then two, then three; then I tried throwing with the first and third finger extended. I experimented with any number of grips, including something close to what a knuckleballer would use. I did pretty well, really; at least nobody out in that lonely back yard got a hit off me.

The best I could do in real life on a sandlot team was to play first base, the least demanding fielding position on the team and a spot where someone as sluggish afoot as I was could do the least harm.

Pitching with a regulation size and weight baseball and from a distance 60′6″ from the plate, I discovered, was something quite different from what I had trained for.

Nor did my magic grip and flawless form dazzle any batter or, for that matter, get the ball up to the plate without taking at least one bounce. It became clear to me that my hands were too small and my frame too fragile to propel me to greatness as a pitcher. I didn't last beyond the summer even at first base.

Young cartoonists face something of the same disappointment when they pin their hopes on certain pen points, special papers, and mechanical shading techniques. These will do little to atone for a lack of drawing ability. The truth of the matter is that someone who can draw well can get by with an ordinary ballpoint pen and cheap typing paper. George Booth, the great *New Yorker* cartoonist, settles for a Bic pen for outlines, a felt-tip pen for shading, and ledger paper to carry his image. Jack Tippit, who does the syndicated panel *Amy*, sometimes uses a toothpick dipped in ink.

Still, some attention paid to the tools of the trade may be appropriate here. They do influence drawing style, if only psychologically, and they can seriously influence the reproduction quality of a drawing.

Ken Muse, an art and photography professor at Macomb County Community College, Warren, Michigan, thoroughly explains the use of countless drawing tools in his *The Secrets of Professional Cartooning* (Englewood Cliffs, N.J.: Prentice-Hall, Inc., 1981).

Muse does not think much of markers as tools for final drawing because their points quickly flatten and the lines fade. Still many cartoonists choose markers because they are so easy to use. They don't have to be dipped continually into an ink bottle, and the lines on the paper dry quickly. Even a nearly dried out nylon tip marker can still serve, provided the cartoonist is willing to settle for grayed lines, not unlike what a pencil might produce. My illustration for a newspaper feature on courtly manners (Figure 3.18) came from a Pentel I tried hard to get extra mileage from. The reproduction for a drawing like this often has to be highlight halftone rather than line.

Figure 3.18

Cartoonists who like lines that are consistent in thickness use a Rapidograph or some other technical fountain pen. When using a Rapidograph or one of those throwaway fine-line markers, like the Nikko Finepoint, you may have better luck with a hold that doesn't allow the instrument to rest in the crook between your thumb and first finger. Force the instrument up so that only your thumb and first two fingers grasp it; it then touches the paper at a 90-degree rather than a 45-degree angle. The valve (or whatever) that allows the ink to escape seems to work better that way. Anyway, the new hold might force you into a slightly different drawing style, and that could be a good thing.

For some drawing I like to use an ordinary fountain pen. I prefer a Mont Blanc classic, with its gold point, possibly because of the aesthetic pleasure I get from just holding it and looking at it. But fountain pens filled with writing ink, even with permanent black ink, can cause problems in reproduction because of grayness that often shows up in the lines. Pens that must be dipped into ink—India ink—are probably a better choice.

Higgin's ink is the old standby, and Pelican ink with its wider bottle neck is widely used, too. Muse's favorite ink is Artone extra-dense black. Muse says he likes to use it because he doesn't have to give black areas extra coats.

Flexible pen points such as the Gillott's 1290—the so-called "brush pen"—and the Gillott's 170 and 290 are favorites with cartoonists, but when they do lettering, as in balloons, cartoonists turn to firmer points of the kind made by Speedball. Or they use a Hunt Globe Bowl Pointed point. The Iserlohn point, made by

Brause & Co., has a reservoir at the top that makes frequent dipping unnecessary.

These pen points come in a variety of tip shapes and flexibilities. Art stores offer a bewildering choice. Cartoonists should try as many of the points and as many other drawing instruments as they can afford before settling for one. They should also investigate newly available tools from time to time to keep their drawing styles fresh, contemporary, and unpredictable.

Often a combination of tools can be used to make a single drawing. Dave Gerard, who does the syndicated panel *Citizen Smith*, uses a speedball B-6 or B-5$\frac{1}{2}$ pen and a Winsor & Newton No. 1 or 2 brush.

For some cartoonists nothing beats a red-sable watercolor brush. A quality brush of the kind made by Winsor & Newton is expensive, but with proper care it can last for years. A brush changes from making thin lines to making thick lines with just a little extra pressure, and it can move up the page as easily as down the page. Some cartoonists do everything with a brush, including lettering.

A brush should dip into an ink bottle only about halfway up the bristles, and the bristles should be reshaped to a point after each dip by rolling the brush against the inside neck of the bottle or on a piece of scratch paper.

A cartoonist involved in brush work needs, say, a No. 1 (fine point) for a general drawing and a No. 4 for filling in black areas. Not that you can't fill in black areas in other ways. Ed Sullivan uses a blunt, felt-tip black marker to fill in his black areas. He finds that the marker lays down the blacks faster than a brush would do, and he loses no time afterwards washing and reshaping a brush point.

A cartoonist tends to draw more rapidly when using a brush than when using a pen, and the cartoon tends to be looser. I often redo a section or two of a brush-drawn cartoon several times and paste the best pieces together. This means using lots of cheap paper. An expensive piece of illustration board intimidates me.

Paper and board choices make a difference. Smooth-finish sheets are best for fine-line, detailed work; rough-finish sheets are best for looser styles, especially when the work is done with a brush.

Bristol boards come in a kid finish (textured) or a plate finish (smooth). Illustration boards come in a cold-press finish (textured) or a hot-press finish (smooth). A textured finish accepts washes while still providing a workable surface for pen and ink. A smooth finish provides a surface for intricate pen and ink lines.

You can get Bristol boards in various plys, from 1 to 5. You can draw on either side. Sometimes one side has a different finish from the other. Illustration boards are really sheets of drawing paper mounted on stiff backing boards. You work only on one side. Illustration boards come in either single or double weights.

starting with a pencil

A pencil is best used for laying out a drawing prior to inking. Art gum, a Pink Pearl eraser, or a kneaded eraser eliminates any pencil lines after the ink has dried. Every cartoonist has made the mistake, at least once, of erasing too soon and bringing smudges to the drawing.

Sometimes an artist submits a pencil-only drawing to an editor and almost always feels disappointed at the weak showing the drawing makes in reproduction. If anything, the reproduction process weakens the already too-gray, partly shiny lines an ordinary lead pencil makes. If you choose pencil for your final drawing, choose one that has a grease-crayon lead, such as General's Layout Pencil No. 555. Or do what Jim Berry of *Berry's World* does. He uses an ordinary pencil to scrub on his lines, which are thick and uneven. Then he makes an office-machine copy of the drawing, a copy that drops out the middle tones. The result is a drawing with strong, crude lines that reproduce well when the work finally goes before the plate-maker's camera.

Some cartoonists rough in their drawings with a blue-lead pencil. Blue—or at least light blue—does not reproduce. There is no need to erase such pencil lines after they have been inked over.

Ed Sullivan uses an ordinary pencil to rough in his drawings on tissue sheets, then places them on a light table. He puts thin Bristol-board sheets over the roughed-in tissue sheets and draws directly in ink. This, too, means no pencil lines to erase.

Some cartoonists trace their pencil lines exactly. Cartoonists with looser styles use the lines only as rough guides. The finished drawings may be a far cry from the original sketches.

technique

Anything that makes a mark or that simply stands there in three dimensions, waiting to be photographed, qualifies as an illustrator's medium.

Pen and ink remains the most popular medium, especially in humorous illustration, because it yields so many effects and reproduces so clearly. Most editors and artists think of lines when they think of pen and ink, but there are other possibilities. Robert Mankoff, a gag cartoonist for the *New Yorker,* uses mostly dots to make his drawings. He derived his style, obviously, from the pointillist paintings of Georges Seurat and Paul Signac.

A scratchboard drawing represents another interesting variation from a pen-and-ink drawing. The scratchboard drawing of Lenin (Figure 3.19) by an anonymous artist illustrates the strength and flow of the medium. Such a drawing requires a coated, slick paper or board over which a coat of black ink has been painted. The artist uses a knife or sharp tool to scratch away the black to expose the white. The artist makes a drawing first on a sheet of tracing paper, then marks the back with white chalk, then traces the drawing on the scratchboard. Some scratchboard sheets come already inked. You can buy tools that

have a series of parallel points so that when you pull or push the tool across the black surface it makes several parallel lines at once.

The depressed couple at the right of Lenin represents scratchboard drawing of a different order: less formal, with stippling instead of lines. What lines there are, as in the man's arm, are scratched in haphazardly, in short strokes rather than long ones.

Some of the best humorous illustrations are done as paintings, with oils, acrylics, designer colors, or watercolors as the medium. A painting can sometimes carry humor more effectively than a line drawing can, mostly because we do not expect it in that medium.

Editor Gary Olsen of *Tracks,* an employee magazine published by John Deere for employees at Dubuque and Davenport, Iowa, wanted to show the home computer as the new member of today's family, so he commissioned Bill Ersland to paint the picture that appeared on the cover shown in Figure 3.20. Note that the computer, instead of saying "cheese," as a person might do, carries the word on the screen.

Figure 3.19

THE HOME COMPUTER—NEW MEMBER OF THE FAMILY?
THE UNPREDICTABLE ECONOMY—AN INTERVIEW WITH JOHN LAWSON
WE BUILD ONE FOR MR. JOHNSON

Figure 3.20
Courtesy of John Deere Company.

Figure 3.21

The style is painterly, with a kind of a Cézanne feel. The photo-album corners give the cover even more of a family feel, as though the picture were a snapshot in an album. A painting such as this usually runs in color, but it can also run in black and white, as it does in this reprinting, without losing a lot of its detail.

Pen-and-ink artists often work from their imaginations, but painters work from nature or from photographs. My own painted scene in Figure 3.21, although it has a cartoon feel, started with a long look at a printed photograph.

The most common painting technique used by cartoonists—especially gag cartoonists—is the wash drawing, which is nothing more than a watercolor, but done only in grays for black-and-white printing.

You begin a wash drawing by squeezing a tube of lampblack pigment onto a tray and mixing what you squeeze out (a small amount) with water. You want to establish several puddles, varying from light gray to dark gray. Or you can build your puddles with India ink. The trick is to move fast over the drawing, first applying light tones, then darker tones, trying not to overscrub or overpaint. Of course you ink in the outlines first. Erase any pencil lines before you begin the washes.

Wash tones in the newspaper illustration shown in Figure 3.22 help establish the idea of a light source over a too-talkative prisoner, although in applying the washes I didn't worry a lot about establishing shadows correctly. I was more interested in roundness and substance for the drawing.

Many artists approximate a wash-drawing technique by using gray felt markers. They are quicker, and they offer a more even tone. They come in both warm and cool grays. The warm grays reproduce best.

Still another technique involves paper cutting. You can use ordinary scissors on black paper or you can cut black paper with a sharp, fine knife and paste the result on white paper. You can also make stencils, and press ink through them onto paper for art with a strong, crude look.

Glenn Hanson, a journalism professor at the University of Illinois, creates shadow areas on his sketch of Paul Sullivan (Figure 3.23), professor at the University of Evansville, by cutting scraps of

47

Figure 3.22

Figure 3.23
Courtesy of Glenn Hanson.

printed material and pasting them down at various angles. The technique is appropriate in that Sullivan is involved in the graphics end of journalism education.

A tool that has regained some of its earlier popularity is the airbrush, which allows for superrealism and tones with polished softness. *Esquire*'s famous Vargas girls were executed with an airbrush. (See Alberto Vargas' and Reid Austin's *Vargas*, New York: Harmony Books, 1978.) In using an airbrush you must first cut friskets to mask those portions of a drawing you don't want influenced by the spray.

Robert Grossman, the caricaturist, often—but not always—uses an airbrush technique to create his faces. The technique seems particularly appropriate in his portrait of Hugh Hefner, founder of *Playboy*. Hefner's head is nearly buried between two huge breasts, with only his thin mouth and jutting jaw and pipe showing. The nipples act as eyes. Airbrushing

made the skin smooth and centerfold-like.

Grossman, a man of many techniques, did his Fats Domino caricature for the "Cooking with Fats" album cover in clay. He also did a caricature of a walking, smiling piano in clay for the back cover.

Franz Xavier Messerschmidt, who created his works in the late 1700s, was one of the first to do caricatures as sculptures. Such works, when they serve as illustrations, must be photographed; the photographs are run as halftones.

Alexander Calder, who invented "mobiles" in the early 1930s, created caricatures by bending wire. (He drew more ordinary caricatures for the national *Police Gazette* in the 1920s.)

The medium used is one thing; how it is used is something else. Henry Major, a caricaturist of the 1920s and 1930s, used a soft-lead pencil or grease crayon and sketched from life, not from photos. That was common enough. But he kept his eye always on the model, never looking down at the paper.

I used an ordinary nylon-tip marker to draw the jogging woman who changed into her sweat clothes in too much of a hurry (Figure 3.24), but I held the tool palm down, fingers above, thumb below. You lose a little control that way, but you get more sweep

Figure 3.24

to your lines. It is a good way to loosen your style a bit.

The texture of the paper can also affect the drawing style. Alan E. Cober, magazine and book illustrator, likes to work on textured paper. This slows his pen so that it doesn't get ahead of his thinking.

I used quick strokes, sometimes letting the brush nearly run out of ink before re-dipping it, on Glarco, a textured paper, for a newspaper illustration (Figure 3.25) that accompanied a feature on parolees and the supervision they get. That's a parolee you see saying No to a drink, with his supervisor peering around the corner. The shading comes from a chunk of lithographic crayon pulled quickly across the paper's surface, without much regard for the figure's outlines. This gave them a roundness and informality that seemed appropriate.

Figure 3.25

the willingness to experiment

What makes Saul Steinberg so admired by other cartoonists is his compulsion to experiment, not only with style but also with subject matter. It is impossible to describe his work (you see it in the *New Yorker* and in book collections), but it deals with surrealism and parody and even puns.

Steinberg is the dean of experimentation among humorous illustrators, but there are—and were—many others.

Figure 3.26 goes back a long way—to a 1908 issue of *Judge*—to show an illustration experiment: doing it all with a single line, presumably never lifting the pen from the paper. The drawing is called "The Line Up." That's the

way baseball players looked back then. "Baseball is not considered a dangerous sport," said an article above the illustration, "although it causes a gigantic mortality among grandmothers each year." The artist's first name is Harvey. (It is impossible to make out the last name, but you can see that the signature is part of the single-line drawing.)

In Figure 3.27 Georg Goedecker uses geometric or partly geometric shapes and perfectly straight lines to draw two faces. These shapes are placed in a carefully controlled pattern. Facial elements, including wrinkles, are

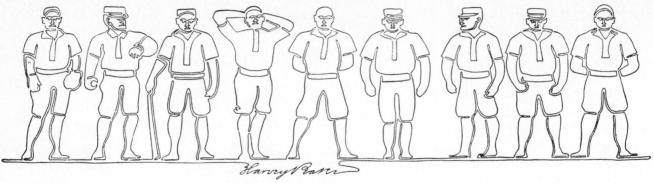

Figure 3.26
From *Judge*.

Figure 3.27
From *Advertising Art in the Art Deco Style*, Dover Publications, Inc., New York, 1975.

Figure 3.28
From Harry Furniss's *The Confessions of a Caricaturist*, T. Fisher Unwin, London, 1901.

Figure 3.29

reduced to simple and repetitious forms.

Harry Furniss, a late nineteenth and early twentieth century British caricaturist for *Punch*, created faces by drawing smaller versions of them and using the smaller versions for noses, ears, etc. He called his sketches "puzzle-headed people." Figure 3.28 shows one example. The miniature faces appear in the background and on the clothes as shading.

Figure 3.29 shows another experiment—by an anonymous Soviet artist—in which the main art is constructed with a pattern of its miniature versions.

changing a style

Having finally developed a style, a cartoonist tends to stick with it. This could be a mistake. Times change, and so do editors' preferences.

To shake loose from a style that has grown stale or gone out of date, you might want to try drawing with tools you have never used before. If you're a Rapido-graph addict, switch to a nylon-tip marker. If you are a pen-and-ink artist, become a brush-and-ink artist. If you've drawn everything in line, try washes.

Bill Gallo, sports cartoonist for the *New York Daily News*, advises cartoonists to go into oil or acrylic painting—not that your paintings necessarily will be reproduced, but doing them will broaden your basic drawing skills and heighten your sense of design. Learning to paint can result in a looser drawing style.

To get even further away from a style you've lived with for a long time, try making a drawing with your eyes closed. Or try drawing without lifting your pen or pencil from the paper. Right-handed Saul Steinberg sometimes draws with his left hand because the unexpected is more likely to happen.

You might want to try an experiment outlined by Betty Edwards in her *Drawing on the Right Side of the Brain* (Los Angeles: J. P. Tarcher, Inc., 1979). Try drawing the figure and props as though they were upside down. Wait until you have completed the entire drawing before turning it right-side up and then marvel at the distortions you have achieved. Deliberately distorting things in a drawing for some people is as hard as deliberately singing off-key.

Another way to achieve a different feel is to draw the space around the figures and props rather than the figures and props themselves.

A style should be always evolving, the drawing improving. Jeff MacNelly, the editorial cartoonist and comic-strip artist, told students at the University of Oregon that a cartoonist who can look back at earlier work and not be dissatisfied with it probably is not "going places."

Not that changing a style always pays off. Sometimes an artist disappoints an editor because what's offered is not the expected. John Geipel, British author and cartoonist, tells of a cartoonist friend in London who enjoyed a long engagement as a political cartoonist on the *Evening News*. Geipel says in a letter: "During the late 1960s, his style, which had previously been very realistic, began to evolve into the much simpler—and much funnier—style he uses today. The editors, sensing the stylistic change, became incensed by the increasing simplicity of [his] drawing—although his gags were as amusing as ever. His attempts to reason with them—that the new style was much wittier than the old—had no effect, and he became torn between the urge to develop his new style (which his fellow cartoonists admired) and the need to earn his crust by pleasing the editors, who demanded more lines for their money! Eventually, the poor chap had a minor breakdown and left the *News*. Luckily, he's continued to enhance his reputation—by giving his own, intuitive style full expression, but his case can hardly be [considered] unique. . . ."

Geipel himself, while a cartoonist on Fleet Street, found it necessary to give in to the "inflexibly philistine attitude of many editors" by putting "as much detail as possible into my drawings merely to enhance the illusion that I was giving my clients their money's worth."

4

attention to detail

Kenneth Bird, who signs his drawings "Fougasse," said of Gluyas Williams that he was "a superb noticer." It is a quality all cartoonists try to cultivate. Persons in the company of cartoonists are likely to feel they are always being sketched, whether or not the cartoonists hold pencils in their hands and sketchbooks in their laps.

What cartoonists see is likely to be different from what other people see. When gag cartoonist Virgil Partch—better known as "Vip"—visited the University of Oregon to deliver a series of lectures on comic art he was bemused by a mobile and pool outside the art school. Figure 4.1, a brush drawing, registers his reaction.

Cartoonists often carry sketchbooks with them to record what they see. The sketchbooks are used later as reference. Occasionally a rough sketch can be used as the final art for an assignment.

Some cartoonists feel embarrassed to sit in a public place making sketches. Some people, no doubt, resent being used as models. One way of getting around the problem is to use a small notebook and appear to be writing rather than drawing.

A student putting up with large lecture classes has a marvelous opportunity to fill a sketchbook with useful poses. The unwary instructor, seeing the furious activity with a Pentel or Rolling Writer, can only conclude that the student is caught up in an enthusiasm for the course material and eager to do well in an upcoming examination. I am not fooled, however, by students in my Caricature and Graphic Humor class who appear unusually eager to record my every word. Having spent a good part of the term celebrating artists who look hard and draw mean, I know I stand at the front of the classroom, a near-perfect nonmoving target. The likenesses slipped surreptitiously

under my door after class confirm it, and only a well-developed sense of modesty prohibits my showing some of those sketches here.

It can work the other way around. Students make inviting targets for teachers to draw. Eric May, who teaches art at Kent State, using a Rapidograph on tracing vellum, shows in Figure 4.2 what students look like to him as he struggles to impart knowledge at 7:45 in the morning. (They get up early in the Midwest.)

Cartoonists not only do primary research, sketching from life, but also do secondary research, working from photographs and newspaper and magazine halftones clipped to build up their "morgues." True, much of what cartoonists produce for publication bears little resemblance to reality; still, they need a base from which to take flight.

Figure 4.1
Courtesy of Virgil Partch.

Figure 4.2
Courtesy of Eric May.

Whatever their degree of zaniness, cartoonists still are bound by certain accuracies. Rowland B. Wilson endured criticism from a *Playboy* reader after his cartoon involving a plane landing on a Monopoly game was published. Wilson showed houses and hotels on the board which were, the reader said, in violation of the game rules. Douglas Borgstedt's depiction of President Reagan as a right-hand pitcher in *Editor & Publisher* brought a quick letter of reprimand from a reporter/reader. The President, the letter said, was "a born and bred southpaw."

Borgstedt, it turned out, had done his homework well. The letter-writer was wrong. A member of the White House staff wrote Borgstedt that Reagan *does* throw—and write—with his right hand. Borgstedt was moved to observe, then, that his critic had been "way off base, and I'm afraid we must send him to the showers."

the figure

A few cartoonists enjoy drawing props and scenes as much as figures, but figures remain the staple of most humorous illustrations. To do them justice—to distort them properly—the artist needs to deal with them first realistically. Nothing helps more than drawing from life.

Quick sketches of the figure in action or near-action benefit the cartoonist most. What's important are general shapes and thrusts. Details can be ignored, as in my sketches in Figure 4.3, some taking no more than seconds to do.

The three sketches in Figure 4.4 took a bit more time to do, with just a little more attention paid to form and dimension. In a case like this an artist does not first pencil in the lines and then trace over them in ink. The idea is to work directly with pen on paper, feeling the figure more than tracing it, drawing more with eye than with hand, allowing a few false starts to remain with those lines that are more definitive.

After such warming up exercises, the artist spends a little more time

Figure 4.3

Figure 4.4

Figure 4.5

with each sketch, but still no longer than a few minutes. A fine nylon-tip marker produced the sketches in Figure 4.5.

The artist comes close to converting serious drawings to humorous ones by becoming more fanciful in the handling of the tool. Proportions begin to expand and contract more for interest than for accuracy. The artist begins to pay more attention to the quality of line, which, in the sketches in Figure 4.6, grow thick, then thin, and take on a good deal of character of their own.

Drawing from life is a little like taking notes for a class. The very act of putting what you see on

Figure 4.6

paper impresses it upon your mind. When called upon later to produce a near nude, you don't have to look for a model, check an earlier life drawing, or consult a book on anatomy. The figure rolls easily off the tip of your drawing instrument.

The figure is fun to draw, but unfortunately for the artist the market for true nudes limits itself mostly to the skin magazines—to gag cartoons there. But the market expands to all media when the nudes are at least partially dressed, as in my gym scene in Figure 4.7.

RoyPAUL

Figure 4.7

A familiarity with the figure is evident here, even though the sure, tight brush strokes eliminate a lot of detail. Male figures—or muscular figures—come off best with short, angular strokes; female figures deserve longer, rounder strokes.

Knowing the figure helps greatly in dressing it, especially in deciding where to put the folds and wrinkles. For some drawings wrinkles are best pressed out. They only add clutter. For other drawings, wrinkles provide a necessary dimension. Looking at such drawings you can feel the pulls and pileups of cloth. The stance taken by the gentleman in Figure 4.8, for instance, becomes more dramatic because of the pull of the suit at the waist and the pileups at the shoulder and legs. The wrinkles help tell us the man is leaning backwards. Perhaps he is getting ready to surprise someone with a gift. If you had to illustrate the line, "Which hand?" this might be the way to do it. (Presumably, the author would have made some reference to a big nose and a jutting chin.)

Figuring out where wrinkles go is a matter of logic, but turning to a "Standing Figures" file in a cartoonist's morgue helps get things right. A clothed figure makes use

Figure 4.8

of two kinds of wrinkles: those resulting from tension or pulling of the cloth and those resulting from too much cloth loosely gathered. The cartoonist using wrinkles on a figure sets up a contrast between the two. You can't have one without the other.

A cartoonist takes all kinds of liberties with the human figure. Nor do clothes get in the way of what the cartoonist wants to say. The build on Miss Buxley in *Beetle Bailey* is important enough to

Figure 4.9

Mort Walker's gag that he keeps her in an outdated miniskirt, the better to torment the poor general.

The feeling-good gentleman of Figure 4.9 flexes his muscles, and they show through his coat sleeves, as though the sleeves were not there.

Because the figure was used as a small-space newspaper illustration, I made little attempt to define the coat's lapels or even its bottom edge. Using a dry-brush technique, I allowed the black to run dry in a few places to give the figure some roundness and dimension.

the head

In a life drawing class, the head gets only scant attention. Taking only a seventh or an eighth of the body's total height, it turns out to be little more than a rough oval in the drawing. The artist is too far from the model to see it clearly; nor is there time to concentrate on it. The entire sweep of the figure is what's important.

In a cartoon meant for publication, the head becomes important.

Many cartoonists make it much bigger than it would be in real life. A cartoon figure may be three heads or only two heads high.

Heads get even bigger in proportion to body size as you draw children and babies. The heads on these young citizens are mostly

Figure 4.10

circular, and, like their arms and legs, bulge with fat. Stubby fingers and peculiar poses for hands are part of the picture, too. If a baby must cry, you should really open the mouth, close the eyes, raise the eyebrows, and tip the head backwards, as in Figure 4.10.

Only in sports cartoons and in some editorial cartoons is the head smaller than in real life. It is small on a cartoonist's athlete so the viewer can concentrate on the remarkable body motion provided. It is small on the politician shown in an editorial cartoon so the viewer can appreciate the fact that the politician is a pinhead.

Adult heads of whatever size in a cartoon exist often without foreheads and chins. The idea is to use all available space for eyes, noses, and mouths, important as emotion indicators. Younger faces, though, need plenty of forehead space. That space suggests youthfulness. The eyes, then, go about halfway down from the top of the head on a child. Intellectuals also show up in cartoons with large foreheads.

Most of the how-to-draw-cartoons books suggest that, to draw heads, you should start with a circle and build from there. Such instruction goes back at least to the nineteenth century. F. Opper in an 1894 issue of *Puck,* the comic weekly, provided some "Easy Lessons in Caricature, for Little Learners." Figure 4.11 reproduces a few of the sixteen heads that went with the feature. The first few are generic; the last four belong to well-known people of the time: Joseph Pulitzer, the newspaper publisher; Charles A. Dana, editor of the New York *Sun;* a Senator Peffer, and a Senator Hill. This series of sketches shows how a few lines can completely change a face.

An elongated oval, a triangle, an upside-down triangle, or a combination of these can also serve as the basic shape for a face. Then, with all the hairdos available, you have any number of possibilities. David Levine, the caricaturist, thinks of a head (and its face) as landscape, with all the possibilities

for twists and turns that a landscape presents.

What kind of eyes, nose, mouth, and ears you put on a face makes a difference; *how* you place them on the head makes an even bigger difference. The eyes and their placement are particularly important. Dots alone often are enough for eyes; the eyebrows do most of the work in defining the expression. Raised, they indicate fright or surprise. Lowered, they indicate anger.

Charles Addams does a lot with round circles, drawn with a bold line, the pupils small—almost lost—inside. The look he gets with these eyes is sinister. Don Wright, editorial cartoonist for the *Miami News,* used Addams-like eyes on an official of the Tobacco Institute shown sitting at his desk, the window of his office revealing a graveyard with tombstones extending far into the distance. The official, looking smug, is saying, "Prove it!" (The cartoon was prompted by the 1982 Surgeon General's Report linking, more clearly than ever, cigarette smoking with cancer and other diseases.)

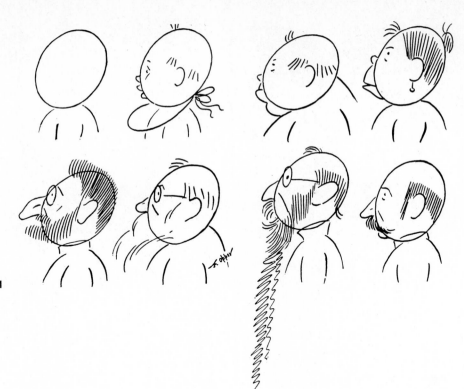

Figure 4.11

Perhaps the most famous comic-character eyes belong to Little Orphan Annie: those pupil-less ovals. Though they bear Harold Gray's imprint, Tom Bloom appropriates them for the faces of the figures he puts into his *New York Times* illustrations.

Facial expressions, where possible, should be implemented with hands. You say more with hands, sometimes, than with the mouth and eyes. The cartoonist believes in body language.

Figure 4.12 shows an I-couldn't-help-it fellow and an Oh-my-God! lady, both depending on hands to convey their expressions more fully.

The timid illustrator (Figure 4.13), drawn for one-time showing in a column I do for *Communication World,* a publication of the International Association of Business Communicators, advertises his shyness not only by a worried expression but also by the finger he puts in his mouth.

In the drawing in Figure 4.14, a man who's "had it up to here" uses his right arm and hand to demonstrate. The lowered, straight-across eyebrows and the turned-down mouth establish his

disgust. Well fed and well dressed, with his hair closely cropped, he appears to be pure Republican, and you get the impression that high taxes may well be what's bothering him.

Figure 4.12

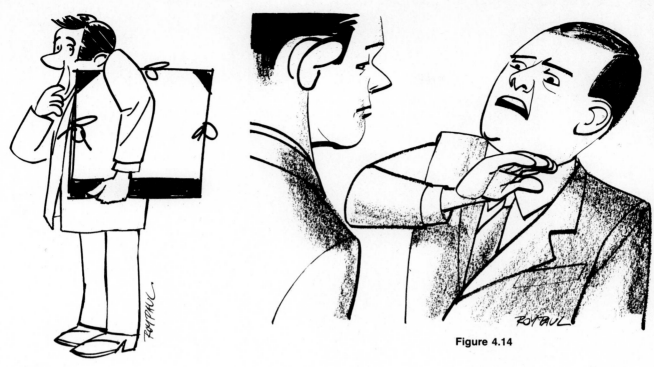

Figure 4.13

Figure 4.14

the hand

Its complicated configuration and its great flexibility make the hand difficult for some artists to draw. There are ways around the problem, of course, but as an artist you can't go through life indefinitely putting hands in pockets.

Once you've put aside your awe, you can as an artist have as much fun with the hand as with the figure itself. The two sketches in Figure 4.15 depend to a considerable extent on the handling of hands. For the dancing couple, I have set off the hands against the pure black background of the man's suit. I have made the violin player's hands bigger than normal, even though the sketch is reasonably realistic, in order to help the reader savor the detail of the fingers and thumb.

In drawing hands, as in drawing figures, it is a good idea at first to stay as close to reality as time allows. Your own nondrawing

hand serves as a willing model. You should use your drawing hand as a model as well, studying it in a pose first, then drawing it from memory, coming up with a sketch, say, like the one in Figure 4.16, done in bold brush strokes and grease crayon.

Figure 4.17 shows hands as they are used in several actions. The hands here push away, grasp, point, and lift. Note the simple, almost abstract shape the cop's hand takes. Hands must be drawn with conviction. They should grasp firmly.

Figure 4.18 shows hands used for holding books. In poses such as this, some of the hand is hidden. Sometimes it's the thumb, sometimes it's the fingers that don't show.

Figure 4.15

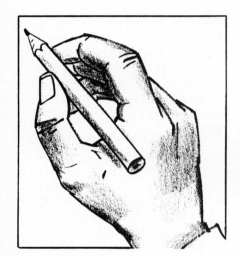

Figure 4.16

Figure 4.17

PovPAUL

Figure 4.18

call
for action

Nobody moves routinely in a cartoon. People sit, stand, walk—with character. Cartoonists can do a lot with walking because they have so many walking styles to choose from. Figure 4.19 shows a man—not necessarily an old man, but see what happens when you put a beard on somebody—walking while using his arms as though they were wings. The walk is all the more interesting here because it comes as front view.

Figure 4.19

That the figure has but three digits on each hand should bother no one by now. Film animators, to cut down on drawing time, went to under-fingered hands many years ago, and many print-medium cartoonists followed suit.

One mark of the professional is a willingness to provide front views rather than easier-to-draw side views. To do front views, the cartoonist has to solve the problem of making noses, arms, and legs appear to protrude. That's done through foreshortening: cutting down on perceived lengths and making what's up front much bigger than logic tells you it should be.

As an assignment in one of my Caricature and Graphic Humor classes at the University of Oregon, I asked students to depict a middle-aged man reacting to a political speech by Jane Fonda on TV. I wanted action in the picture, no matter what reaction was depicted. Figure 4.20 shows Brian Christ's handling of the assignment.

It works for a number of reasons. In the first place, Christ has converted the man's body and limbs to a series of diagonal planes. The angry facial expression and the sweat marks add to the mood. The man has a strong grip on the rolled up paper, seen clearly because of the oversize hand. A series of overlaps unites the props and figure, and they arrange themselves to form a strong basic silhouette.

Figure 4.20
Brian Christ

Christ shows us what is essentially a front view, and concentrates on the back rather than the front of the TV set. He thus avoids drawing Miss Fonda herself.

Action in a cartoon does not confine itself to walking, throwing, or other activities designed to work up a sweat. It belongs to standing or sitting figures as well. Anyone at a desk pushes papers around with enthusiasm. Someone playing a musical instrument plays it as though it were a wild animal to be calmed. Note the energy expended by the fellow mastering the cello in Figure 4.21.

Action often comes from the correct coordination of one part of the body with another. To depict the high-octave singer of Figure 4.22, I put arms to work as well as mouth. Pulling against each other horizontally, the arms here are meant to contrast with the vertical pull of the lady's generous mouth. This is a high-pitched operatic singer at work, of course; I'd handle a country singer or a rock musician quite differently.

Figure 4.22

Often a series of diagonal thrusts in a drawing gives it the action it needs. Diagonal lines convey a sense of falling. Horizontal lines suggest repose. Vertical lines imply dignity or stateliness.

Straight swish lines, puffs of smoke, and short, slightly curved lines can help the action, but these should be considered as crutches, to be avoided if possible. Another more effective device is partially to redraw a figure several times, letting the sketches appear one right after the other. This is as close as a print-medium artist can come to imitating the animator's technique.

Paul Kim and Lew Gifford, in an ad selling their animation service (they've been partners in New York since 1958), imitate animation technique—and suggest the passage of some time—in a single panel (Figure 4.23). That's Kim walking behind Gifford.

A running figure would be shown with legs more widely spread and lifted up off the ground. You do this, of course, by putting down a shadow well below the figure. You'd keep the figure's feet well off the ground.

Action involving throwing or swinging a bat or racket works best when shown at the beginning of the throw or swing, the figure leaning well back in readiness, or at the end, possibly with the figure off balance. Showing the action in the middle of its arc usually does not work. The figure appears to be frozen in awkwardness.

Figure 4.21
From an early issue of *Harper's;* artist unkown.

Figure 4.23
Courtesy of Kim & Gifford Productions Inc.

the value of props

Add a prop or two and you have all the ingredients you need to make a cartoon statement in a closeup.

Take smokers (please). There are many ways to portray them. One of Mort Walker's great contributions to cartoon art is the cigarette stuck to the lower lip of a character with his mouth wide open. You've seen people like that. When they pull the cigarette away, part of the skin of the lip goes with the cigarette.

The two smokers in Figure 4.24 may also be familiar to you. The fellow on the left is one of those deep-suckers who almost turn inside out while smoking. He scratches his cheek absently while he waits for the draw to be over. The other fellow, his age showing, does his thinking with a cigarette, propping up his chin with his thumb. No doubt sales at his discount office-supply store are on the skids.

The props can be but vaguely suggested. You don't have to draw everything in the scene with precision. Nor do you have to make room for props in their entirety. Just the hint of a prop will do. By keeping the props in weak lines and light tones, you can make figures stand out. The church background in Figure 4.25, by an anonymous artist, serves as an example; the scene is ready for a firm drawing of a priest.

My sketch for a newspaper feature on early times (Figure 4.26) suggests a wooden boardwalk with the edge of two or three boards. It also suggests recent rain, with a kidney-shaped puddle and several parallel reflection lines.

Props in cartoons often lag behind real-life props in their design because modern versions of familiar objects often smooth themselves out, losing some of their character. An old Underwood No. 5, for instance, looks more like a typewriter than a modern, low silhouette plug-in.

Even cartoon buildings may seem to some viewers as dated. What should you show to represent a church, for instance? Around the nation the various denominations

Figure 4.24

65

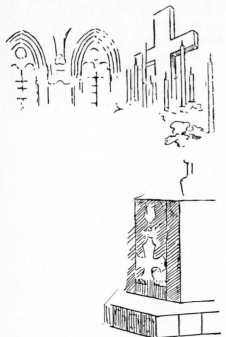

Figure 4.25

Figure 4.26

Figure 4.27

were putting up some remarkably un-church-like buildings in the 1980s. But in a humorous illustration would any of these say "church" to the unsuspecting reader? Could a cartoonist afford to show something other than a building with arched windows and doors, steep steps, with a glassed-in bulletin out front announcing the sermon? Can the cartoonist, without including a robe or a turned-around collar, show a minister out on the street with ordinary citizens and expect readers to recognize the man's calling?

Trees often play a role in cartoon scenes, if only to say "outdoors." A cartoonist tends to draw the same tree, scene after scene. That's unfortunate, because trees come in so many varieties. A few sketching trips, just to observe trees—their trunks, their foliage— can be useful to a cartoon-

ist. Figure 4.27 offers a tree sampling.

The first, a detail from a drawing in *Bizarre Magazine,* is a simple line drawing that anchors the narrow trunk to the ground, like a hand with its fingers spread out. The branches high on the trunk move out at uneven intervals. Leaves are like lips or narrow lemons, and they overlap.

The second tree is a study in pattern: stripes and catacombs. Together, they form a recognizable tree silhouette.

The third, the most abstract of the three, is really an early American stencil. It is strong, simple, crude, with a weeping-willow look.

the magic of drawing

You suggest distance by drawing people in the foreground bigger than people in the background, by putting darker tones into the foreground, by including more detail, and even by using darker, firmer lines.

When an item thrusts itself forward toward the viewer, you make the part that's close more massive than the part that remains in the background. James

Montgomery Flagg's World War I "Uncle Sam Wants You" poster showed a large, pointing hand on an arm that was shorter than normal, an arm that grew thinner as it receded to the shoulder. We call such a phenomenon "fore-shortening."

To give an item all three of its dimensions, despite the fact that it is shown on a two-dimension surface, and also to suggest distance, you establish a horizon line (it need not be shown). If the item is cube-like, its parallel lines, if they were extended, would merge at vanishing points, one at the left, one on the right, on the horizon line. This is only a simplistic explanation of perspective; to go into it more deeply would require too much space. Ernest W. Watson's *How to Use Creative Perspective* (New York: Van Nostrand Reinhold Company) is one of the most useful books on the subject. Although published originally in 1955, it is still in print as a paperback.

Perspective lines in most drawings move toward vanishing points on a horizon line at the middle or upper middle of the scene. The drawing in Figure 4.28 by an anonymous artist shows that lowering the horizon line (it runs through the fence) can make a drawing more dramatic. The viewer of this drawing looks up at the house, making the house more imposing. Such a view is called a "worm's-eye view."

Alan Rose's gas-line drawing done in washes (Figure 4.29) provides a good example of a bird's-eye view with a *high* horizontal line. The drawing, published here for the first time, could serve as an illustration for a feature on gasoline consumption or the gasoline shortage.

Rose's drawing makes use of a different kind of perspective. Instead of extending to two vanishing points on the horizon line, the

Figure 4.28

Figure 4.29
Courtesy of Alan Rose.

67

lines of the building and the lot extend to a single vanishing point. This is because it's a head-on shot instead of a three-quarters view.

A gag cartoon which Harley L. Schwadron did for an American Bar Association journal showed a judge with a wedge-shaped sign on his desk. From the front it said: "Your Honor." From the back it said: "My Honor." How to show the front and the back? Schwadron did it by focusing from above—using a bird's-eye view.

Sometimes in a humorous illustration you may want to ignore the rules of perspective by showing a full, flat front view of an object as well as one of its sides. Do your drawing as you would if you were in a mechanical drawing class, with parallel lines never converging at a point on a horizon line. Let design and pattern overshadow reality.

Sometimes you ignore true scale. The more realistic the art, the more effective wrong scale can be. People expect things to be out of whack in a cartoon; when they find distortion in a photograph or a realistic painting they are surprised. Figure 4.30 shows some realistic halftone art with unusual scale. You can feel the limpness of the undersized character, the enormity of whose job has plumb tuckered him out.

Figure 4.31 makes a family riding in a small car outrageously over-

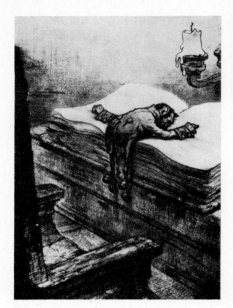

Figure 4.30
From *Album: Fifty Years of Soviet Art*, Graphic Arts, Moscow, n.d.

size, but the drawing, for a newspaper feature, pointed to the move to small cars back when most people rode around in comfortably large V-8s. My choosing to depict the small car as a convertible made it easier to show the people.

A three-quarters view like this is more interesting than a side view

Figure 4.31

because more of the car shows and the car has a solid look. Three-quarters views—and front and back views—may be harder to draw, but the extra effort is worth it, whether you're showing objects or people—or animals. Figure 4.32 shows a rear three-quarters view of a dog given roundness by shading that allows lightness at the outside edges. The drawing is rather loosely and hastily drawn by an anonymous artist, but you sense a real professional at work here.

Figure 4.32

A humorous drawing can show things that more conventional art pieces cannot. One way to show the impossible is to rely on printed sound effects. Jeff Mac-Nelly in a *Shoe* episode needed to show soggy cornflakes. He simply drew a bowl and lettered "SOG" above it, allowing a short wavy line or two to run from the bowl to the "SOG."

optical illusion

Optical illusions can be useful to the artist wanting to create double-take art or art that stands out from other pieces. An anonymous artist for an eighteenth century engraving shows "The Isle of Man" as a sleeping woman (Figure 4.33).

Artists and editors interested in optical illusions should study the surrealistic, eccentric work of M. C. Escher, the Dutch artist (1898–1972) who often offered the reader several viewing points in a single beautifully drawn scene. *The Graphic Work of M. C. Escher* (New York: Ballantine Books, 1971) is one collection.

Escher has provided the inspiration for many modern insignias and illustrations. Editorial cartoonists, for instance, have borrowed his never ending staircase to show that wages and prices keep going up.

Figure 4.33

composition

Artists who draw well and humorously are easy enough for an editor to find, but artists who put what they draw into pleasing and useful arrangements—artists who *design* their drawings—are rare. It would probably profit a would-be cartoonist at an early stage to put more time into design studies than in drawing classes.

The elements in a cartoon drawing should fit together like the elements in a fine painting. Too often cartoonists on assignment begin to draw aimlessly, without worrying about how one figure relates to another and how the figures and props fit into their settings. The best cartoonists plan their settings first, then work in the figures and props. These cartoonists have in mind a light source, and they know, early in the drawing, where the horizon line will be.

Good cartoonists follow long established principles of design. For instance: contrast. Every drawing needs contrast to make it interesting. The contrast comes from showing something large along with something small, something straight along with something wavy, something dark along with something light. Figure 4.34, drawn by an anonymous artist, contrasts the black of a woman's eyes with fine lines that define the remainder of the face, the hair, the neck. As a bonus we get a middle tone in the horizontal fine-line shading that gives a third dimension to the nose.

Figure 4.34

69

The contrast can startle. In Figure 4.35, an unlikely woman sits in a French rococo arm chair, spilling ashes, probably unaware of the antique's value. The chair dates to the eighteenth century. That's a rare tapestry upholstery she's possibly spilling ashes on. Two different styles of drawing make the contrast more severe. (Actually, the chair comes from public-domain art; I drew the figure separately and patched it on the chair.)

Figure 4.35

Another design principle asks that you put the elements in the drawing into some kind of balance. Nearly always you would use informal balance. You'd place the biggest or strongest element off center, balancing it with several lesser elements on the other side of the picture. Occasionally, though, you would try formally balanced composition, as in Figure 4.36, a drawing by an anonymous artist.

Figure 4.36

In this drawing the boat and the seaman, main elements, are on or near a center line running vertically. The style of drawing in this example of formal balance is itself informal (or loose), not formal (or tight).

Good design further asks that you tie things together somehow to make them appear related, and that the viewer observe things in their correct order, seeing first things first. The illustration involving a young boy soliciting lawn-care work (Figure 4.37) makes use of circular composition. I arranged everything to follow roughly the contours of an "O," with eye travel moving in a counterclockwise direction. The blackness of the shirt occurs at, roughly, the optical center of the drawing, to take advantage of where the eye normally starts. The lawn mower's large size helps

Figure 4.37

establish it in the foreground. (An advantage a drawing has over a photograph—at least a photograph taken with a large lens opening—is that things both in the foreground and background can appear in sharp focus.)

Irwin Caplin also uses circular composition in his drawing for a newspaper ad sponsored by The Westin Hotel, Seattle (Figure 4.38). His eye travel is clockwise. The viewer starts at 9 o'clock, moves around past the hotel to the couple, then, appropriately to the hotel again. Those are some

Figure 4.38
Courtesy of Irwin Caplin and The Westin Hotel.

Seattle landmarks you see in the picture.

An important way to hold things together in a drawing is to overlap them. Overlaps also help establish distances and scale. An artist who keeps figures and props completely separate from each other ends up with chaos.

Each overlapping in a drawing should be substantial. Barely overlapping or stopping a figure where a prop begins suggests a balancing act that may detract from the drawing's central idea.

shading

Shading helps establish the source of light for viewers and gives roundness and dimension to the figure or object being depicted. The shading can be in solid black or in texture.

A good artist puts thought into the shape of a shadow, treating it as though it had a life of its own. The *sum* of the shadows in a drawing take on a meandering, interesting shape. One technique has the artist *outlining* the shapes of shadows and filling in the shapes with Zipatone rather than with black.

Just a hint of shadow often is enough. The fiber-tip pen I used to create the cab hailer in Figure 4.39 produced the scribbled shading you see as well as the outlines. The shading becomes a little more intense on the briefcase because it is closer to the "camera." An outline defines the edge of the shadow under the briefcase because it is a *cast* shadow rather than one that simply molds the figure.

Paul G. Donelan, a freelance illustrator with clients in the Mas-

Figure 4.39

71

sachusetts area, shows that it is not necessary to go out to the edges when applying black to a garment to make it stand out (Figure 4.40). In fact, allowing for a halo of white between the outline and the black area gives a figure roundness.

Putting an extra touch of black near the head of the figure in the stained-glass window makes it stand out, too, and helps unite it to the aroma coming from the cooked bird.

Figure 4.40
Courtesy of Paul G. Donelan.

texture

Texture comes from pulling or pushing a grease crayon across a rough-surface paper, from applying sheets of Zipatone or similar shading on a finished drawing, or from brushing a chemical solution over the surface of a special paper or board of a kind used by many of today's editorial cartoonists. It also comes from the painstaking marks and strokes put down by a fine-point pen, as in the pastoral scene in Figure 4.41 drawn by an anonymous artist.

Humorous drawings as a rule get by with much less texture than in this scene, and some get by without *any* texture, but the scene is

worth studying to see what an ordinary pen dipped in ink or a Rapidograph or similar pen can accomplish. If you count the carefully drawn tightly-packed leaves, the billowing clouds, the rolling-hills background, the stone fence, the twisted-bark tree trunks, the stippled grass just this side of the fence, and the detailed blades of grass in the foreground, you have at least seven distinguishable textures that contrast with the pure white of the paper.

Figure 4.41

stereotypes and clichés

Charles Addams did a gag cartoon for the *New Yorker* showing businessmen playing on a baseball field. One disgruntled fan in the stands says to another that the game has "gotten too damn big-business, if you ask me." Addams showed that the players were businessmen by putting them in dark suits. Each was wearing a hat.

Now some businessmen do wear dark suits, and a few still wear hats; but many businessmen dress differently from what Addams showed. Addams obviously could not explore the possibilities within

the confines of a single panel. Avoiding sameness in dress would have ruined the effect of the cartoon and made the point less obvious. So Addams, like most cartoonists, relied on a stereotype. Discredited elsewhere in publications, the stereotype still plays an important part in cartoons and humorous illustrations.

Just a few touches in dress or a prop or two can establish a person's occupation. You know that

73

Figure 4.42

Figure 4.43 (far right)

the woman in Figure 4.42, out to rescue someone hurt at the county fair (she is a detail from a larger drawing illustrating a newspaper feature), is a nurse by the cross on her hastily drawn cap and the items she clutches. She appears happy to have discovered a potential patient. The farmer at the right wears the overalls we associate with that business, plus a cap that seems appropriate, and he carries part of his harvest. He appeared originally as a small spot drawing in a farm story in a newspaper.

The typical thug in a cartoon wears a cap, a sweat shirt, and baggy pants. In Figure 4.43 he carries a nasty club with a nail in it and waits just around a corner for his victim. I used brush and ink to make this newspaper drawing.

The shading—part black ink, part grease-crayon shading—gives the drawing a sinister touch and helps hold it together. The shading extends roughly to three of the four corners, strongly defining the drawing's dimensions and keeping it from becoming a silhouette.

Possibly less defensible than stereotypes in cartoons are clichés. But clichés sometimes represent the only solutions to visual problems. A light bulb over a character's head, for instance, has long suggested "idea," and because it has so firmly established itself as a recognizable symbol it still works today. One way to minimize its cliché quality is to put the light bulb into an abstraction instead of drawing it in comic style.

The sweat mark is perhaps the most common of cartoon clichés— and one of the most versatile. It can help suggest nervousness as well as exhaustion and an over-heated condition. When used with a laughing face, sweat marks emphasize the mirth.

Still, the artist who can move a comic figure through space without resorting to sweat marks (and swish lines and clouds of smoke) shows a mastery of the art of humorous illustration that the ordinary artist does not have. The most discredited of the clichés takes place in the last panel of a comic strip where, after hearing the joke, a main character falls backwards, his feet going up in the air. An all-caps "PLOP" appears nearby.

everyone (almost) a victim

Cartoons and humorous illustrations are, if anything, democratic. Everyone has a chance to look ridiculous. The woman who poses for us in Figure 4.44 fits into the cartoon world very nicely. With those oversized glasses and pampered eyes she tries hard to look at least fashionable, but she is eminently forgettable. She probably chews gum and licks her fingers to turn the pages of a book.

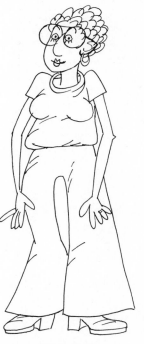

Figure 4.44

In Cartoonland, most people are hopelessly arthritic. Not a few are bowlegged. The overemphasized left elbow is only one more insult the woman in Figure 4.44 must endure. She makes her appearance without benefit of solid black or shading. The only texture she exhibits is in her Uniperm. That she is antiqued with just a few short interrupting lines gives her a roundness she would not otherwise have.

Cartoonists delight in physical deformity, although they generally shy away from the blind and the lame. The fat and the oversize, though, come in for enthusiastic cartoon treatment. The belly of a fat man, for instance, becomes so huge the poor fellow must carry it in front of him in a wheelbarrow.

Faces on fat people end up with features squeezed to the center by rolls of flesh. There is no neck on a cartoonist's fat man, but there are several chins. Face and shoulders form a triangle, as the anonymous drawing from *Simplicissimus* shows (Figure 4.45). Heinrich Kley supplies (at the right) a sideview of the head of

Figure 4.45

another fat man. He emphasizes the bulging neck with a series of short vertical lines where the neck stuffs itself into the collar.

Cartoonists and humorous illustrators find old people especially vulnerable. But then, old people don't fare very well anywhere in the mass media. You remember Tim Conway on the *Carol Burnett Show* portraying an old man who moved only by shuffling? A rug on the floor stopped him cold. He couldn't lift his feet high enough to move at rug level. His only recourse was to keep shuffling, making waves of the rug and, apparently unaware of what he was doing, taking it with him.

In a TV sketch in which Bob Hope played an old man, an interviewer asked what he ate to live so long. Hope answered: "Bourbon and junk food."

"Do you drink your bourbon straight?"

"No. Bent over."

In commercials old people hold fast to outworn ideas about which soap to use only to be put into their places by smart-aleck married daughters who have stumbled onto new, improved versions of the product. Silly old men in ridiculous bathing suits from the past sit around in inner tubes talking about nothing but old-fashioned lemonade taste. A reporter friend of mine, Dan Sellard, wrote a newspaper column on turning sixty, complaining bitterly about young reporters referring in their stories to people in his age bracket as "elderly." That Sellard can hike the highest mountains and run the roughest rapids has made no impression, apparently, on those on the sweet side of thirty.

In the hands of a cartoonist an old person suffers from excessive stooping, wrinkling, and sagging. Take the lady in Figure 4.46 moving, however slowly, down the street. The feet are big enough to show her all too firmly rooted to the ground. Her right hand makes a feeble effort to pull her forward. (Texture in the hat and

Figure 4.46

on the scarf adds a bit of interest to a fine-line drawing, which is made with a technical pen with a 00 point. The drawing is shown actual size, almost a necessity with fine-line drawings. Lines this fine do not take well to reduction.)

Figure 4.47 shows an old couple head-on in a kind of a blind-leading-the-blind routine. The woman's posture has a lot to do with establishing the mood. She seems to be in a little better shape than the old man, but not by much. The excessive wrinkles in the man's pants are a necessary part of the cartoonist's shorthand for "old." (Texture this time is provided by a pattern of Zipatone in the man's suit, by the brush's outline, and by a bit of pattern in the woman's blouse. The outlining comes from a Gillott pen point, more flexible than a technical pen point and capable of stronger, more varied rendering.)

A rocker becomes an essential prop in a drawing involving an old person. If it's a man involved, you give him a pipe, of course, and around his mouth you draw some tiny vertical lines, to suggest a lack of teeth. Figure 4.48 shows such a specimen, who carries a "Who, me?" expression because he was used to illustrate a newspaper feature about birthday surprises being arranged for people in a nursing home.

Children, along with well-endowed young women, seem to enjoy the best press, so far as cartoonists are concerned. Mostly they come out looking cute, if not adorable, as in the grouping in Figure 4.49 clipped and rearranged from an art nouveau drawing by Ethel Larcombe.

Figure 4.48

Figure 4.47

Figure 4.49
From *The Studio*.

Figure 4.51
From Timothy Shy's *The Terror of St. Trinian's*,
Max Parrish, London, 1952.

Figure 4.50

My collage of assorted youngsters (Figure 4.50) explores the use of various media: the dancing couple in brush and grease crayon, the innertube girl in pen and ink and brush for the solid blacks, the firecracker thrower in a medium-point marker.

Not all children are this cute. A few cartoonists take their cue

from Len Norris of the *Vancouver* (Canada) *Sun* whose old-faced, no-neck kids are among the world's ugliest. Cartoonists who can't make them ugly can make them mean, as Ronald Searle does in one of his book illustrations (Figure 4.51).

reaction
to the art

In the early 1900s, a man on a train reading a H. T. Webster cartoon about the Chicago School Board went into convulsions and had to be carried off to a hospital, where he was listed in critical condition. Webster never knew whether the reaction the man had was one of laughter or anger, but he was gratified nevertheless that one of his cartoons could so move a reader. (Webster was in a class with Clare Briggs and J. R. Williams with his charming style and homespun humor. You can see a sampling of his work in *The Best of H. T. Webster,* New York: Simon and Schuster, 1953.)

People sometimes react strongly to cartoons. Older readers of newspapers complained to editors and cartoonists in the 1980 election that cartoonists were unfairly concentrating on Ronald Reagan's wrinkles. Wrinkles aren't funny to those who have them. When Don Wright of the *Miami News* drew an editorial cartoon showing all Republican candidates but Reagan throwing their hats in the ring (Reagan was throwing in a cane) the howls from old people (whose numbers are legion in Florida) became especially loud.

Some of the most violent reaction comes not from the victims themselves but from their champions, many of whom are too single-minded to appreciate the humor or too preoccupied with their causes to even recognize it. Jules Feiffer, certifiably liberal, felt the rage of the self-righteous in 1979 when one of his cartoons in *The Village Voice* made fun of rednecks given to using "fag," "dyke," and "nigger" in their talk. People took the cartoon in the opposite way from what was intended. "We find it not only

offensive but far from funny and not in the least illuminating," read one of the complaints. Harry Stein, recounting the uproar in an article in *Esquire,* observed that the temptation of critics to assume a morally superior position is often overwhelming when it comes to cartoons. But it is a temptation to be resisted. "In the end," he said, "the humorless slug is usually more irritating than whatever it is he's railing against."

Some reaction from victims establishes the point, quietly and convincingly, that the cartoonist or storyteller is truly off base. Charles Potter, resident of a retirement home, asks in an article in *Northwest Magazine,* "Whatever gives people the idea that getting older causes people to lose their sense of humor?" He tells about arthritic people around him referring to their place as "Happy Achers Retirement Home." One resident reported to Potter, "I never eat Jell-O because I just don't eat anything that shakes worse than I do." Someone who worked at the hobby shop, which serves residents with repairs, said, "We are prompt, no matter how long it may take." One lady had a sign on her wheelchair: "Old Age Is Not for Sissies."

One story that made the rounds in the early 1980s must have bolstered the aged. It is the kind of story you hope is true but you are afraid is merely made up. An old lady in a Mercedes drives into a parking lot. Just as she steers into a space, a shiny sports car driven by a young and pampered punk scoots in ahead of her. As the driver leaves, he says, "That's what you can do when you're young and quick." He walks away with his giggling friends; then they turn to watch in horror as the old lady starts banging into his car with hers. She backs up and pulls forward repeatedly. As he comes running, she says, "That's what you can do when you're old and rich."

A surprising number of victims of humorous art are mature enough—or thick-skinned enough—to request cartoonists' originals to hang on their walls. This is especially true of politicians. To be ridiculed becomes a badge of recognition.

5

illustrating
the magazine piece

Before you respond to Figure 5.1 with a "My four-year-old child can do better than that," look carefully. The drawing is *supposed* to have a child-like feel, for it accompanied an article in *Education Week* on book burners and people who wildly criticize the education system. Illustrator Salvador Bru worked hard to imitate the style of youth while still controlling the composition and line.

Fred Schrier uses a much different style—tighter, busier, funnier—for his view from above of a busy Sohio service station (Figure 5.2). The art accompanied an editorial on "Marketing Merits Our Attention" in *Sohio News*, employee publication of The Standard Oil Company (Ohio).

This is another interesting drawing to study for all that it contains. Its bird's-eye view allows the il-

Illustrations for magazines run the visual gamut, from the slapstick to the abstract, taking in a whole scene or moving in for a closeup. Sometimes a single illustration does the job. Sometimes it takes a series of them.

To illustrate a *Saturday Evening Post* article on "The Sounds of Sleep," B. B. Sams did a Robt. Crumb-like full-color cartoon that had the kind of exaggeration

Figure 5.1
Salvador Bru
Courtesy of *Education Week.*

Studying the drawing, you begin to appreciate its artistry. The lines have character, and the shapes adhere to the principles of interesting composition. The black area, extending from in back of the fire to the coat of one of the book burners, is carefully planned for its placement and shape, and it nicely unifies the work. One final touch concerns the scraps of actual text matter cut out and placed inside the books, as though this were a collage instead of a mere ink drawing.

lustrator to summarize the many jobs performed on a typical day. Schrier exaggerates the sweep of the scene by rounding the horizon line, as though what we see here were really a sizable chunk of the globe. The figures in the drawing are remarkably similar—short and squat—so that the reader does not look for types but instead notes all that's going on. The figure sameness is like the device of parallel structure used by a writer to make a series of points.

you'd expect to find in one of the underground comic books of the 1960s. In the illustration a hysterical woman sits up in bed holding her ears, her eyes bloodshot, her toes curled, while the man beside her, mouth wide open, snores all kinds of word sounds that look as though they came out of the comic strips, along with lots of "Z"s. The racket is so loud, one sees, that it shakes a box of earplugs and a box of sleeping tablets off the night table.

Laurie Adams's illustration for an article on junk food in *Playgirl,* at

Marketing success depends on doing many jobs well. This sketch shows the multiple tasks a station employee may perform in a typical day.

Figure 5.2
Fred Schrier
Courtesy of *Sohio News.*

the other end of the magazine spectrum, was a closeup of a woman eating a cream-filled cookie with a skull-and-crossbones insignia on the dark chocolate top. The drawing was closely cropped with only part of the face, the cookie, and part of a hand showing. Adams figured that there was no point in involving the reader in hair style, dress, and other matters that were beside the point.

Sometimes symbolism turns out to be the best approach for a magazine illustration. For a *Harper's* cover advertising an article on "The Double Lives of Homosexuals in Politics," Melinda Bordelon, through a painting, showed two briefcase-carrying men, safely apart, eyeing each other warily. In the background was the capitol. Also in the back-

ground were the two shadows of the men, coming together in a tentative embrace.

Figure 5.3 shows samples of symbolism made with small, closeup, abstract pieces of art. The bomb, of course, suggests war; the fingerprint, crime; the propped-up storefront, facade (or Hollywood).

Figure 5.3
From Rudolf Modley's *Handbook of Pictorial Symbols,* Dover Publications, Inc., New York, 1976.

Symbolism can be the most powerful, the most direct way to communicate a visual idea. But it can also quickly deteriorate into a cliché. Using a photograph of a doll, with its head partially cracked open, has become standard for articles these days deal-

ing with child abuse. The cliché has developed for two reasons: getting photographs—and releases—of real children who are beaten is not always easy, and the damaged doll is less grisly and more arty.

Aside from its being overworked, the photograph of the battered doll has the additional disadvantage of saying not so much "child abuse" as "abuse by a child." Some unthinking child has not taken very good care of her toy. That could be the viewer's reaction.

the magazine editor

"Editor" is an elastic term in journalism. I discovered this back in my college days when, as editor of the yearbook and a senior, I recruited eager freshmen from the sororities to paste down and caption row upon row of mug shots and to perform other journalistic chores holding no challenge for a person of my station. These people pasted and performed for the "activity points" they could rack up. Their houses assigned points on the basis of time spent in various good works on campus, and the yearbook was one place eligible for good works. The points were necessary, apparently, if one were to wear a house pin and learn the secret handshake.

As editor I earned a token salary. I was swept with guilt, therefore, when I saw my charges doing all that work and getting nothing in return but a little organizational security. I hit upon the idea of passing out titles. "Executive Editor" sounded good to me, so everybody on the staff became one. There was an Executive Editor in Charge of Captions, an Executive Editor in Charge of Pasteup, and Executive Editor in Charge of the Index, and many others. I am happy to report that no one who worked on that book faced the indignity of writing merely "yearbook writer" or "yearbook pasteup artist" or "yearbook indexer" on her résumé when, three years later, she set out to look for a job.

I have since learned that the idea of fancy titles was anything but original. In American journalism, titles come universally in lieu of impressive salaries. You see this when you go through the masthead of a publication looking for Indians among all the chiefs. You find, in addition to the editor, executive editors, managing editors, associate editors, assistant editors, news editors, copy editors, production editors, and other editors. Writers not even on the scene turn out to be contributing editors on many magazines.

Just plain "editor" is the title above all others, of course, and the person who holds that title is the person to whom other editors answer. But even the editor often does more writing than editing. On company magazines—magazines published for public relations reasons rather than for reasons of profit—the editor is likely to do it all: write, edit, take pictures, and lay out pages. About all a company magazine editor doesn't do is draw and paint the illustrations, although on a few of the magazines editors do that, too.

Gary Olsen runs such a magazine—*Tracks*—for John Deere Dubuque Works, Dubuque, Iowa. For one of his issues, Olsen wrote a feature on retirees, a feature that concluded that with their years of experience and special skills, they are a valuable resource for their communities. Olsen depicted them as superpeople, and that's exactly how he decided to show them in an illustration. He hired Greg Manchess to draw a mature man and woman in Superman garb (Figure 5.4). Appropriately, Olsen had his artist put the title for the spread in Superman-like lettering. A bold frame held the two pages together.

Olafur Hauksson, editor of *Samuel,* a general-circulation magazine published in Iceland, does his own writing, editing, and designing and occasionally his own humorous illustrations. Established in 1973, his lusty magazine enjoys the highest circulation in Iceland (14,000), but it is a circulation low enough to prevent Hauksson's buying much art from outside. Anyway, Hauksson finds that freelancers "are not keen on keeping deadlines."

FANTASTIC RETIREES!

They possess years of experience and special skills. Truly, they are the community's most valuable talent resource.

Story by Gary Olsen
Illustration by Greg Manchess
Photography by Max Winter

If every John Deere person who promised they were going to "do a lot of fishing" when they retire actually did just that, there wouldn't be a fish left alive in any of the local rivers, lakes or streams. The fact of the matter is most retirees eventually discover they don't have time to fish. They're too busy pursuing other less-than-sedentary lifestyles.

It's been said that retirement is the end of one career and the beginning of another. After several casual conversations with retirees in various stages of their post-John Deere careers, I have come to believe that this is true in most cases. One of my jobs in preparing *TRACKS* Magazine is publishing retiree announcements which include a photo session involving the soon-to-be retirees and me. This personal contact reveals many interesting things about these people, some of which never really get published in the highly structured and somewhat formal retirement announcements you see on the bulletin boards or in the pages of *TRACKS*. For one reason or another, many of these retirees don't want a lot of this "special" information in

their announcements. News about service organizations, volunteer work, hobby/businesses make the retirement announcements, and one usually reads about the old standby's like "fishing, traveling, woodworking, gardening and relaxing." Perhaps telling the truth about retirement plans would be too much like bragging for some of them. Modesty seems to be the rule for most retirees. They like to maintain a "professional low profile" so to speak.

One of the greatest resources our community has is its retired people—craftsmen, professionals, individuals with vast knowledge of business, manufacturing, and possessing skills and experience that could be very useful in a society that is becoming more dependent on volunteerism and less dependent on government handouts and federal programs. However, many retirees don't pursue activities anything like their work-a-day lives. It's more common for a retiree to go in an entirely new and different direction from their careers. What follows are a few illustrations of community service work involving John Deere retirees:

Marguerite Connolly has a very constructive attitude when it comes to discussing her many and varied roles in the community. "I feel we as a group *must* do something in the community, particularly now with so many people in need." Marguerite, along with fellow Dubuque retiree, Helen Holz, hold positions on the Mercy Medical Center Gift Shop staff, proceeds of which go to defray the medical costs of needy children at the hospital. Both Marguerite and Helen belong to a whole host of other organizations in their city.

For many retirees, their church not only serves as a spiritual refuge, but as a tremendous outlet for creative energy. Dan Mihal, a recent retiree from the Product Engineering Center, is very active in his local parish of the Greek Orthodox Church. "Our parish is very small (less than 20 families), but we have a lot of enthusiasm," explains Dan. "I'm a chanter during regular services, and this work has inspired me to start taking piano and voice lessons now that I'm retired." The small church is involved in many successful money raising projects in the Dubuque community, the biggest of which is

(continued)

Figure 5.4
Gret Manchess
Courtesy of Tracks.

the magazine article

Early in their history, magazines served largely as repositories of short stories, with little room for nonfiction. Now the opposite is true. Few magazines run fiction of any kind. The illustrator working with magazines works mostly with articles.

Magazines publish several kinds of articles, including those loaded with inspiration, those that expose corruption, those telling us how to perform our tasks more expeditiously, those telling us what to think of celebrities or introducing us to quirky people, and those recounting first-person or third-person adventures of various kinds. Typically, the article, of whatever kind, takes an unpopular stand or gives the appearance of doing that, at least at the beginning. The article means to shake the reader up a bit.

It is reasonable to expect the accompanying art, especially if it is meant to be humorous, to shake up the reader, too. Our old friend, the visual surprise, is back.

For an article suggesting that the United States is a colony to the rest of the world in that, among other things, "Control over the American economy by non-American powers is growing," J. C. Suares used surprise by combining two different kinds of dress on one man. The man, representing the United States, wore a suit coat and tie but, below the shirt, he had on only a loincloth. His hairy legs showed and he carried a spear. The implication was that the country may be advanced but it has some of the marks of a barely emerging nation, too.

package deals

A person usually overlooked in all the plans for displaying an article is the author. Seeing an article finally in print, the author may feel that the art fails to capture the spirit of the piece or, worse, actually makes a point that is the antithesis of what has been written. Ideally, the author should be able to see a spread before it goes to press, but the pressures of deadlines preclude that. Besides, editors have found that some authors nitpick too much about art that has been chosen. The editors would rather field complaints when it is too late to make expensive changes.

Some authors offer art and even layout suggestions at the time they submit their manuscripts. Many submit photographs with their manuscripts, and a few submit drawings.

A surprising number of writers draw as well as they write, and the package deals they offer are wel-

come because they save editors time and effort. An author/artist enjoys the feeling of being in full charge of a product, with copy and art perfectly integrated.

Betty Swords of Denver is one such author. She provides her own illustrations for many of the lighthearted articles she sells, but she never does the illustrations until an article is accepted. Instead, she reminds the editor that she does illustrations and includes a sample of her published work if she hasn't sold to that editor previously.

Other author/artists send everything at once, hoping that the package will prove so impressive, so readily available, that the editor won't be able to resist buying it.

Swords does not query an editor before sending in an article. You can't sell humor by describing it, she points out. You sell it by showing it. Her steadiest market for a time was the *Christian Science Monitor,* a national daily newspaper that, apart from its newspaper look, has many qualities of a magazine. "After they bought a piece, I would draw a *gag* cartoon," she says. "It illustrated the piece but added an amusing gag on the subject as well. [The editors] trusted that they would like what I drew; they never requested a rough first, nor a written description, nor did they ever reject an illustration. It was an ideal setup."

It is perfectly natural for a cartoonist to write as well as draw, Swords believes. "If you are a [gag] cartoonist, you're already a humor writer: captions are short, short, short pieces of humor." She adds that "Once you expand your cartoon thinking to include humor-writing, you will see that some ideas can be better expressed in words, and enhanced with pictures. . . ." She suggests that humorous writing, to sell, should inform as well as entertain. "Space is tight and . . . editors don't want to 'waste' a big chunk on just humor."

If you deal with company magazines, one subject area likely to interest editors, Swords observes, is plant safety. Editors periodically have to run safety campaigns. "Any such editor will bless the

artist with a new and amusing way to do one. I've usually humorously exaggerated the pitfalls of the wrong way; the text contains the warning underneath." Of course you have to know the industry and plant before you can effectively preach safety and show the equipment and machinery.

Swords also puts together cartoon features or spreads, with little or no copy other than the captions. Her most successful venture involved a spread for *Changing Times,* in 1972, on "the new look in politics: the woman candidate." She submitted fifty-four gags for the editor's consideration. "It was so simple! All I had to do was reverse every tired old cliché about women and politics." The cartoons chosen formed the magazine's first two-page spread of cartoons in three colors. Swords got all kinds of response on the spread. One woman politician in Texas enlarged the cartoons and used them in her election campaign. Swords, who calls herself a "born-again feminist," says, "It was a good feeling to have both my professional and personal interests combine."

Swords has illustrated works by other writers, too. "I've found the pay for illustrations to be from two to nearly *ten* times that for [gag] cartoons, for the same amount of work. It annoys me, because I think [gag] cartoons should be better paid."

Swords particularly likes illustrating her own writing. "After all, who knows the subject better?"

she asks. "And I definitely like almost doubling my pay." She offers this advice to other writer–illustrators: "Keep reminding editors that you 'usually' do your own drawings; tell them how soon you could have the drawing back to them (and see that you do it)."

She also urges beginners to "cultivate your editors. When you find one who likes your work, make sure you keep her supplied. If you are selling [gag] cartoons, and the magazine uses humor-illustrations, ask if you can be considered for that job. Or the editor might ask you, but don't wait for that."

One of Swords' most reprinted illustrated articles appeared originally in *Rocky Mountain Medical Journal.* Titled "What to Do When the Doctor Leaves," it dealt with the problem of following the doctor's directions, including the problem of giving medicine to an ailing child. Figure 5.5 shows the illustration she supplied with her article.

Figure 5.5
Courtesy of Betty Swords.
© 1958 Colorado State Medical Society.
Reprinted with permission.

magazine formats

Magazines come in a variety of formats or page sizes, ranging from tabloid size down to pocket-book size. The most common size is 8½ by 11.

A tabloid-size magazine is sometimes called a "magapaper," be-

cause at that size a magazine begins looking like a newspaper. Like a newspaper, it can contain pages that are not bound.

Large-size magazines allow editors and artists a chance to give art

Figure 5.6
Courtesy of Chris Pontrelli.

Figure 5.7
Jean Francois Allaux
Courtesy of *Gracescope.*

more impact, as though the art were posters. Bright colors and bold lines, executed with brush and crayon instead of pen or Rapidograph, are possible. Small, *Reader's Digest*-size publications can pursue an aggressive art program, too. A full-page piece of art in a small magazine can be more impressive than art that same size in a magazine with larger pages.

Magazine-like publications that can't afford a magazine format turn to a newsletter format: a few 8½-by-11 pages stapled together or larger sheets folded down to an 8½-by-11 size. Often an ordinary typewriter is used for the wide, single columns of ragged-right copy. The only real typography is confined to the nameplate at the top of page one.

Newsletters can be enlivened with pieces of line art in the usually wide margins—art similar to what you see in Figure 5.6. As a student in a School of Architecture, Chris Pontrelli faced "review week" with trepidation. He showed how he felt in a cartoon published in the school's newsletter for students, making appropriate use of a T-square as his symbol.

Some newsletters are designed with the same flair that is used to design magazines and printed in several colors on quality stock.

They are "newsletters" only because they do not have enough pages to qualify as magazines (sixteen or more) and the pages are not bound. Such a newsletter is *Gracescope*, a newsletter for management people of W. R. Grace & Co.

To illustrate a *Gracescope* feature on a retail educational program, Jean Francois Allaux combined a classroom setting with a cash register to come up with the fanciful crosshatch drawing in Figure 5.7. The keys of the cash register made ideal seats, as Allaux envisioned them, and the pulled-out drawer a good platform for the speaker.

two-page spreads

An article that is to be illustrated often spreads out over several pages in the magazine. The article may start on a right-hand page, then continue as a series of two-page spreads. Or it may start on a left-hand page. The opening it-

Figure 5.8
Brian Smith
From *Aramco World Magazine.*

IS IT EXTINCT? OR JUST HIDING?

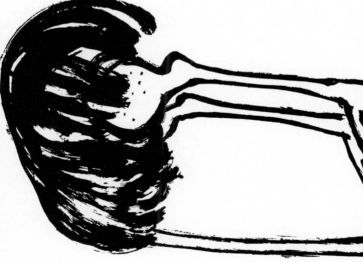

THE CAMEL BIRD OF ARABIA

WRITTEN BY CAROLINE STONE   ILLUSTRATED BY BRIAN SMITH

I n February 1966, flood waters north of Ma'an, in Jordan, brought down into the Hasa Valley near Petra a single dying specimen of the species called *Struthio Camelus Syriacus* – the ostrich or, as the Chinese call it, the Camel Bird of Arabia. Since no ostriches had been seen on the Arabian Peninsula since 1941, the unexpected appearance of even one specimen gave hope to some optimists that these ostriches – which once roamed freely through Arabia – were not extinct but in hiding.

Ostriches were well known in the ancient world. The Egyptians, for example, took their feathers as the symbol of justice – because the vanes are exactly equal in width on either side of the shaft – and the Pharaohs were cooled with ostrich-feather fans; one fan with a handle made of gold was found in the tomb of an Egyptian queen of about 1700 B.C. And in Mesopotamia, ostriches, usually being sacrificed to the gods, were carved on seals. Mesopotamia also made ostrich eggs into cups, and eggs found in Etruscan graves, and in those at Mycenae, suggest that they were articles of trade in early times.

Many of the classical writers provided good descriptions of ostriches and their habits – indeed, it was Pliny, some 1,900 years ago, who first called them "camel birds" – and they seem to have cropped up in all sorts of surprising ways. Apicius gives recipes in his cookery book for preparing ostriches and one emperor had himself drawn by an ostrich team in the hope it would look as if he were flying. Ostriches also made their appearance in the amphitheater, taking part in the games – not as odd as it sounds, since ostriches, kicking backwards, can bend an iron rail into a right angle.

Ostriches also appear frequently in the poetry of Islamic verse and especially from Arabia itself, where the birds were common. The pleasures of ostrich hunting, for example, were extolled, and large numbers of ostriches and eggs were considered an indication of prosperity.

In one of the great Arabic romances, "the Deeds of the Bani Hilal" – a story of the conquest of North Africa – one image describes Tripoli as a "city of merchants, proud and wary as the she-ostrich guarding her eggs."

Arab naturalists also focused on the ostrich – and often described it quite accurately. The following passage, for example, comes from Qazwini, whose *Cosmography*, written in the mid-13th century, includes a long section on birds:

When the ostrich has laid her eggs, 20 in number or more, she buries them under the sand, leaving one third in one place, exposing another third to the sun, and hatching another third. When the chicks have come out, she breaks the last third on which vermin will collect, and this serves as food for the young until they are able to graze.

Not all writings on the ostrich were accurate. The belief that ostriches are bad parents, for example, probably goes back to Lamentations: "... the daughter of my people is become cruel, like the ostriches of the wilderness ... " and to Job, where the ostrich "leaveth her eggs in the earth and warmeth them in dust and forgetteth that the foot may crush them or that the wild beast may break them. She is hardened against her young as though they were not hers ... " And this is quite unfair. Ostriches, at least in the wild, are excellent parents, the female incubating the nest by day, the male by night.

A case recorded in the Nairobi National Park in 1960 illustrates this. A male ostrich was sitting on a clutch of 40 eggs, when he was driven off by a pride of lions. The cubs played with the eggs as if they were balls, dribbling them all over the surrounding area. When they had gone, the he-ostrich came back and laboriously succeeded in rolling the eggs back into the nest. Amazingly enough, they hatched.

Ostriches are the largest living bird and have existed in almost their present form for at least a million years, and though their origins have been much disputed, there is an Arab myth to explain why they cannot fly. Once upon a time, the falcon and the ostrich had a wager as to which could fly

the best. The falcon said, "In the name of God!" and flew straight up towards heaven while the ostrich, who forgot to invoke his Creator's blessing, was scorched by the sun and fell to earth, never to fly again.

The present-day ostrich is two to three meters tall (seven to nine feet), weighs about 136 kilos (300 pounds), lives up to 70 years and has a number of physical peculiarities which set it apart from all other birds. The ostrich, for example, is the only bird that yawns, and, having an extraordinarily efficient heart, can run at 30 miles an hour for an hour at a time without showing distress, and can manage 40 miles an hour for 15 minutes.

M any of the popular stories about ostriches have an element of truth. They do swallow metal and stones – although not to the extent described by writers in the past – and the idea that they hide their heads in the sand to avoid being noticed isn't quite as silly as it sounds. Originating with the Arabs and passed on by the Romans, this legend is based on the fact that ostriches stretch their necks straight out on the ground to sleep and, when pursued, will suddenly throw themselves down flat, preferably with their head in a bush – to apparently vanish before reaching the horizon.

In the Arab world, the ostrich was hunted for pleasure. As a by-product of the sport, the feathers were used as decoration and the skins for cuirasses and the handles of knives. The skins are beautifully marked and very tough, although heavy, and now serve to make extremely elegant luggage. The eggs were sometimes blown and hung in churches, as ornaments where all kinds of legends came to be attached to them.

In early Islamic times, there was a lively trade in live ostriches. The Arabs, for example, sent them to China from Aden and Hormuz, and T'ang sources record that "the camel bird who inhabits Arabia is four feet and more in height, its feet resembling those of a camel; its neck is very strong, and men are able to ride on its back; the birds thus walk for five or six miles. Its eggs have the capacity of two pints."

The ostrich had a much more serious role in Africa, since it was hunted not for sport but for food. The Kalahari bushmen were particularly adept at this – disguising themselves in ostrich skins in order to lure the birds into traps – and buried the eggs in the sand full of water, providing small reservoirs that permitted them to hunt far out in the desert. Women also used them as containers and would carry great grass nets full of them to and from the pools or springs. In the Kalahari and by the Orange River, rock carvings and paintings of unknown age have been found showing ostriches and the hunt. In other areas of Africa, such as the Sudan, ostriches were kept semi-domesticated as food and for their feathers, which in many regions were simply pulled out in handfuls at a time and sold as the owner of the bird needed cash.

Towards the end of the 19th century, ostriches became rare. This was partly because of changing patterns of agriculture and urbanization, and partly because of changing fashions. The demand by European women for feathers for hats and boas – exports from South Africa rose from about 9072 kilos (20,000 lbs) to nearly 453,590 kilos (one million lbs) in 50 years – might well have led to the ostrich becoming extinct. Fortunately, ostrich farming was introduced and proved successful all the way from Australia to Florida.

In Arabia, the introduction of firearms caused a great decline in the number of ostriches. On April 14, 1914, a British explorer, Captain William Shakespear, bought an ostrich chick when he was encamped near Jawf in today's Saudi Arabia, and about the same time a customs officer at the Allenby Bridge in the Jordan Valley reported that he had an ostrich that used to follow him about. But these were rare examples, and when, in the early 1920s, a hunter in Jordan discovered a clutch of ostrich eggs, they were rushed to England and incubated in the London Zoo. In 1941, though, the ostrich was declared extinct. Now, with the discovery of the ostrich near Ma'an, hope has revived that the Arabian ostrich may still be strutting about somewhere in the Middle East.

Caroline Stone writes regularly for Aramco World.

self, in that case, becomes a two-page spread. Sometimes the two pages are enough to present the entire article, plus its title and art.

Art incorporates itself with the title of the article by adopting a style that matches the look of the typeface used. Bold letters, for instance, call for bold brush strokes in the drawing.

Figure 5.8 shows a two-page article on the ostrich—the "camel bird," as the Chinese have called it—that appeared in *Aramco World Magazine*. The article explores the possibility that the bird may not be extinct in the Arab world, as has been thought. Brian Smith's strong dry-brush drawing dominates the spread, providing its only art. The typeface chosen for the titles and for the two initial letters match the bird itself with its tall, awkward look. The subtitle, in slightly smaller type, appears above the main title.

Because the art is not signed, and because the art takes up about a third of the assigned space, the artist gets his name set in a byline the same size as the writer's (just below the main article title). The even billing is mitigated somewhat on the table of contents page (not shown), where only the writer is credited and where a picture of her is shown.

With their smaller page sizes, magazines, more than newspapers, like to run art across the gutter to unite two facing pages and give the art more impact. Not all art lends itself to gutter crossing. The part of the art that falls into the gutter can't carry an element vital to its understanding. Often it's merely a patterned area you find in the gutter.
It is not a good idea to center the art at the gutter, placing as much of it on one side as on the other. The art should go *mostly* on one page or the other. But enough of the art should cross over to make the crossover worthwhile.

These considerations are less important when the art is to appear in a saddle-stitched magazine, where the gutter is shallow compared to the gutter in a side-stitched magazine. The centerfold of a saddle-stitched magazine contains no gutter at all, but the staples that show could create a problem.

Sometimes the editor may want to run the art so large that it not only crosses the gutter but also bleeds (runs off the page) at the top, sides, and bottom. Bleeds are effective, but you can't bleed pictures unless your publication is printed on sheets that are to be trimmed slightly after printing. Bleeding pictures is a luxury reserved for magazine editors and book publishers; newspaper editors, because of the way their publications are printed, in most cases can't bleed pictures.

the tie between title and art

The article title itself may suggest the illustration. For an article about "A Town That Decided to Pay for Good Schools," *McCall's* showed in its newsletter section a coin drawn in the shape of an apple. The idea was a takeoff, of course, from two words in the title: "Pay" (the coin) and "Schools" (the apple—for the teacher).

Whether the illustration comes from the article title or the article itself, it should have an obvious tie to the title. The title should not say one thing and the art something else.

Figure 5.9 shows Don Pegler's interpretation of "That Speaking Invitation: It Sounds Flattering,

But—," an article by Ron Hoff in *Advertising Age*. Pegler, an advertising agency executive who freelances as an illustrator, shows the plight of a speaker whose audience is smaller than promised. (A section in the article warns that executives who speak on the last day of a convention seldom get a crowd because people leave early to catch their planes.)

Figure 5.10 shows an unsigned illustration used by *Enterprise*, the Journal of the National Association of Manufacturers, for an article entitled, "Will Congress Really Cut the Budget?" The illustration involves an analogy. You can't

Figure 5.9
Don Pegler
Courtesy of *Advertising Age.*

Figure 5.10
From *Enterprise.*

show a budget being cut, so you make the budget a plot of grass, and you run a lawn mower over it to symbolize cutting. The budget remains, but in a trimmed, more acceptable version. No need to show anyone pushing the mower—that would only complicate things—so you go for a closeup.

The gray you see is a wash brushed onto a paper without the right tooth to accept it, causing the gray to form puddles. This is not a bad thing. It makes for tone and texture different from the ordinary.

captions

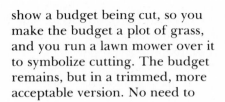

Drawings dealing broadly with themes—drawings not illustrating sentences or incidents from articles—do not require captions. Even when illustrations stem from specific references, they can run without captions. Let the illustrations intrigue or even puzzle the readers, many editors argue. And why add typographic clutter to pages already burdened by titles, subtitles, bylines, credit lines, initial letters, blurbs, subheads, and folios? Newspaper editors and even book editors feel the same way.

Captions are necessary where art is not clear without them, as in a chart or graph. Captions are also necessary where real people should be identified. Of course, photographs, dealing with reality as they do, need captions.

When captions are necessary, illustrators type them on separate sheets of paper that can be turned over to the typesetter. Editors mark these to be set in a typeface usually different from the face used in regular textmatter, in a smaller size, perhaps, or in italics or boldface.

Most gag cartoons require captions. Artists submitting gag cartoons simply letter their captions underneath their drawings. Editors type them out on separate sheets and have them set in type.

Editors use gag cartoons in the backs of their magazines as fillers to break up gray areas of type. The cartoons usually have no relationship to the articles around them. Some editors now contract for gag cartoons dealing with specific subjects and use them with articles on that subject, as though they were illustrations and not self-contained cartoons.

some examples of magazine illustrations

In one of his "On Language" columns in the *New York Times Magazine,* William Safire cited the emergence of the word "wimp" in the 1982 political campaign. "Wimp" had replaced "comsymp," "egghead," "kook," and "little old lady in tennis shoes" as a term of derision. Kimble Mead for his illustration showed a little old lady in tennis shoes kicking sand in the face of a wimpy man—a beach weakling looking unable or unwilling to defend himself. The illustration traded on the once widely seen comic-strip advertising for Charles Atlas, a body builder.

Sometimes a humorous illustration in a magazine turns into a kind of puzzle, inviting reader participation. Charles Saxon's full-color, across-the-gutter illustration in *McCall's* for "Eight Wasn't Enough," an article about a family with ten kids, showed a busy kitchen scene with a mother feeding a baby in a highchair and a father reading the morning paper. It was difficult to keep from searching out all the other children there in the kitchen, finding one digging into the cupboard, another making toast, another talking on the phone, etc.

"Billions Down the Drain" read the title over an article in *Enterprise,* the journal mentioned earlier. The piece dealt with the volume and cost of federal regulation of business. One section measured the amount of paper work involved. The accompanying simple line drawing, signed only Carol (Figure 5.11), showed a whale, looking worried, not in a sea of water but in a sea of sheets of paper.

When *Aramco World Magazine* ran an article on "The Nairn Way," a post-World War I bus business

that crossed the Syrian Desert, it commissioned Penny Williams to do the illustrations. She did a series of nine, two of them in full color. Just one of the drawings can teach you a lot about pen technique. Figure 5.12 shows one of the cars used, with luggage attached. The solid black areas, carefully placed to suggest the source of light, nicely sets off the crosshatching. There is plenty of pure white in the drawing, too. Williams resists the urge to put her pen down everywhere. The pure white, especially in the suit, helps establish the feeling of desert heat, as does the black shadow cast by the big-brimmed hat.

Focus, a publication of the graduate students in communication at CBN University, Virginia Beach, Virginia, ran a two-part article on "Saints of the Smile: Two Masters of the Art." It started one part, about G. K. Chesterton, on a left page, and the other part, about C. S. Lewis, on the facing page. John Lawing, Jr., associate professor of journalism, got the call to provide the art. Poor reproductive quality of the available photographs for the page sent Lawing to his drawing table, where he hastily sketched likenesses by putting tracing paper over the photographs (the editors were up against a deadline, as usual). One photo was smaller than the other, which meant that the one sketch (of Lewis) had to be enlarged slightly. That accounts for the cruder pattern in that one.

Lawing calls these sketches "just renderings," but they have strength and character, and they ran big enough to give the spread plenty of visual impact.

Figure 5.11
From *Enterprise.*

Figure 5.12
From *Aramco World Magazine.*

Figure 5.13
Courtesy of John Lawing, Jr.

the magazine cover

The plum among assignments for a humorous illustrator is the magazine cover. So glorious a display space is it that an illustrator may be willing to do the assignment at a pay scale far below what an illustration for an advertisement would bring. The cover drawing appears on a stock usually thicker and of a higher quality than the stock used inside the magazine. The illustrator can use various paints or dyes. The cover is likely to be printed in process colors.

On some magazines the cover drawing is independent of anything inside the magazine. The only requirement may be that it is appropriate to the season and that it shows a slice of life or carries a touch of irony. The best current examples of self-contained covers can be found on the *New Yorker*. People collect the covers and even use them to paper rooms. The old *Saturday Evening Post* used to run memorable self-contained covers that, in reality, were cartoons: full-color whimsical paintings.

A more common kind of cover is the one that carries a piece of art relating to an article inside. Sometimes such cover art is repeated at the beginning of the article, but more often the cover art acts as a companion piece to art inside.

Often such covers carry blurbs printed in neutral areas of the art. One blurb refers to the article the cover art illustrates; other, smaller blurbs refer to other articles. Such clutter is necessary to sell magazines at newsstands. Non-newsstand magazines, like company magazines published for public relations reasons, can get by without blurbs.

company magazines

Nobody has a clear record of exactly how many magazines are published in this country. A number of directories list magazines, but no one directory could possibly include them all. The big newsstand magazines are easy enough to count, but what about all the others? It is difficult to think of any special interest group, organized or not, that doesn't have its own magazine. Putting specialized magazines with general-interest ones, you could produce a list with tens of thousands of entries.

Among the groups of magazines to make the best use of humorous illustrations are company magazines, once called "house organs" until their editors balked at the designation. "House organs" as a term does not reflect the sophistication of many of these publications. But then "company magazines" doesn't say it all, either, because many of them come from governmental agencies, educational institutions, hospitals, and other organizations. "Organizational publications" has lately been used to categorize the magazines.

The International Association of Business Communicators represents some 11,000 editors of these publications, and there are many others who do not belong to the organization.

The beauty of these magazines, from the illustrator's standpoint, is that usually there is no advertising in them to detract from the editorial art. An illustration, humorous or otherwise, lounges on the pages, sometimes basking in a second color if not full color, surrounded only by columns of editorial copy and maybe a little white space. The editors in charge of copy might admit that the subject matter in some of the articles is a little on the dull side, making the art, by comparison, even more interesting than it would be otherwise.

When *The Bulletin* of the American Society of Newspaper Editors devoted most of an issue to the phenomenon of liberals dominating the mass media, it got Chris Armstrong of the *Florida Times-Union* to do an illustration to give the opening pages some visual impact. Armstrong produced a detailed line drawing of a conservative at his typewriter typing away, apparently unaware that a janitor was standing behind him, brushing his bald head with a feather duster. You could tell that the depicted reporter (or editor) was a conservative because (1) he was using an old typewriter, not a VDT; (2) he was wrinkled and tending toward fat, with a bow tie and wire-rim glasses; (3) there was a bottle of rubber cement nearby, not a waxer, and his chair and desk and artifacts were all from an earlier era. It was not an unkind portrayal, but it did suggest that conservative newspeople are something of an oddity.

Figure 5.14 shows one of a number of drawings Marty Garrity made for a series of articles in *The Strategist*, a magazine published by Aerojet Strategic Propulsion Company, Sacramento. The articles told employees how they could make better use of company benefits. Garrity provides a multiple-mailbox motif to establish the fact that the woman has just received a medical-plan check and that she lives in an apartment complex. He uses a Zipatone sheet with an irregular pattern to bring tone to her skin. The irregular pattern works well with the hasty, strong brush strokes that define the figure.

Figure 5.14
Courtesy Martin E. Garrity and *The Strategist* of the
Aerojet Strategic Propulsion Company.

Not to be confused with company magazines are trade and professional journals, published not for public relations reasons but to make a profit, like most other publications. They do not confine themselves to the employees of one company; they go out to people throughout an industry. That they contain advertisements—and many of them—cuts down on the impact of their illustrations. The ads are often more exciting, visually, than the articles. People who read trade magazines read them for the ads as much as for the editorial matter. Even so, trade magazines represent a market for illustrators, too.

opinion magazines

Even the opinion magazines, those usually deadly serious butcher-paper journals operating always on the edge of financial disaster, are beginning to dress their pages with funny pictures. *National Review,* a journal that has always been able to merge outrage with wit, has long included drawings on its pages. Some of them are funny, although the drawings are often reprints from other publications syndicated by an outfit called Rothco. Other opinion journals are following suit. *The Nation* and the *New Republic* carry a number of cartoons in each issue. *The Progressive* carries so much art and typographic display you have to return to the cover occasionally to remind yourself you are in progressive-politics territory (Midwest Division).

book-review sections

What do you use to dress up a book-review page or section or a publication devoted exclusively to book reviews? Some editors settle for reproducing book jackets covers. A few run photographs of authors. *The New York Review of Books* for years has run exquisite caricatures by the much imitated David Levine, with his marvelous crosshatching and keen eye for facial and body aberrations. The magazine has also run public-domain art from old magazines.

The *New York Times Book Review* (don't confuse it with the *NYRB*) runs a variety of art pieces, some drawn or painted, some in photographic form, some put together as montages or collages. It is obvious that a picture research department reads hard, thinks deeply, and researches imaginatively to come up with art pieces that nicely complement the excellent design of this square-format publication.

When a book being reviewed is itself well illustrated, it is easy enough to reproduce one or two of the illustrations to run with the reviewer's comments. As in any illustrated piece, it is good to pick art that illustrates the headline that runs above the review. Most review pages or publications use headlines different from the titles of the books reviewed. Book titles are run small, just before the reviews' opening paragraphs, along with book authors' and publishers' names.

The easiest books to illustrate in a book-review section are cartoon collections. A sample cartoon and caption plucked from the book and surrounded by a bit of copy describing the book, perhaps boxed, makes a nice change of pace on a page.

A book-review editor should not fall into the trap of using art that duplicates the art used in an ad for the book that might appear in the same issue.

spot drawings

The *New Yorker* holds onto a tradition of inserting small, charming illustrations into columns of type just to bring some graphic relief, however unrelated, to its pages. Some of the illustrations show up again and again, but because the subject matter is so innocuous, readers do not notice or object. The "spots," as they are called, allow readers to admire the beautiful scratchboard drawings of Mario Micossi and the careful line drawings of Judith Shahn, to name two regular contributors. What you can expect to see are street scenes, buildings, pieces of furniture, occupations, recreational activities, table settings—almost anything. Some of the spots are unsigned, or signed only with initials. An occasional spot bears the signature of a regular contributor of gag cartoons—of a Charles Saxon, for instance, or a James Stevenson.

Doing spots used to be a nice sideline activity for gag cartoonists, but with the *New Yorker* almost alone among magazines using them, spots represent an almost lost art. It may be time to resurrect them among the magazines.

6

the light touch
for newspapers

With the coming of age of each new mass medium—radio just after World War I and television just after World War II, to name two—people have predicted the end of newspapers, a medium that traces its origins back several hundred years. We do have fewer newspapers today than at the turn of the century, but the decline leveled off during the 1940s, leaving us with many one-newspaper cities, but also with roughly 1,750 daily papers and 8,000 weeklies, most of which serve as outlets for cartoon art. The economic conditions of the 1980s forced some notable newspaper closures, but a number of new papers appeared to keep the totals constant. Newspapers computerized their typesetting in an effort to stay competitive and gave more atten-tion to the way they looked. The move to offset lithography, now generally complete, made the reproduction of art easier and less expensive.

Most of the art comes from photographers, but illustrators, especially humorous illustrators, have made something of a comeback on newspapers. Before photography, all the art came from a stable of artists and cartoonists. Then photographers took over. A steady diet of photographs over several decades has made artwork an attractive if not frequent alternative.

Not all newspaper artwork is humorous. Some of it comes close to qualifying as fine art. Many newspaper artists turn out both cartoons and serious illustrations. Frank Hockaday, who heads *The Oregonian*'s art department, is such an artist. Figure 6.1 shows a fluoro wash drawing he made for a feature built around several dance programs. (When the paper was still being printed by the letterpress method, wash drawings that were to appear as highlight halftones had to be painted with a pigment mixed with a fluoroscopic solution rather than with plain water.)

Hockaday's dance-program art commanded attention because it stretched all the way across a six-column newspaper page. Hockaday planned it so that an arm reached out of the art's rectangle and into the area of the paper reserved for headings: an interior logo (name of paper) and the section name ("Leisure").

Figure 6.1
Frank Hockaday
Courtesy of *The Oregonian*.

the
art staff

A small paper has people around who both write and take pictures for publication. On bigger papers the jobs are separated; typically, several people do nothing but take and process photographs.

A small paper often uses one person on a part-time basis to produce occasional sketches or cartoons. A big paper maintains a staff of several illustrators. *The Oregonian,* for instance, a big daily in Portland, has a graphics editor who, with an assistant, is in charge of twenty-one photographers and six staff artists, some of whom do cartoons. Hockaday says the job of the artists there is to "give the reader a chance to discover there's something worth reading."

Although newspaper artists are allowed to sign their drawings, few earn the recognition that their counterparts in the comic-strip world earn. Some newspaper artists and cartoonists are as good as the best in any of the other media. Brad Holland, whose work appears on the op-ed page of the *New York Times,* is one of the most respected of the newspaper illustrators. Holland started out as an artist in a tattoo parlor, then moved to a greeting-card company, then to the underground press. For a time he drew for *Playboy.* Lately he has illustrated books. You can see a collection of his intricate crosshatch drawings in *Human Scandals* (New York: Crowell, 1977).

what
to show
in the art

As in any other medium, the idea behind the illustration is more important than the style or tools used. What to show? An illustrator can spend more time figuring that out than pulling a pen or brush across a paper surface.

Consider Tom Bloom's assignment to illustrate a *New York Times* feature on traveling at Christmas time instead of spending it with family. The feature outlined a number of possibilities, apparently to inspire single people adrift in the city without ties. Christmas "can be an especially rewarding time to travel." How to show that a person was traveling during the Christmas season? Bloom put the traveler in a Santa Claus suit, put a lei around his neck and a plane ticket in his hand, and had him carry a suitcase, but not an ordinary suitcase.

It was shaped to hold a Christmas tree.

For the same paper Charles Waller drew a living room scene for a feature on economic affairs: "Relax, Social Security Is Doing Its Job." He constructed a rocking chair out of a bent social security card, and that piece of furniture dominated the pleasant, traditional room.

For a feature on federal consumer protection—or the lack of it—in another issue of the *New York Times,* Niculae Asciu, using a style possibly influenced by Tony Auth, showed a man being held up by someone nonchalantly going through his pockets. Uncle Sam with a gun, nightstick, and walkie-talkie was walking by, but with dark glasses and a white cane. He didn't see.

Figure 6.2
Ned Levine
Courtesy of *Newsday.*

Figure 6.3
Courtesy of *Newsday.*

Figure 6.4

Figure 6.5

For a review of Mildred Klingman's *The Secret Lives of Fat People,* a book criticizing fat people for deceiving and excusing themselves, Pat McLelland in *The Oregonian* showed a fat person reading a book with an arm jutting out from the pages, finger pointed at that reader in accusation.

To illustrate Lou Cottin's *Newsday* feature on the problems and joys of young couples moving back home with their parents, Ned Levine made use of a nursery rhyme image: an old shoe for a home (Figure 6.2). With fine-pen lines, he created a pleasant series of patterns and a nice feeling of roundness and dimension. He put smiles on the faces of the old folks waiting at the open door and expressions of apprehension on the faces of the suitcase-carrying couple coming up the walk. Figure 6.3 shows how the drawing fit into the tabloid page.

Often the illustration works a lot like an editorial cartoon, with some kind of a symbol making a strong point. David G. Klein, using a scratchboard technique, took the rocking-chair image we have given the elderly and turned it into a weapon. The *New York Times* feature that he illustrated said that politicians fear the clout of old people organized into pressure groups. In Klein's illustration, a giant woman in a giant rocking chair was about to rock into—and smash—the U.S. Capitol.

As in humorous illustrations elsewhere, humorous illustrations in newspapers take liberties with reality, even when the illustrations go with serious stories. Figure 6.4 shows a small, brush-stroke illustration for a newspaper feature on tourism and what it means to the hometown. Few ride around in convertibles in this hometown, where mostly it rains, and certainly tourists do not spend so wildly, but the drawing was meant more to decorate than inform.

size and shape of the art

Sometimes the illustrator gives a literal interpretation to a word or phrase taken from the headline or story. Figure 6.5 went with a story on a proposal for reducing the number of counties in Oregon. "Erasing the boundaries" was mentioned.

With those giant pages in a newspaper—even a tabloid newspaper—the illustrator has a chance to create visual impact not possible in other media. Once in a while a whole page goes to the illustrator, as when the *Chicago Tribune* turns Jeff MacNelly loose on one of his special creations. During the 1982 race for governor, MacNelly took a full page to present his illustrated "letter" to his parents, written by a country boy from Virginia (that's Mac-Nelly) new to the big city and awed by its crazy—and suspect—way of counting votes.

A newspaper illustration can be as big as a poster or as small as a postage stamp, depending upon how much impact the editor wants to give it.

As with any print medium, a newspaper likes to run an occasional piece of art in a severe horizontal or vertical shape instead of the usual rectangle or square. A drawing that isn't very deep can stretch all the way across a page, for instance, without taking up a lot of space.

Jack Barrett of the *St. Petersburg Times* demonstrates this space-saving technique in a severely horizontal drawing (Figure 6.6) for a story about conflicts between renters and landlords. That he puts his figures in a shallow setting not only saves space; it also emphasizes the pull between the two opposing forces.

What if the space assigned to the artist is strongly vertical instead of strongly horizontal? Could the same people participate in a tug-of-war drawing just as dramatic? Of course. The focus then probably would be from above, with the renters at the bottom of the vertical rectangle, the landlord at the top. It would be a harder drawing to execute, but an artist as experienced as Barrett would have no trouble bringing it off.

Figure 6.6
Jack Barrett
Courtesy of the *St. Petersburg Times.*

humorous art for serious stories

That a newspaper story is deadly serious does not necessarily preclude its being illustrated with humorous art. My editor at the *Eugene* (Oreg.) *Register-Guard* had no art for a story featuring interviews with child-rearing authorities on the effects of toy guns on the thinking of the young. At the last minute, he turned to me. There was no time even to show me the story. My drawing had to be generic. Although only a toy is involved, the gun-user takes on a jaded appearance in contrast to the innocence of his youthful victim. The upward wrinkles in the pants help add to the illusion of reaching. My inclusion of a cute dog makes the action more poignant or pathetic.

My illustration in Figure 6.8 for another *Register-Guard* story drummed up a little sympathy for court reporters (official stenographers, not people associated with newspapers) who were being replaced by electronic equipment. That accounts for the worried look on the face of the long-time public servant.

I used solid black here to relate the man to the machine at the right. The black on the machine helps give it a third dimension. The black in the suit provides a good background for the expressive hands. In brushing in the black I made no attempt to define

Figure 6.7

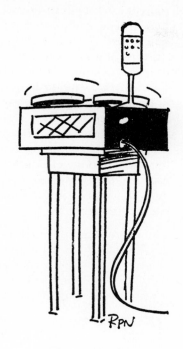

Figure 6.8

the lapels of the suit, the inside edges of the arms, or the wrinkles. Nor did I bother to fully define the cuffs, socks, or shoes; I ran them together with the brushed-on black. These things are penciled in to begin with, and we artists hate to give up all that preliminary drawing; but, as chapter 3 pointed out, clarity and simplicity can contribute more to a drawing than tedious detail.

With the popularity of jogging and the plethora of books and articles extolling its virtues, you could expect a few warnings from physicians. The sketch in Figure 6.9 accompanied a *Register-Guard* feature that treated the dangers of jogging for some people. To bring some action to the scene, I

put the doctor out on the jogging trail rather than behind his desk. The poor jogger, properly suited out and sweating just a bit, expresses his bewilderment.

A number of years ago, what students wore greatly distressed teachers and administrators, and local papers like the *Register-Guard* ran features on the controversy. My drawing in Figure 6.10 shows an unconcerned young woman walking past her principal, a man not in a good mood for what he sees. The one book carried in her right hand was enough to identify her as a student. The feature made special mention of the trend then to walk the halls barefooted.

Figure 6.9

Figure 6.10

with an emphasis on quickness

Illustrators working for newspapers work against tight—even impossible—deadlines. A few quick brush strokes, and the drawing is sent to the offset cameraman. No time to reconsider. Laura Dirksen might have wanted to do a bit of retouching on one of her illustrations for the *Baltimore Jewish Times*, maybe even put more work in on the lettering, but she had only a few minutes—less than thirty, it turned out—to draw the near-destitute family you see in Figure 6.11.

The ink and grease crayon drawing illustrated a feature about the Hebrew Free Loan Association of Baltimore, founded in 1898 to aid Jewish immigrants. Baltimore Jews today who are in need of money can turn to the association for interest-free loans. Those getting the loans are people who, like those shown in the drawing, would probably be turned down by conventional loan companies and banks.

A half-hour is often par for the course. That's the time illustrator Bill Kresse reports having on the *New York Daily News*. In that time, he must read the story and come up with an idea that has to be approved by the editor. That gives him fifteen minutes to do the drawing, if he's lucky.

Figure 6.11
Laura Dirksen
Courtesy of the *Baltimore Jewish Times*.

eliminating ambiguity

A drawing of a man midway between a sitting and a standing position, a chair just below his rear, can say either that he is getting up or that he is sitting down. A slight adjustment in the drawing can make a big difference in what's said. If the man grasps at the crease in his trousers, as men in trousers are wont to do, the viewer knows then that he is sitting down. If the person pictured is a woman in a skirt, she can be made to clutch at her bottom with both hands to keep the cloth from wrinkling in the sitting. And that will say *she's* sitting down instead of standing up.

A drawing of a woman, her hand holding something just over an open purse, can say either that she is putting something into the purse or that she is taking something out. With her hand firmly grasping it, she would be taking it out of the purse. With the item slightly away from her hand and between the hand and the open purse, she would be putting it away. Were she looking away from the purse while this was going on, with a worried expression on her face, the woman might qualify as a shoplifter.

Is the action in a drawing taking place indoors or out? A simple

Figure 6.12

prop or two can erase any ambiguity. In Figure 6.12, a rack of coats, barely shown, tells the viewer that the woman is inside a store, and the coat and purse

mark her as a shopper and not a clerk. The glasses suggest that she is going to look the merchandise over carefully, prices being what they are.

The drawing is one of a long series of spots I did over the years to illustrate newspaper features on the increased traffic in the stores before Christmas. What is the mood of the typical shopper this year? would be the theme of a typical feature. What are people buying this year? would be another. How fussy are they? Do they have specific items in mind, or are they moved by point-of-purchase displays? What are the latest things in toys—for grownups as well as children? A reporter interviewed store managers, clerks, and customers to find answers. The story that resulted each time called for several small drawings to relieve the several columns of type.

localizing the artwork

Much of what a daily or Sunday newspaper runs in its news columns comes from wire services and syndicates, and some of the material comes already illustrated. But sometimes a newspaper wants to illustrate a piece that comes in from a wire service or syndicate unillustrated. Or maybe the paper wants to discard the illustration that comes in and substitute one that stresses a local angle. The paper may also feel that its local artist has a better style than some far-away artist has.

For a New York Times News Service feature published in its Sunday travel section, Portland's *Oregonian* called on staff artist Ted Reeves to supply an illustra-

tion. Reeves' line drawing (Figure 6.13) picks up on a warning carried in the feature that travelers should read contracts carefully now that airlines are including contracts with tickets. Some contracts are pretty long, outlining as they do all the liabilities and special services. Reeves gets plenty of action into a setting that, in lesser hands, wouldn't have much. (When not illustrating stories and features for the paper, Reeves designs the paper's Sunday magazine section.)

In some respects a small, weekly newspaper is in a better position

Figure 6.13
Ted Reeves
Courtesy of *The Oregonian*.

to use local art than a big-city daily is. Usually a weekly produces all of what it runs in its columns. It doesn't have access to the wire services (all of its news is local), and only occasionally does it find room for anything supplied by syndicates. The weeklies (and small dailies) were the first to jump on the offset lithography bandwagon, and so were able to avoid the costly photoengraving charges big-city newspapers faced when processing local artwork.

dealing with history

Many newspapers like to reach back into history for features designed to interest older readers. The feature may dwell on what the town was like, say, near the turn of the century. Perhaps some old-timers are interviewed so that what they remember about the place and the people can be recorded.

A newspaper running an historical piece often has trouble finding photographs to illustrate it. If photographs are available they may be too faded to reproduce well. But they can be of use to an illustrator—even a cartoonist—as reference.

Memory alone can be enough for the cartoonist creating a contemporary scene, but research becomes necessary when old times are involved. What was the cut of the clothes then, the shape of the furniture, the nature of the artifacts? As a newspaper illustrator I faced the problem often, because my newspaper delighted in its annual progress editions that celebrated the past or which, for

Sunday sections all year long, recalled events that had shaken the lives of older readers. Some stories went back even further, like the story of how news reached the West that Lincoln had been shot.

Tight deadlines prevented my doing the kind of research one would do to illustrate a magazine piece or a nonfiction book, but I had time at least to pull down an encyclopedia volume from the shelf or pick out my "Historical" file from my morgue. Figure 6.14, a Pentel sketch, is more a rough sketch than a finished drawing, but, run small, it was adequate for newspaper reproduction. The portrait of Lincoln on the wall, the old wall clock, and the roll-top desk were enough to set the scene, and the message on the floor and the bowed heads were enough to convey controlled despair.

Note that the props are kept close enough to the figures to form one major unit and that the major unit, at least at the top, takes on an irregular rather than a rectangular shape.

Unlike a serious drawing, a humorous drawing needs just a hint of the past to become appropriately dated. The baseball scene (it illustrated an anecdote involving an early-part-of-the-century picnic) is made old through use of an old-fashioned baseball cap, suspenders, knickers, and a few other touches that involved no research. Sometimes there is not enough time even to go to an illustrated encyclopedia. But a cartoonist memorizes details of costume and scene in off hours much as a writer memorizes quotations and figures of speech. In rough form, the material is always there when it's needed.

Figure 6.14

Figure 6.15

facing
the holidays

What's left to say about the holidays? They tick off with monotonous regularity, and each time the editor or feature writer looks for a fresh angle. After a few years the humorous illustrator, too, wishes they would go away.

I don't know how many times I looked for some new gag or gimmick to celebrate St. Patrick's Day (to name one of the holidays that had to be recognized). I stooped low enough one year to putting an "O" in front of my signature to give it an Irish flavor. The one joy the holiday brought me was an invitation to use a second color where mostly throughout the year I was stuck with black alone.

Holiday features lately seem more sophisticated and even useful, making them more worthy of illustrations. When the *Oregon Daily Emerald,* a campus paper, ran a feature on "How Not to Burn Your Bird" for students who couldn't get home for Thanksgiving and who had to cook their own turkeys, it turned to Jane Hart Meyer for art. Figure 6.16 shows what she produced. She used a technical fountain pen to

Figure 6.16
Jane Hart Meyer
Courtesy of the *Oregon Daily Emerald.*

capture the frustration of a person not overly familiar with cooking procedures. Seeing the nostrils and looking deep into the cook's mouth, the reader gets the impression that the cook is howling in grief. The hands firmly grasp the legs of the turkey, the better to crowd it into the too-small pan.

helping
the reader
make
comparisons

Whenever there are two or more items to be compared, they should appear in the same form, preferably right next to each other on the horizontal. They should be shown from the same angle and in the same size. This makes it easy for the reader to make necessary comparisons.

Jack Barrett of the *St. Petersburg Times* illustrates the principle with his well-dressed, well-heeled ciga-

rette smoker on the left (Figure 6.17) and his down-and-outer on the right with his cigar butt, probably picked up off the street, held together by a toothpick. The discarded, opened tin can further established the cigar smoker's credentials. The drawing accompanied a *Times* feature on apparel.

Figure 6.17
Jack Barrett
Courtesy of the *St. Petersburg Times*.

making statistics bearable

Dr. Ridgeway Trimble of Johns Hopkins University likened statistics to a bikini. "What they reveal is enticing but what they conceal is vital." That's statistics from the standpoint of agencies and organizations releasing them to impress or propagandize people. An editor's job is to report them and to reveal as much as possible. Art can help and humorous art can help even more in relieving the tedium.

A newspaper—or any publication—dealing with statistics makes use of three kinds of charts: line charts, bar charts, and pie charts.

A line chart shows a zigzag line on some kind of grid, with amounts calibrated on a vertical axis at the left and units of time calibrated on a horizontal axis below. A bar graph shows the amounts as solid bars of varying lengths, arranged either horizontally or vertically. A pie chart deals not with amounts but with percentages, various slices of the pie adding up to 100 percent. The cartoonist comes in here to dress up the charts, keeping them accurate but making them into metaphors if possible or at least adding some decoration.

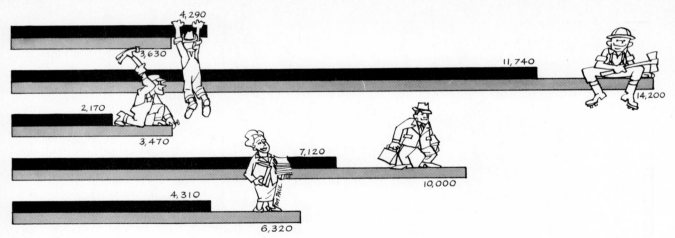

Figure 6.18

A good way to dress up a line chart is to go ahead and plot the zigzag line, then study it to see what its course suggests: a valley, a hill, a slope, whatever. *U.S. News & World Report,* recognized for its imaginative charts and graphs, showed one that measured the millions of dollars in fraud over the years in unemployment benefits. The graph line suggested an easy chair, and so the chartmaker placed a workman in it, feet propped up, eyes closed in contentment, a hand holding onto a glass.

The *New York Times,* for a feature on toy sales in its business section, showed a line chart with the line built with Tinker Toys. A round connector marked each new year. Toy blocks spelled out the chart's title.

One way to dress up a vertical or horizontal bar chart without converting the bars themselves to drawings is to overlap the bars with drawings or put drawings nearby to decorate the bars but, more important, to help identify them. The chart (Figure 6.18) showing employment in the county where I live carried the words "Agriculture," "Wood Products," "Construction," "Wholesale-Retail Trade," and "Public Education" in front of the bars along with appropriate num-

bers at the ends. A cartoon farmer, logger, carpenter, businessman, and teacher posed on the bars to help in the identification. The black bars represented jobs for one year, the shaded ones jobs five years later. Readers could quickly compare numbers of jobs in the county and see that in at least one category (at the top) they had decreased over the five-year period.

Hope Hornbeck, while a student at West High School, Iowa City, and a staff artist for *West Side Story* there, dressed up a feature on grade inflation with a bar chart of a clown being progressively raised off the ground by a balloon grown too inflated since 1969 (Figure 6.19). Why a clown standing in for the student? Hornbeck explained that many students could get good grades even while clowning around.

To show what goes where in Bucknell University's operating budget, Newton Art/Advertising, Selingsgrove, Pennsylvania created a bar chart that was really a mortarboard cut into appropriate sections (Figure 6.20). This was an interesting concept because the odd shapes meant that the areas representing the various percentages had to be estimated rather

than measured. The drawing is flat and abstract rather than realistic and three dimensional, but artist Stephen Newton included a detailed tassel as a decorative and identifying artifact. The chart appeared in a fund-raising brochure.

Pie charts can take imaginative treatment, too. To illustrate a feature on the Disney organization, the *Los Angeles Times* devised two pie charts that made use of Mickey Mouse's ears. One ear/pie was cut into slices to represent revenues for 1966; the other to represent revenues for 1981. The chart showed a proportionate increase in revenue from the theme parks and a rather substantial decrease in revenue from theatrical films and TV.

Flow charts, which show how products are made; organization charts, which show chains of command; and ordinary lists and tables look more inviting when small, decorative drawings are included. Maps can be improved by putting them into perspective, placing three-dimensional props in them, and peopling them. Such maps necessarily distort distances and scale, but they are interesting to look at and in the end, perhaps, more revealing than ordinary maps.

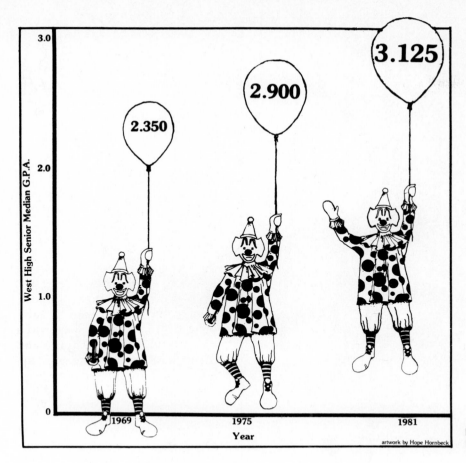

Figure 6.19
Hope Hornbeck

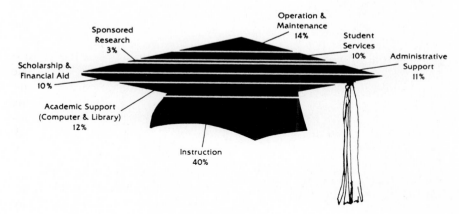

Figure 6.20
Stephen Newton

special pages and sections

Some of the most satisfying illustration assignments for a newspaper involve special pages, such as the editorial page or the op-ed page, and special sections, such as the sports section.

An editorial cartoon usually dominates the editorial page. Smaller illustrations can give the page even greater visual vitality. The lead editorial can profit from an illustration, and so can the letters-to-the editor column. The op-ed page, which takes more of a magazine approach than the editorial page takes, is especially receptive to innovative artwork.

Some of the bigger newspapers, for their Sunday issues, devote a

113

Figure 6.21
Paul Kolsti
Courtesy of the *Dallas Morning News.*

Figure 6.22
Courtesy of the *Dallas Morning News.*

full section to editorials, thought pieces, interpretive stories, and roundup stories summarizing the week's news. Newspapers' most imaginative artwork often appears in these sections. (See, for instance, the Sunday *New York Times.*)

To illustrate an opinion feature on illegal aliens in the *Dallas Morning News,* Paul Kolsti, using a crosshatch technique, showed Uncle Sam sweeping the problem—and the aliens—under the "rug," which is actually the United States itself (Figure 6.21).

Figure 6.22 shows how the cartoon appeared on the page to bring graphic relief to the guest-

written feature, which dominated the page.

Kolsti was honored in 1982 with the second annual Scripps Howard Foundation/Charles M. Schulz Award as the nation's most promising new cartoonist.

People working on the art staff of a newspaper also get assignments to do cover art for the locally edited magazine section, for any number of special tabloid sections, and for the weekly guide to TV programming. Jack Barrett's cover art for a *St. Petersburg Times* TV guide (Figure 6.23) puts his portraiture ability to work. The sketches of Johnny Carson and his sidekicks, despite the large heads, are more serious sketches than Barrett's Woody Allen car-

icature shown earlier, but Carson's money bags, McMahon's beer can, and Severenson's loud shirt are cartoon-like touches. This art easily accommodates itself to a second color to be put in the box surrounding Carson's head. The color would have to be light enough to allow the black type to overprint clearly. A dark color would require the letters to be reversed (printed to read as white).

The illustrator in this case, not the art director, decides on the placement of the type and actually pastes it into place, so that the type and the illustration are treated by the platemaker as one piece of art.

114

Johnny Carson:
A comedic
Rolls Royce

Page 3

Times Art By Jack Barrett

Figure 6.23
Jack Barrett
Courtesy of the *St. Petersburg Times.*

sports cartooning

Compared to what it was in the pre-TV years, with the likes of "Tad" Dorgan and Willard Mullin at their boards, sports cartooning is now almost a lost art. A few cartoonists still enliven the sports pages of metropolitan newspapers. One of the best is Karl Hubenthal, just retired from full-time work with the *Los Angeles Herald Examiner* but available for an occasional assignment. In the cartoon shown in Figure 6.24, Hubenthal, true to the trade, both writes and draws a cartoon essay on an upcoming baseball series between the New York Yankees and the Los Angeles Dodgers. See what he does with the Yankee pin stripes. Notice, too, that he makes a vacuum sweeper out of the Yankee slick-fielding third baseman, Graig Nettles.

Drew Litton, another sports cartoonist, draws sports cartoons five days a week for the *Rocky Mountain News,* Denver. Unlike other sports cartoons, his express opinions. They are like editorial cartoons.

Figure 6.24
Karl Hubenthal
Courtesy of the *Los Angeles Herald Examiner*.

regular columns

A regular newspaper column dealing with life's foibles, such as something local that is written in the manner of Erma Bombeck, can benefit from a small cartoon inserted near the beginning each time. The cartoon can involve the writer, so that the character becomes familiar, almost like a comic-strip character. Say the writer works for the college paper and, in one column, advocates doing away with P.E. as a requirement for graduation. The cartoon might show a flabby reporter with a pot belly pounding away at the typewriter and looking the worse for the exertion.

What kind of a cartoon to use would depend on how a column is worded. If it has a surprise or ironic ending, you would not want the art to give it away.

Some columns, like some humor, do not lend themselves to art of any kind. The trouble with column illustration is that once you start it, you have to keep it up. Some days an illustration will be easy to come by; other days there will be nothing there. Contrast this with the assignment to illustrate occasional feature stories. If the feature cries out for a drawing, it gets it. If it doesn't, the piece gets published without illustration. No problem.

When he was a reporter for the *Oregon Journal,* a Portland daily, Jack Ostergren in 1956 started a weekly column dealing with how he faced life's irritations. It was a light-hearted column, the kind that often ended with a surprise twist. It was also a column that could benefit from a humorous illustration, and Ostergren was enough of an artist to do the drawing himself. In fact, when the paper's full-time staff artists were swamped or vacationing, he turned out an occasional illustration for other reporters' feature stories.

When the paper merged with *The Oregonian* in 1982, Ostergren and his column moved to the bigger paper, and it continues to appear there each week. Figure 6.25 shows a sample illustration with his headline for that day.

This particular column discusses his gentle nature and describes a typical day's pleasant start that degenerates, because of unreason-

Morning drive turns pussycat into tiger

Figure 6.25
Jack Ostergren
Courtesy of *The Oregonian.*

able traffic, as he drives to work. The art, executed in rough, strong lines, is ideal for newspaper reproduction, even when it is greatly reduced, as it is here.

spinoff publications

A newspaper recognizing it has a good thing in a local cartoonist may choose to publish an occasional or an annual collection of cartoons. This is especially true of papers with good editorial cartoonists. Few of these cartoonists get to see their work published in book form by New York publishers. A locally published paperback book, even if it's only on newsprint, turns out to be a reasonably good substitute. The newspaper may use the book for promotional purposes if not to make a profit.

The *Minneapolis Tribune,* proud of its own Richard Guindon (who has since moved to the *Detroit Free Press*), a sophisticated gag cartoonist with a style not unlike that of George Price, brought out a wire-bound calendar featuring full-page reproductions of his *Tribune* drawings. Each calendar page covered one week, so there was room for fifty-two drawings on facing pages. Often a drawing was appropriate to the week, especially when the week had a holiday in it.

One of Guindon's cartoons showed a young woman getting gas for her van. She was wearing overalls and a funky cap—clothes that, except for their revealing fit, duplicated almost exactly the uniform of the tired looking, middle-aged station attendant. She said to him: "Hey, I just love your outfit."

freelancers and the newspapers

In the main, only full-time staff members draw local illustrations for newspapers. Freelancers do not look to newspapers as much of a market, although a few editorial cartoonists in recent years have worked out arrangements with small or medium-size papers to submit occasional cartoons commenting on lapses among the local politicians. (The big papers make room on the staffs for full-time editorial cartoonists, of course.)

I worked out a freelance arrangement with the editorial page of the *Eugene Register-Guard,* a medium-size daily, to submit an editorial cartoon once or twice a week, supplementing the ones it got from the syndicates. The arrangement lasted for twelve years, or until the paper's political stands began to differ from mine (or mine from its). I worked out a separate arrangement with the city editor to illustrate news and feature stories. He would drop off stories on his way home from work and pick them up with the drawings on the way to work the next morning. He was impressed by the overnight service, if not by the quality of the work. My prices were right, too, except when he ordered charts, graphs, and maps. I hoisted my rates on those in order to price myself out of the market, for I am desperately allergic to statistics and not particularly comfortable with straight lines.

The bulk of the artwork in newspapers, humorous or otherwise, comes from wire services, which supply "graphics," as they're called, for nonlocal stories, and from feature syndicates, which supply comic strips and other self-contained cartoons (see Chapter 9).

7

art in a permanent binding

In other industries, a company establishes a product and stays alive by manufacturing it year after year. In the book publishing industry, a company must come up with one new product after another, each requiring its own manufacturing and marketing program. Each book issued—some publishers issue several hundred a year—represents a different challenge.

A book manuscript arrives, it is evaluated and either rejected or accepted; if accepted it is edited, then designed, then set in type, then proofed, then printed, then distributed. In the meantime a program of promotion and advertising, however modest, is arranged.

Occasionally a book makes money for its publisher as well as for its author. But most books lose money or just break even, and their authors gain little more than the temporary joy of being published.

No wonder the profit margin is low. Several thousand publishers, ranging from one- or two-person operations to big conglomerates, compete for customers, and to-gether they put out a total of about 41,000 new books each year. Only a small percentage can be reviewed. It is impossible for every book to get its proper notice.

One obvious way to help a book along is to provide it with some illustrations. Even the word-oriented person who buys books responds to the lure of pictures. Where photographs are involved, the author usually supplies them. Where drawings are involved, the author may make suggestions, but the publisher's editor usually arranges to have them done.

Potential book illustrators often call on book editors with portfolios of examples, and the editors note the illustrators' strengths and weaknesses. When the right book comes along, an editor may get in touch with an untried illustrator. Usually, though, the editor calls in an experienced illustrator who has done other work for the house. For humorous illustrations, an editor may line up a famous gag cartoonist, editorial cartoonist, or comic-strip artist, hoping the name, exploited with that of the author, will help sell the book.

Sometimes a book author searches out an illustrator, as Edward Streeter did when he wrote his *Daily Except Sunday,* to be followed ten years later by *Father of the Bride.* The man he lined up was Gluyas Williams, who, with his clean, black-and-white drawings was possibly the best humorous illustrator America ever produced. Not often do mere illustrations get collected in book form, but Williams' did, in *The Gluyas Williams Gallery* (New York: Harper & Brothers Publishers, 1957). The original accompanying stories by such writers as Robert Benchley and Corey Ford were included. (Williams died in 1982 after a long, rich, creative though quiet life. He was born in 1888.)

David McCord, another writer who asked for Williams as illustrator whenever possible, said that "If we [writers associated with Williams] have ever let him down, he has always held us up." Not "held us up" as in missing a deadline but "held us up" as in keeping writers from failing.

the history of book illustration

Most of the early illustrated books dealt with scientific matters. Maps and technical drawings helped readers to a fuller understanding of what authors talked about. One of the most influential of the early illustrated works was Denis Diderot's *Encyclopedia* (Paris, 1751– 72), a seventeen-volume collection accompanied by eleven additional volumes of illustrations.

Illustrations for books go back to the illuminated manuscripts of the fifteenth century and before, when artists decorated handwritten sheets and books with letters, pictures, and designs in gold and silver. After 1450 printing from woodcuts became possible. Elaborate designs often framed pages of type, and occasionally a whole page was given over to an illustration.

The first illustrated books were "block books," with type and illustration carved together. Soon it was possible to carve the illustrations separately and combine them with movable type. The type then could be reclaimed after printing and, reassembled, used for other books. The printing process was *letterpress,* invented by the Chinese and reinvented and perfected by Johann Gutenberg in Germany. Where wood cutters carved their cuts in relief, leaving uncut those areas that were to print, metal engravers *etched out* the lines and areas that were to print. The printing process called for then was *intaglio.* This meant that art had to be printed separately from the type. It made for more detailed art, but it also resulted in greater expense.

In the eighteenth century, artists in England perfected a wood-engraving technique that resulted in reproductions rivaling what was possible from metal engraving. Gustave Doré, the nineteenth century French artist, showed what heights could be reached in wood engravings with his dazzling book illustrations for various classics. Doré made his drawings on the surfaces of the woodblocks, then turned the blocks over to a highly talented staff of engravers he had trained.

The original lowly woodcut survived in some book publishing. It survived because it could be printed along with the type in a single press run. It took on a look that some readers found crude but others found charming.

Joseph Crawhall, an English artist, used the woodcut technique to illustrate a number of his own books published in the last half of the nineteenth century. Figure 7.1 shows one example. Crawhall hand-colored many of the reproductions in his books. He is also noted for the rough sketches, with captions, that he supplied to Charles Keene, a celebrated artist for *Punch.* (Crawhall, who lived from 1821 to 1896, had a father and a son, both named Joseph, who were artists, too.)

Figure 7.1

The process of lithography (invented in 1798) further contributed to the widespread use of illustrations in books. In lithography, the artist drew in crayon directly onto a flat stone surface. The surface was then dampened and inked, and the image then was transferred to paper pressed against it. Doré used this process as well as the wood-engraving process. Perhaps the best-known lithographic artist was the caricaturist, Honoré Daumier, another Frenchman; his work appeared mostly in magazines and as broadsheets and prints.

It was photoengraving, which came along near the end of the nineteenth century, that gave publishers the ideal and inexpensive way to incorporate illustrations into their books. Letterpress was still the dominant printing process, and now metal plates could be made through pho-

tochemistry and combined with type in single—and long—press runs, the plate withstanding all the pressure and the art holding onto all the detail the artist had put into it. The printing could be in either line or halftone form.

By the time Aubrey Beardsley came on the scene (1872–98) most drawings, like his cover for "The History of Ali Baba and the Forty Thieves," part of *The Arabian Nights* (Figure 7.2), went through the photoengraving process. Beardsley enjoyed the luxury of working in pen and ink, a medium remarkably suited to his decorative art nouveau style.

Sometimes publishers found that the imprint or blackness of the plate showed through on the other side, and so back sides of pages with art were left blank. When halftones were involved, publishers often gathered the units into special glossy-paper signatures (groups of pages), which offered greater print fidelity. Stephen Leacock's *Nonsense Novels* (New York: Dodd, Mead and Company, 1923) contained eight scattered full-page, full-color illustrations by John Kettelwell, all on single glossy pages tipped onto regular pages. A tipped-on page is a page with a narrow strip of glue running down the side next to the binding.

After World War II offset lithography, a commercial adaptation of stone lithography, already around for awhile, took over as the principal printing process for book publishers—and most other publishers as well. Offset reduced the costs of reproduction of all artwork, including photographs, and provided finer detail as well, even on poor-quality paper. From a production standpoint, there

Figure 7.2
Aubrey Beardsley

was little to prevent a publisher from filling a book with art.

The woodcut process and other processes from an earlier era continue to intrigue illustrators (Rockwell Kent did woodcuts for a 1930 edition of *Moby Dick*), but today, with offset lithography as the printing process, book publishers, to use woodcuts, need first-prints from the artist. These prints are treated as though they are pieces of original art. The pieces are photographed to make negatives, which are used to make plates.

same book, different illustrator

Some books go through several editions, with later editions being illustrated by different artists from the artists who illustrated the first editions.

A classic that lives through many editions may carry illustrations by several artists in succession. Lewis Carroll's *Alice in Wonderland* started out with illustrations by Sir John Tenniel, familiar to most of us, and over the years has featured illustrations by Arthur Rackham and cartoonist Ralph Steadman, among others. In late 1982, the University of California Press brought out a new edition with illustrations by Barry Moser, called by *Newsweek* "perhaps the foremost wood engraver in America."

But when a publisher approached James Thurber with the idea of a special edition of *Alice in Wonderland* with Thurber drawings, the humorist, amused by what he considered a sacrilege, suggested instead a special edition retaining the Tenniel drawings but carrying new Thurber text.

the two chief book categories

Books tend to fall into two categories: fiction (novels and collections of short stories) and nonfiction (everything else).

Novels of an earlier era used to feature lots of illustrations. With no movies or television programs to watch, illustrations then represented one of only a few visual diversions available. Now usually the only novels that are illustrated are comic novels, and you don't see many pictures there, either. For instance, the comic novels of Peter DeVries appear without illustrations, even though DeVries has spent much of his non-book-writing time polishing the gaglines on *New Yorker* cartoons.

I don't know why some comic novelists have their books illustrated while others do not. No doubt it is the publisher who makes the decision, and no one has been able to fathom the thinking processes that go on in publishers' minds. Perhaps one of the novel's great strengths lies in its ability to involve the reader. It takes more imagination to read a novel, certainly, than to read a piece of nonfiction. Authors and publishers may feel that readers can invent faces and bodies better than artists can. And readers can more easily identify with what they create themselves. Reading novels is a little like listening to radio, while reading nonfiction is a little like watching TV.

But clearly some stories can benefit from the imaginative touch of an illustrator. Figure 7.3 shows what an anonymous artist dreamed up, in two stages, for a book called *Flowers of Happiness for Beloved Youth*.

Were these two sketches to appear together in a sort of before-and-after form, it would be better to have the reader view the bed from the same side both times. The progression in the tree growth would be clear.

Students in my Caricature and Graphic Humor course sometimes illustrate comic novels not already illustrated. Ragnar Askeland, a student from Norway, chose James Kirkwood's *P.S. Your Cat Is Dead!* A character in the story, using a pistol, orders two worried looking people out of an apartment (Figure 7.4). They had recently arrived from a New Year's Eve party, hence the costumes. Unlike other beginning illustrators, Askeland is not afraid to draw hands. The detail of his hands adds considerably to this illustration's worth. The gun toter, for instance, uses one hand to spin the chamber of his pistol. The several illustrations Askeland did for this assignment followed a style of stopping the figures suddenly at their waists.

In some respects the illustrator of a novel is like the comic-strip artist. There is a cast of characters to develop and keep track of. As a sort of warmup for the illustrator it is necessary to draw each character in a number of poses from a number of angles. All this is done before settling on which scattered incidents deserve illustrating. The job of developing characters is complicated by descriptions offered by the author. Some of these descriptions may not come

123

Figure 7.3
From the book edited by Leonard DeVries, Busybee,
Amsterdam, 1958.

Figure 7.4
Ragnar Askeland

124

until later in the story, well after characters have played roles that might be illustrated. This means a thorough reading of the book before beginning to do any drawing.

Nonfiction books far outnumber novels, and they offer a better outlet for the work of humorous illustrators. The nonfiction category includes reference works, textbooks, histories, biographies and autobiographies, how-to-do-it books, exposés, long essays, inspirational and humorous books, and many others, including collections of short pieces.

collections

Short stories, essays, articles, poems, recipes, quotations, excerpts from longer pieces, and other literary units have been gathered together in book form, sometimes for first-time publication, sometimes as reprintings. Any books in these categories could be illustrated. Sometimes the collection consists of art itself, with a limited amount of textmatter.

A collection of cartoons often centers on a single topic, like sports, business, or cats. Especially cats.

In 1981 Jim Davis had three of his *Garfield* cartoon collections on paperback best-seller lists: *Garfield at Large, Garfield Gains Weight,* and *Garfield Bigger Than Life,* all published by Ballantine Books. Several others appeared later.

Cartoon collections inspire collections that answer the original collections. The spate of cute-cat books, including Davis', in the early 1980s brought on a series of I-hate-cat books. Skip Morrow, a singer from Vermont who was scratched by a cat at a friend's house, published *The Official I Hate Cats Book* with Holt, Rinehart & Winston. It became a best seller. *The Second Official I Hate Cats Book* followed. Another cartoonist brought out *101 Uses for a Dead Cat,* with Clarkson N. Potter Inc. as publisher. It had a sequel, and it also inspired some fight-back books, like *Cat's Revenge: More Than 101 Uses for Dead People* and then *Cat's Revenge II.*

Some cartoon collections involve the work of a number of artists. The U.S. Department of Health, Education, and Welfare (it has since changed its name) once gathered a series of editorial cartoons, gag cartoons, and comic strips on air pollution from a variety of artists and put them together in a book called *No Laughing Matter.*

Jack Corbett, who makes his living freelancing gag cartoons to magazines, acted as his own publisher when he put together a collection from among the many he has sold. He picked those that fit a basic outdoors theme and called the book *"Hark! Who's that Yoohooing in My Jungle?"* (Salem, Oregon: JC/DC Cartoons Ink, 1979). As in many collections of this kind, the title stems from the caption of one of the included cartoons. Figure 7.5 reproduces a typical page. The cartoon appeared originally in *Changing Times.*

Corbett used a second color on the cover of his book, but, to keep costs down, only black inside. The several testimonials to his work on the back cover included this quote: "'Jack would do better in school work if he'd quit drawing silly pictures.'—Sixth grade report card."

Trina Robbins provided the illustrations for *Women in the John,* a

Figure 7.5
Jack Corbett

"Better hurry, folks, this may be your last chance to buy this property at any price."

collection of graffiti taken from women's bathrooms. Figure 7.6 shows one of her illustrations. It goes with the line, "Human beings were created by water to transport itself uphill."

Robbins, whose work has appeared in comic magazines and other publications and who contributed earlier to *Titters,* an anthology of women's humor, loves the style and design attitudes of the 1940s, and elements of the 1940s appear in her own more recent work. Her clean, strong lines and solid-black areas reproduce well on any paper, including the better quality stock found in books.

Kim Hubbard created a cartoon cracker-barrel philosopher in Abe Martin and for many years contributed widely quoted Abe Martin sayings to the *Indianapolis News* and other newspapers. On several occasions early in the century, Hubbard gathered his Abe Martin sayings and drawings and published them in book form through his Abe Martin Publishing Co., Indianapolis.

Abe Martin's Sayings and Sketches (undated) carried one-liners like these: "A spectacular career allus ends in stomach trouble," "Ther's been entirely too much said about th' glory o' dyin' for your country by those who've never tried it," and "Quite a lot o' th' folks who are talkin' hard times wouldn' have 'em any other way."

Figure 7.6

Figure 7.7 shows one of his sketches—of Mr. Lester Slocum, "bookkeeper at th' creamery an' first tenor o' the' Baptist church choir . . . . Although Mr. Slocum has a thick, soggy, reddish brown mustache, he does not care fer corn on th' cob."

The "All out!" sketch (Figure 7.8) appeared with a short essay on "Th' Auto." "Now that all doubt has been cleared away an' it appears reasonably certain that th'

Figure 7.7
Kim Hubbard

automobile is an established institution, ther remains but one thing fer us pedestrians t' do—waive our rights, or buy a car an' git in th' game."

Richard Huber, exploring man's fascination with the irrational, put together a book of more than 1,000 of his own drawings recording what other artists had done with beasts, devils, and other creatures in various works of art, from prehistoric rock paintings to the gargoyles of Notre Dame. His *Treasury of Fantastic and Mythological Creatures* (New York: Dover Publications, 1981) became part of the publisher's Pictorial Archive series, meaning that editors clip and use the art, because it is copyright free.

Huber based one of his drawings on René Magritte's 1937 painting "The Therapeutist." (Figure 7.9.) Read into it what you wish. Magritte, a commercial artist and wallpaper designer who became a surrealist painter, was both serious and humorous in what he produced. Many of his paintings, like his blue sky with a hole in it,

explored the paradoxes of life and showed the complexity of what we perceive. Others, such as his woman with a fish's head (the reverse of a mermaid), were like painted cartoons.

In another drawing (Figure 7.9b) Huber depicted a mask painted on the border of a Japanese cloisonné plate, made around 1870. In still another (Figure 7.9c) he showed a seventeenth century stone statue found on a mountain slope of Easter Island. As Huber presents it, it looks like something by the late Basil Wolverton.

Huber's bold, simple style, with his carefully controlled texture, resulted in detail clearer than what he could have gotten through photography, and of course by drawing rather than photographing his art objects he could in many cases work from books instead of traveling long distances. And the drawings are easier for editors to reproduce.

127

ABE MARTIN'S SAYINGS AND SKETCHES

TH' AUTO.

Now that all doubt has been cleared away an' it appears reasonably certain that th' automobile is an established institution, ther remains but one thing fer us pedestrians t' do—waive our rights, or buy a car an' git in th' game. While th' upkeep of an auto has been a big bugaboo t' many of our wealthier friends, not a few o' them have found out that a car has some economical advantages. As a result ther is quite a lively trade jest now among folks who are really able t' own cars.

"All out!"

However, we must not fergit that th' feller o' shallow means made th' industry what it is t'day. Ther kin be no doubt that th' auto cuts down th' clothin' bill. All that one requires in th' way of apparel t' operate a car is a $1.50 linen duster, a cheap cap an' a pair o' $2.00 shoes, although one kin easily manage a car barefooted. Th' wife or chicken may dress in proportion. Inexpensive vacation trips are also possible with a small tent an' a can opener, th' terbacker bill often exceedin' th' outlay fer gasoline. Th' auto also teaches a feller somethin' about machinery, an' often little things come up that exercise all th' muscles o' th' body. Ownin' an operatin' a auto is fer from bein' costly, unless one tries t' go from Seymour to Louisville. If a feller is sane an' of a mechanical turn o' mind, th' expense o' maintainin' a car is only a trifle more'n winterin' a gold fish, when we consider th' exhilaration an' scenery we git out o' it.

———

Professor Taft 'll go down in history as th' best ex-President th' country ever had.

❧

Ther's too many folks layin' somethin' aside fer th' nickel the-ater instead of a rainy day.

❧

We'll never be able t' take th' curves out o' th' road t' wisdom.

❧

Figure 7.8
Kim Hubbard

Figure 7.9a

Figure 7.9b

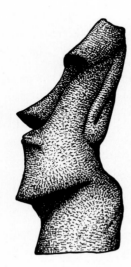

Figure 7.9c

how-to-do-it books

The publishing world seems especially receptive to how-to books and information manuals, many of which profit from the inclusion of humorous drawings, even though the subject matter is essentially serious. *Women: A Book for Men* (New York: Avon Books, 1979), produced by James Wagenvoord and Peyton Bailey, is a showcase of the work of two excellent illustrators: Sandra Forrest and Keith Right. The many lighthearted drawings and decorative initial letters, set off by wide margins, make the book a visual delight. The drawings are at once appropriate and vague. A group is flying a big kite, and the kite turns out to be a woman. A woman knits, and what she knits turns out to be her husband, dog, and surroundings. A woman walks across a room with a wallpaper pattern consisting of assorted hands, all beckoning her in one way or the other. A woman walks a tightrope stretched from an office desk and chair to a bed, all floating in shark-infested waters.

On one page in a chapter on sensuality is a woman's black boot, in a sideways silhouette, looking like a building with a lineup of men's shorts as windows. What are we to make of an illustration like this? What exactly does it mean? It can mean whatever the reader wants it to mean. The best illustrations in books (or anywhere) leave much to the reader's imagination.

Because they are so witty and so outspoken, several of the recent books protesting the abuse of the language come equipped with a generous supply of humorous illustrations. Kimble Mead, for instance, contributed about 100 sketches to William Safire's useful *On Language*.

Student Chip Cannon for my Caricature and Graphic Humor course drew a series of illustra-

Figure 7.10
Chip Cannon

IF THERE'S ANYBODY AROUND WHO HAS THE HABIT OF TELLING YOU NOT
TO TRY BECAUSE YOU'LL PROBABLY BUNGLE THE JOB,...

tions for George Daniels' *The Awful Handyman's Book* published by Avenel Books, New York—a book whose title cries out for some light touches.

In the sample shown, Cannon's "plumber" is bungling the job, all right, and is pushing a woman (possibly his wife) away as he ignorantly proceeds with the job. The waist-high water tells you

that so far he hasn't had much luck. The carefully drawn pipes seem authentic enough, and the water is nicely handled. The parts of the bodies under water are less distinct than the parts above. Cannon uses a nylon tip marker for a strong, steady line.

Like student Ragnar Askeland, Cannon does not find the drawing of hands much of a problem. See how firmly he has the "plumber" grasp the wrench. And feel the push the left hand gives

the woman's face. Nor is Cannon afraid to let the man's hand hide the woman's face. Less sophisticated beginners would feel it necessary to show all her features.

The typing you see at the bottom of the drawing is a sentence lifted from the text. It would be set in type were the cartoon to go into production.

cartoon instruction books

Most of us who like to draw came upon cartoon-instruction books at an early age and savored every drawing on every page. One of the favorites of my youth was *How to Draw Funny Pictures* by, I recently discovered, someone named E. C. Matthews. Not one to read title pages back then (the book was published by Frederick J. Drake & Co., Chicago, in 1928), I had assumed that Eugene Zimmerman (Zim) was the author because almost all of the 200 drawings were his. But he had only *illustrated* the book. (Zim started out as a cartoonist at *Puck* in 1882, then moved to *Judge*, where he worked until the late 1920s. He wrote several cartooning manuals of his own and ran the Zim Correspondence School of Cartooning, Comic Art and Caricature.)

Matthews' advice, I see now, was a bit thin, but I didn't spend much time then with the text. I studied only the deliciously comic Zim creations, most of them drawn on the horizontal to conserve space and all of them displayed on thick, glossy paper of a kind not now found in books. The printing was in vigorous letterpress, and you could run your fingers across the crisp, black lines and enjoy their feel as well as their look.

Figure 7.11
Eugene Zimmerman

Figure 7.11 shows a Zim illustration for a chapter on "School and College Humor." That's a jazz band that you see.

Matthews observed that jazz groups were fun to draw because of "the excessive action and pensive expression," and he mentioned to his cartoonist-readers that "Professional jazz bands will often buy a good characteristic picture of themselves for advertising purposes."

Matthews put the jazz-group drawing where he did because he associated the new and somewhat suspect musical diversion with the nation's colleges. Not much impressed by colleges, apparently (People often ask, "Are you a college man?" "No," is my sad reply. "I was kicked by a mule."), Matthews also showed a motley trio of Zim-drawn college students, each on the seedy side, each with a cigarette dangling from his mouth. "The little fellow in the center can also read and write," was Matthews' interpretation.

How to Draw Funny Pictures, long since out of print, is a book worth looking for in the dusty stacks of your library. Other interesting early cartoon-instruction books include Carl T. Anderson's *How to Draw Cartoons Successfully* (1935), Doug Anderson's *How to Draw* *with the Light Touch* (1954), Clare A. Briggs' *How to Draw Cartoons* (1926), and Richard Taylor's *Introduction to Cartooning* (1947). Carl Anderson created *Henry;* Doug Anderson draws illustrations for major magazines and advertisers; Clare Briggs was the creator of various highly respected cartoon panels and strips, including *Mr. and Mrs.*; and Richard Taylor, famous for his big-eyed beautiful women, was a gag cartoonist for the *New Yorker.* Most cartoon-instruction books are written by less successful cartoonists than these.

Some cartoon-instruction books show mostly or only the work of the cartoonist-writer; others, such as this one, gather works from all over. Collections involve a lot of extra work, because each piece, unless it's in the public domain, has to be dickered for. The author typically spends as much time writing letters as writing the book itself.

approaches to book illustration

Illustrations for books, like illustrations for other media, can pick up details from the text and report them more or less faithfully, or they can deal more with the book's mood or theme. What's shown can be reasonably realistic, or it can be symbolic.

In an illustration created for Arthur D. Morse's *While Six Million Died* (New York: Hart Publishing Company, 1967), Paul Bacon focuses on a familiar subject, the Statue of Liberty, but shows the figure in an unfamiliar pose (Figure 7.12). The torch is out and the arm is no longer lifted. It is the kind of art one might expect to find on a newspaper editorial page, but there it would be done in lithographic-crayon strokes, not in Bacon's photo realism.

Alan E. Cober, who has illustrated quality editions of the novels of Franz Kafka, Albert Camus, and Nathanael West, thinks the best approach in book illustration is to avoid the literal and to conceptualize instead. "Artists are magicians," Cober told students at the Art Center College of Design, Pasadena. The implication was that they should exercise their magic instead of acting as mere visual reporters.

Figure 7.12
Paul Bacon

number and placement

How many illustrations should a book carry and where should they be placed? *Too Many Songs by Tom Lehrer: With Not Enough Drawings by Ronald Searle,* brought out by Pantheon in 1981, had some fun with this problem in the book's title, but the thirty-four songs and the five cartoons were probably a good enough mix, considering that it was Lehrer and his musical satire that was really being sold.

Writer/artist Sandra Boynton in *The Compleat Turkey* (Boston: Little, Brown & Co., 1980), a book dedicated "To whom it may concern," uses the subtitle, "A Comprehensive Guide with Over Three Illustrations," but actually she includes many, and in black plus a second color.

John Simon's *Paradigms Lost* (New York: Clarkson N. Potter, Inc., 1980), a witty collection of essays on good English and clear thought, profits from about twenty humorous illustrations done in wash by Michele Chassare. The illustrator gets a credit line on the jacket and title page and notice in an author's acknowledgment: "The author wishes to thank . . . Michele Chessare, for illustrations that will amuse him long after he has forgotten this book."

Some books give over a few full pages to large illustrations, using an average of one per chapter. Other books scatter various sized illustrations throughout, burying them in the text, sometimes running them narrower than the text and letting type fit around them.

George Moran's simple line sketches for Gyles Brandreth's *The Joy of Lex* (New York: William Morrow and Company, Inc.,

1980) are confined to the beginnings of each of the fifty-two sections examining word usage and word play. For the section on "Crosswords" (to describe one of the illustrations), Moran shows an addict, holding out a pencil, chasing a man in a checkerboard suit.

In illustrating *Improving Newswriting,* an anthology edited by Loren Ghiglione and published by the American Society of Newspaper Editors (1982), Richard Mayer supplied a front cover drawing (a knight carrying a large pen for a sword and riding a horse covered with a blanket in the form of a newspaper) and a full-page drawing as a cover page for each of seven main sections. For a section on "Writers' Tools," he showed a man emptying barrels into a truck labeled "Journalistic Garbage." The barrels were labeled "Subject and Verb Argument," "Blurring of Fact and Fiction," "Jargon," and "Lack of Balance."

It need not be the goal of the editor to scatter illustrations evenly. Some chapters could go with none; other chapters could use several. The subject matter rather than even placement should dictate what's illustrated. Cartoon collections with lots of explanations and juveniles (children's books) can be half text and half illustrations, but books work better usually when they are *mostly* text or *mostly* illustrations. The text in a book of illustrations—cartoons, photographs, whatever—might well be nothing more than captions.

bringing unity to a book

I am working on a book of quotations with comic-strip artist Ed Sullivan. Sullivan is doing the illustrations, most of them in a horizontal dimension to keep them from occupying too much space. The several that you see here show how a clean, crisp style like Sullivan's can relate drawings to give oneness to a book.

Figure 7.13 illustrates a Gilbert Highet quotation from *The Art of Teaching* (1959), which holds that it is impossible to have children without teaching them, that a parent, aware of it or not, always acts as an example. Sullivan interprets this idea to show that even the house pet is affected.

Figure 7.14 shows Sullivan's illustration of a Malcolm Muggeridge remark (in *Chronicles of Wasted Time,* 1973) that future historians may show that "the road to world revolution is paved with best sellers." Muggeridge was commenting on the tendency of radicals and other would-be world-changers to take time out to cash in on the book market with trendy diatribes. The tops of books for Sullivan make an ideal roadway, and the well-armed if motley collection of soldiers seem appropriately single-minded.

In *The Arts* (first published in 1937; republished in 1974),

Hendrik Willem van Loon observed that to "kill time" is "perhaps the most objectionable expression in the whole English language." In a highly imaginative interpretation, Sullivan (in Figure 7.15) shows the ultimate danger in trying to kill time.

In *Practicing History* (1981), Barbara Tuchman says that a good ear is an essential element in good writing. As a writer, "One must *listen* to the sound of one's own prose." In Figure 7.16 Sullivan shows a writer following Tuchman's advice—in stereo yet.

Alexander King was a charming if cantankerous editor, artist, and writer who, with frequent appearances on "The Tonight Show" when Jack Paar was host, was able to write several rambling autobiographical bestsellers. With the freedom that comes to one who knows he is near death (like Oscar Levant, he enjoyed dwelling on his infirmities), King confounded his readers when he couldn't shock them. A master of several languages, he loved playing with words. The following King-written sentence deals with the subject of inspiration: "Just think of all the music, all the painting and all the poetry that

Figure 7.13
Ed Sullivan

Figure 7.14
Ed Sullivan

Figure 7.15
Ed Sullivan

Figure 7.16
Ed Sullivan

Figure 7.17
Ed Sullivan

have come to festoon the amorous doings of mankind since the beginning, and you will learn to stand in proper reverence before the miracle of the Maidenform Bra" (from *May This House Be Safe from Tigers,* New York: Simon and Schuster, 1960).

How would you illustrate that one?

Sullivan took his cue from "since the beginning," showing a scene

of bra worship before bras probably were thought of. The incongruity of the scene gives it some of its humor. It is interesting to see how, from a drawing technique standpoint, Sullivan is able to help the viewer distinguish between a stone carving (short, angular strokes) and real-life people (curved strokes).

Usually one person does all the illustrations in a book. A single style helps hold the book together. Books like the one you are reading, though, because they act

as art showcases, profit from a variety of illustrations. Anthologies and textbooks need variety, too. When Dover Publications brought out *Benchley Lost and Found* (1970), a collection of thirty-nine forgotten essays that appeared in the defunct *Liberty* magazine in the early 1930s, it reprinted the illustrations that accompanied the essays originally, even though several illustrators were involved.

front matter

Some book publishers allow their artists to exercise their skills away from the body of the books, on the title page, for instance, and on other front-matter pages. For some books the publishers' insignias, like Simon & Schuster's man sowing seeds, or Random House's house, get cartoon treatment. The

redrawing is close enough to the original to be recognized, but a light touch comes in.

For the dedication page of his *Cartoons by Homer Davenport,* the artist drew the following cartoon that, with the inscription, was

135

Figure 7.18
Homer Davenport

printed with all the other cartoons. When the book was published in 1898, Davenport had been with the *New York Journal* for just a couple of years; yet he was widely known and admired. Davenport in turn greatly admired his father, a respected Oregon politician and statesman.

Stephen Leacock's *Nonsense Novels* carried a sort of monogram (Figure 7.19) on the title page, which showed Leacock both as a McGill University professor of political economy, which he was, and a clown. The book also carried silhouette art on the end sheets.

Figure 7.19

book jackets and covers

The jackets of hardbound books and the covers of paperbacks offer splendid opportunities to illustrators, for color is usually available and the paper stock is fancier and heavier than stock used inside the book. Often the illustrator acts also as designer. That requires a familiarity with typography. The person who creates the design and art for the

jacket or cover may be someone different from the person handling design and art inside. Jackets and covers are essentially advertisements, meant to act largely as posters. They call for bold handling and often some symbolism.

In doing his sketch of Carry Nation for the jacket design of Robert Lewis Taylor's *Vessel of Wrath,* Paul Bacon noticed a similarity in the shape of the figure of the famous saloon wrecker and the head of the hatchet she carried, and this repetition of shape shows up in his final drawing. The hatchet, which was Mrs. Nation's chosen symbol as well as her weapon during her crusades (she sold small reproductions of it as souvenirs to finance her crusades), provides a recurring design device throughout the book.

The back cover of a jacket or cover deserves some art, too, if nothing more than the author's photograph. A self-portrait makes a good substitute for the photograph if the author is a cartoonist. Orlando Busino's *Good Boy!* collection of animal cartoons (Andor, 1980) carried the sketch shown in Figure 7.20. His later *Oh Gus!* (1981) about "America's Favorite Canine" showed a sketch of the dog, Gus, at an easel just having completed a sketch of Busino.

The sketch shown here is worth studying for its line quality, clean and brimming with character. Notice the separate texture Busino manages for the beard, for the shading on the shirt, and for the pattern on the pants. Notice, too, the solid construction of both the chair and drawing table. Such structure, along with the feeling of roundness Busino achieves through shading, gives the drawing an authenticity it would not otherwise have.

Figure 7.20
Orlando Busino

the versatile book illustrator

Not many illustrators make it solely in book publishing. The field is high in prestige but low in pay. Cartoonists wander in and out of publishing with seeming ease.

Robert Osborn, whose strong, sweeping brush strokes and economy of line influenced many cartoonists in the 1940s and later, spent several years during World War II illustrating training manuals for the Navy. He estimates he made at least 30,000 drawings. After the war his work appeared mostly in *Harper's* and *The New Republic,* but he also produced a number of cartoon commentaries in book form, like *On Leisure* and *The Vulgarians.*

Before launching her comic strip, *For Better or for Worse,* with Universal Press Syndicate, Lynn Johnston put together three good-selling cartoon books, including *David, I Think We're Preg-*

nant. Her obstetrician, impressed by drawings she did for his office, had urged her to put them into book form. Later, when she quit her job with an advertising agency, she published *Hi Dad, Hi Mom. Do They Ever Grow Up* followed shortly afterwards.

Bob Johnson's illustrations for a couple of dozen books led to his launching of a comic strip in 1980, *Hello Carol,* which is distributed by the Los Angeles Times Syndicate. That he drew—and designed—well enough to be a book illustrator shows in the strip, one of the most interesting ones around from the standpoint of style. Judd Hurd in *Cartoonist Profiles* calls the style "sophisticated," a good description. It has a woodcut feel with lots of closeups.

The late Bill Crawford, an editorial cartoonist syndicated by Newspaper Enterprise Association, illustrated more than twenty books during his career, including books written by the humorist Max Schulman. George Price illustrated books in the 1920s before becoming a gag cartoonist for the *New Yorker*, where some 3,000 of his drawings have appeared.

the writer/ illustrator

People who both write and illustrate their books not only enjoy the satisfaction of producing complete packages but also earn royalties untouched by fees that must be paid out to others, agents excluded.

Sandra Boynton found how rewarding producing a book can be when she picked a favorite subject—chocolate—and celebrated it in both words and drawings: *Chocolate: The Consuming Passion* (Workman, 1982). "A delicious little book," observed the *New York Times Book Review*. One of her charming line drawings showed animals at a lecture. A turkey rises to ask the speaker, a pig, if chocolate is available "in nicer colors than brown." (Workman publishes many great and odd cartoon collections, including the works of B. Kliban.)

One of the most successful writer/illustrators was Hendrik Willem van Loon, whose popular histories (*The Story of Mankind, The Story of the Bible*, etc.), written in the 1920s and 1930s, carried many of his own scratchy but witty illustrations. Of course, James Thurber's humorous books carried many of his own lumpy but sophisticated illustrations.

When Harry Graham under the name Col. D. Streamer published his *Ruthless Rhymes for Heartless Homes* in 1899 he apparently provided his own illustrations (the title page credited the illustrations to a "G.H." or an "H.G."; it was hard to tell which). Thirty-one years later, after a career as a successful poet and playwright, he came back with a sequel, *More Ruthless Rhymes for Heartless Homes,*

for which he lined up someone else to do the illustrations: someone identified only as Ridgewell. Ridgewell had a slicker style, all right, but the drawings didn't have the charm of the ones done by Graham himself. They were tighter than Graham's. Figure 7.21 shows a detail from a Graham drawing for a rhyme about a nurse who peppered a baby's face instead of the muffin she was about to eat.

Figure 7.21
Harry Graham

You can compare the two styles in a Dover reprint bringing the two books together in a single thin volume. You can also appreciate the sick humor of an earlier era. Consider this:

Billy, in one of his nice new sashes,
Fell in the fire, and was burnt to
*   ashes;*
Now, although the room grows chilly,
I haven't the heart to poke poor Billy.

Some books go to press with author-drawn illustrations a little on the amateurish side. If the book is lighthearted, and if the illustrations are right there, ready to go, it may be difficult for a harried editor to say No to them. Accepting them, the editor escapes the hunt—and the wait—for outside talent. And what's crude to one person may be charming to another. Shirley Cook, who does books such as *Diary of a Fat Housewife* for Harvest House, a religious and inspirational publisher of Eugene, Oregon, supplies her own line drawings that are, er, not impossible. Her clear lines reproduce well, and that is a good part of the battle.

The idea for a book is more important than the writer-illustrator's drawing ability. Hans Wilhelm, whose drawings can best be described as fragile, neverthe-

less put together *Your Chinese Horoscope,* a book that Avon Books thought enough of in 1980 to publish under its imprint. Wilhelm explained the idea in an opening section: "Today we can seek plausible answers [to our problems] in the ancient Chinese mythology, which was for centuries locked behind the Great Wall of China." The Chinese horoscope, he pointed out, has twelve signs, like the Western Zodiac, but the signs cover twelve-year cycles instead of twelve-month years. The sign of an animal marks each calendar year.

Wilhelm listed birth years and animals from 1900 to 1990 (no reason to hinder future sales) and invited the readers to find their animals and turn to the proper

section, which included drawings and observations. ". . . every man and woman has inherited certain characteristics of the animal which ruled the year of their birth." It is not clear whether Wilhelm expected readers to take any of this seriously.

To illustrate the solicitude of the cat—or the person born in the Year of the Cat—he used a worried cat holding a fish bowl (with fish) up to a faucet to fill the nearly empty bowl. In the goat section, one goat stood with his horns curved to form a heart to illustrate the line, "There is lots of love in the mind of a goat."

collaboration

It is one thing for an illustrator to be called in after a book is already planned or even written. It is something else for the illustrator to be in on the book at the start, perhaps even to originate the book's idea. When two people— writer and artist—are equally involved, sharing royalties evenly, the project is a true collaboration.

Bill Nye's comic *History of the United States* (Philadelphia: J. B. Lippincott Company, 1894) was as much dependent on the numerous illustrations by F. Opper as on the words of the author. In fact, author and illustrator both signed the preface, which argued that they both "respect facts. We have never, either of us, said an unkind word regarding facts. But we believe that they should not be placed before the public exactly as they were born. We want to see them embellished and beautified. That is why this history is written." The preface ended on this note:

"If we succeed . . . , and administer historical truth in the smooth capsule of the cartoonist and commentator, we are content. If not, we know whose fault it will be, but will not get mad and swear about it."

One F. Opper illustration for the book (Figure 7.22) showed "Columbus at Court." It appeared near a paragraph that began, "The interview was encouraging until the matter of money necessary for the trip was touched upon. His Majesty was called in and spoke sadly of the public surplus. He said that there were one hundred dollars still due on his own salary, and the palace had not been painted for eight years."

Another Opper illustration showed "Balboa Drying His Clothes" shortly after discovering the Pacific Ocean. "It was one of the largest and wettest discoveries

Figure 7.22
F. Opper

COLUMBUS AT COURT

Figure 7.23
F. Opper

BALBOA DRYING HIS CLOTHES.

ever made, and though this occurred over three centuries ago, Spain is still poor."

F. Opper deserves a note in passing. He illustrated many books besides Nye's history. A cartoonist with a remarkably long career, he was *Puck*'s leading political cartoonist until hired by William Randolph Hearst in 1899. He did political cartoons for the Hearst newspapers then, but he is best known for his creation of *Happy Hooligan, Maud, Alphonse and Gaston,* and other comic strips. Failing eyesight closed down the Opper factory in 1932, five years before his death.

A new collaboration involves an ad man, Jack Roberts. Recently retired from Ogilvy & Mather, Los Angeles, Roberts is one of those advertising people who can do it all. With Ralph Carson, he founded Carson/Roberts in 1947 in Los Angeles and made it one of the hottest agencies on the West Coast, an agency known for its creative and often lighthearted approach until it merged with the bigger O. & M. in 1971. It was Carson/Roberts that talked Mattel toys into advertising directly to children instead of to adults. It was Carson/Roberts, too, that through institutional advertising helped bring the Dodgers baseball team from Brooklyn to Los Angeles. (". . . We Had Baseball Weather in Los Angeles Yesterday" was the headline on an ad in the *New York Times* following a rained-out game in New York.)

While writing and directing successful advertising campaigns for Baskin-Robbins, Learjets, and other O. & M. clients, Roberts put his cartooning talent to work on a humorous how-to-play-tennis book, beautifully illustrated with cartoons, that sold 100,000 copies.

His latest book, *Who Needs Mid-Life at Your Age?*, a survival guide for men written with Dick Gunther and Stan Gortikov, uncovers "new evidence of life after thirty!" Figure 7.24 shows a Roberts' drawing that was pruned from the book during the editing process. The befuddled fellow is contemplating the difference between what a man does and what a man is. (What you do is not what you are.)

Figure 7.24
Jack Roberts

children's books

Children's books or "juveniles" represent an important segment of the book-publishing industry. Publishers bring them out to serve various age groups. We are interested here in the books for children not quite ready—or just barely able—to read. These books are better described as children's picture books.

Picture books were already common in publishing in the sixteenth century. In 1658, John Amos Comenius in Nuremberg published the first picture book designed especially for children. The Piermont Morgan Library in New York houses probably the most important collection of early children's books in the United States.

Some children's picture books are written and illustrated by the same person; others are the product of collaboration. A person who starts out only illustrating children's books may end up both illustrating and writing them.

Perhaps the best-known person in this field is Dr. Seuss (Theodore Seuss Geisel), who worked for fifteen years for Standard Oil drawing cartoons to illustrate the caption, "Quick, Henry! The Flit!" before he quit to devote himself full-time to writing and illustrating children's books. Dr. Seuss' books are marked by nonsense and rhyme.

Illustrators of children's picture books vie each year for the Caldecott Medal, named for Randolph Caldecott (1840–86), an English illustrator. The Newbery Medal, named for an English bookseller, John Newbery (1713–67), an early publisher of children's books, similarly honors the *writers* of children's books. There's also a Hans Christian Andersen Illustrator's Medal.

In looking through the many children's books issued each year—and there are plenty of them—you get the impression that some of the best commercial art anywhere is being harnessed for the children, or, more correctly, for the parents, teachers, and librarians buying the books.

For sheer artistry, it would be hard to beat the work of Mitsumasa Anno, the Japanese artist and teacher. His *Anno's Journey* (New York: Collins, 1978), a sort of scroll painting, is a series of two-page spreads in full color celebrating the architecture of Europe but containing all kinds of people and scenes and even visual jokes and puzzles. You can also see simplified versions of some of the great impressionist paintings incorporated into his busy scenes. There are no words. You make up your own story as you marvel at the art. It is a children's book too good to waste on kids.

Many of the books have the kind of humor grownups can enjoy. With Harry Allard writing and James Marshall drawing, a family in *The Stupids Step Out* (Boston: Houghton Mifflin Company, 1974) all get in the tub with their clothes on to take a bath. ("But where's the water?" "Don't be stupid. If we fill the tub our clothes will get wet.") Then they go out for the evening, where the children are advised not to watch

themselves in a mirror because it's impolite to stare. At the end of the evening they end up at home in one big bed, their feet comfortably on pillows, the rest of their bodies, including their heads, snugly tucked away under the blankets.

Most of the books educate young readers while entertaining them. Figure 7.25 shows a sample spread from *Why Does It Rain?*, a tall-page (4½-inch-by-9-inch) "Just Ask" book written by Chris Arvetis and illustrated in full color by James Buckley. The book, with its text put into comic-strip balloons as bits of conversation, beautifully and clearly dramatizes how clouds are formed and why rain comes. The writer paid more attention than usual to the art for his book: he is vice-president and art director at Rand McNally, the publisher.

It is not unusual for both people in a collaboration to work on the art. In *We Hide, You Seek* (New York: Greenwillow Books, 1979) Jose Aruego did the outlining of the figures and props and Ariane Dewey did the art research and painted in the colors, textures, and patterns.

A writer/artist needs a unique story angle—a gimmick—to do a successful children's picture book. Dahlov Ipcar for *Lost and Found* (New York: Doubleday, 1981) decided on animals and their camouflage, hiding them in appropriate backgrounds and bringing them into light in succeeding pages. All with rhymes. "Where, oh where, can my zebra be? I know he's there, but he's hard to see."

All kinds of styles and approaches seem to work. The field is open to all media. Gabriel Lisowski, an

Figure 7.25
Courtesy of Chris Arvetis. © 1983 by Rand McNally & Company.

Austrian illustrator and author of children's books, uses a pen to create beautifully composed panels of sensitive lines and crosshatching. His figures and animals are drawn with great character and humor. (See, especially, his *Miss Piggy*, New York: Holt, Rinehart and Winston, 1977.)

Like Lisowski, Marie Hall Ets, an American illustrator/author, works in black and white, but her bolder, simpler drawings have more of a woodcut look, with plenty of texture.

Jose Aruego, a Manila-born illustrator/author who studied at the Parsons School of Design, paints rather than draws his illustrations, using what advertising people would call "decorator colors." Like most people doing children's books, Aruego often features animals; his animals, designed with great simplicity, nevertheless tend to resemble people he knows.

Lydia Dabcovich in *Follow the River* (New York: E. P. Dutton, 1980) uses thick lines to outline her figures and props and fills in with color that appears to come from crayons. The drawing is sure and sophisticated, but the effect is almost as though a child—a talented child—had produced the art.

For some books, color—if it is used—must be produced in a simple form, to keep costs down. The artist does overlays on frosted acetate. These overlays are used to make plates to print the second color (the color other than black). The original drawings are done in black and white.

The books use a variety of formats. Some feature pages with holes in them or pages that vary in width so that parts of succeeding pages can be seen. Tomie de

Paola's *Giorgio's Village* (New York: G. P. Putnam's Sons, 1982) is a pop-up book which, when opened, reveals three-dimensional buildings with doors and windows that open. Perhaps his most popular of his more than 100 books is *Nana Upstairs, Nana Downstairs,* about the death of a great-grandmother, an unlikely subject for a children's book but handled gently enough to work.

Looking through children's picture books you are likely to find a number written and illustrated by big-name gag cartoonists. You gain new appreciation for their work. The *New Yorker*'s Mischa Richter, for instance, has never looked better than in the several children's books he has illustrated with great looseness and boldness. Shel Silverstein, the *Playboy* cartoonist and country-music song writer, is at his best with children's books such as *The Giving Tree* (1964), *Where the Sidewalk Ends* (1974), and *A Light in the Attic* (1981), all published by Harper & Row's Junior Books Division. Ed Frascino, a *New Yorker* cartoonist, has illustrated a couple of dozen children's books, including E.B. White's *Trumpet of the Swan*, a classic. He wrote and illustrated *Eddie Spaghetti*, based on his childhood in the 1940s.

Roy Peterson as a political cartoonist built an appreciative following among adult readers of the *Vancouver* (Canada) *Sun* before he turned to illustrating children's books. He had also done covers for *Time-Canada, Maclean's,* and other magazines. He illustrated a highly popular series of satirical children's books written by Stanley Burke.

Of course what's done in a children's book may be quite different from what's done away from that field. Gahan Wilson modified the morbidity in his work to write and illustrate children's books, including *The Bang Bang Family* and *Harry, the Fat Bear Spy.*

Jack Kent, a talented self-taught artist, drew the comic strip *King Aroo* for a number of years before discovering, in 1968, "the picture-book crowd" and publishing his first children's book. Since then he has written and/or illustrated close to a couple of dozen of them. His *Knee-High Nina* (New York: Doubleday, 1980) involves a little girl who wishes herself big and grownups small, and discovers she's better off being small after all.

William Steig, the *New Yorker* cartoonist, by 1979 had done twelve children's books, receiving the Caldecott Medal in 1970 for his *Sylvester and the Magic Pebble.* He takes about a week to write a book, about a month to do the illustrations.

People who create these books and the publishers who bring them out try to choose topics, locales, and art approaches that do not go out of style. Thus children's books remain for years on a publisher's back list. People who buy them don't worry about the copyright dates.

With success as a book writer/illustrator often goes a travel program to promote books. Steven Kellogg, who has created *The Mysterious Tadpole, Can I Keep Him?* and *The Island of Skog,* among other children's books, visits some 100 schools each year, earning space in local newspapers, which report his visits and interview him. Kellogg studied at the Rhode Island School of Design and in Florence, Italy, before writing and illustrating children's books for a living. He sees a renaissance today for this "true art form," and credits part of the new interest to the entry into the field of the serious artist Maurice Sendak.

143

8
advertisers
with a sense of humor

Advertising means a lot to humorous illustrators. Not only does it provide the revenue that keeps newspapers, magazines, and other media alive to employ illustrators; it also provides an outlet of its own for the work illustrators do. By many estimates, it is the most lucrative market of all.

Interest in humor as a selling tool varies from decade to decade and even year to year, but the 1980s saw it more firmly established than ever before. Advertisers who previously might have been expected to shun humor as inappropriate now seem to embrace it, even for institutional advertising meant to polish images.

Advertising is any kind of sponsored communication meant to sell products, services, or ideas. The best and most elaborate of the ads are prepared by advertising agencies, but many ads originate in advertising departments of advertisers as well. Some ads originate in the media that run them. For instance, a newspaper's display advertising department prepares ads for stores not big enough to employ advertising agencies or maintain their own advertising departments.

This means that illustrators can choose advertising agencies, advertisers, and the media as outlets for their work. They can also work for organizations such as art studios and printers, which supply specialized services to advertising agencies.

The most likely markets for illustrators doing advertising work are the advertising agencies. The person at an agency who works with illustrators is the art director, a person in charge of all the visual aspects of the ads. Big agencies employ a number of art directors.

Illustrators discover that working for an advertising art director is different from working for an editorial art director. The editorial art director is more flexible, more willing to allow experimentation. The advertising art director has more bosses to answer to, including the client, and usually calls in the illustrator only after several meetings with creative types at the agency. Everyone by then is agreed on what must be shown in order to do a proper selling job. The illustrator's job is to come as close as possible to supplying what these people are looking for.

Of the major advertising agencies, Doyle Dane Bernbach, mentioned in an earlier chapter, stands out for popularizing the light touch in advertising. Its campaign in the 1950s and 1960s to establish a place for the unlikely small and ugly VW Bug is still remembered. *Is the Bug Dead?* (New York: Stewart, Tabori and Chang, 1982) reproduces all of the great VW ads.

the advertising illustrator

Humorous illustrators working in advertising soon learn that, like copywriters in the agencies and clerks in the stores, they are there to do a selling job. There is no room in advertising for people who think art is there for its own sake. It is there to serve the client.

The illustrator in most cases works anonymously. The advertiser does not want to be upstaged by an artist's signature in the corner of a piece of art. Nor is there room in an ad for a credit line. (Nor, of course, does the copywriter get a byline.) The anonymity helps explain the large prices often commanded by an advertising illustrator, who, unsung, cries all the way to the bank.

If an illustrator is already well known, however, the advertiser looks differently at the matter of signed work. A *New Yorker* cartoonist, for instance, would always be allowed—even directed—to sign an illustration. One of the most used of the *New Yorker* cartoonists is Charles Saxon, a sophisticated stylist whose signature on a drawing no doubt brings added prestige to an advertisement. He often sits in with creative people at the agency as the idea for an ad evolves. The idea is often his.

Jack Davis, who made his mark on *Mad* and who for a time drew

Heavy-duty muffler now at a lightweight price!

© 1982 Maremont Corp

Playboy's Little Annie Fanny, is another popular humorous illustrator for advertisers. His is a tighter style than Saxon's. Maremont Defender Heavy-Duty Muffler uses Davis to depict "Defenderman," a cartoon character created in 1981 to sell the product. You see Defenderman in Figure 8.1, lifting a car to illustrate the headline, "Heavy-Duty Muffler Now at a Lightweight Price!"

This ink drawing with its carefully executed line and crosshatch shading appeared in newspaper advertisements across the country. A version painted in full color appeared on the cover of a folder going to muffler shops. The headline there read: "Maremont Helps You Muscle Out Competition."

When small cars were still something of a novelty in the United States, Volkswagen arranged with a group of big-name gag cartoonists to produce cartoons gently prodding the Bug. *Think Small,* a book distributed by VW dealers to customers and potential customers beginning in 1967, featured the work of Charles Addams, Virgil Partch, George Price, and many others. Each page or spread showed a cartoon or two by an artist along with his photograph. The book has become something of a collectors' item.

Sometimes an advertiser makes use of an already published cartoon, making special arrangement for reprint rights. The New Chrysler Corporation and its agency, Kenyon & Eckhardt, was so pleased by a cartoon by Richard Wright of the *Providence Journal-Bulletin* that it reproduced it as part of a full-page ad in *Advertising Age.* "The Reports About the Death of Chrysler Were Greatly Exaggerated" was the cartoon's caption (and the advertisement's headline). The cartoon showed a Chrysler car roaring out and up from a grave marked "Chrysler RIP." Chrysler had just announced a turnaround; it had just finished a selling season with a profit.

national and local advertising

National (or brand-name) advertising almost always originates in big advertising agencies. Local (or retail) advertising originates in smaller agencies, in the advertising departments of retailers, or in the advertising departments of local media. Local advertising often makes use of stock art supplied by houses that specialize in that sort of thing. The art is slick and inexpensive, but it is not exclusive and often it doesn't quite fit. The local freelancer steps in then to fill a void.

A nursery is an unlikely user of cartoons, but Lakeview Farms of Mt. Airy, Maryland, through its advertising agency, The Image Makers, Inc., Upper Marlboro, called on Kimberly Lord to do a series of humorous illustrations for ads selling trees, shrubs, plants, and flowers. The ads, with their light touch, stood out from

Looking for a Good Home

Figure 8.2
Kimberly Lord

ads placed in newspapers by other nurseries.

Figure 8.2 shows how Lord interpreted the headline, "Looking for a Good Home." The bag tied to a pole helps make the point that these two examples of plant life are, indeed, ready to settle down. The copy talks about "lots of plants" available at the nursery. "They need good homes. How about yours?"

exaggeration in advertising

Advertising is known for its exaggerated claims. The exaggeration often extends to the art. Sometimes, as when cars in an ad are made to appear sleeker than they really are, the exaggeration can be charged to overenthusiasm by the advertiser. Other times the exaggeration is meant to amuse or entertain readers and make them more receptive to a serious message. Everyone knows the advertisers are just kidding. Ads like these make use of the work of humorous illustrators.

From its start, advertising resorted to exaggeration in art. An excellent example comes from Germany's F. H. Ehmcke, who in 1907 produced a catalog of 314 trade symbols. Figure 8.3 is one example, a piece of art designed

to be used by advertisers, book publishers, and others who needed something symbolic to represent viticulture: the science of grape growing. Ehmcke's bold, classical drawing style was influenced by William Morris, who fostered in England a revival of interest in Renaissance art following the excesses of the industrial revolution.

One of Mobil's "Observation" ads, run in the magazines, discussed the use of energy by farmers. It made the point that "Farming . . . requires *more petroleum products than any other industry.*" Consider the energy to fuel seeders, spreaders, and harvesters— plus the natural gas used in fertlizers. But because of all the energy used, each American farmer, said the ad, grows enough to feed sixty-seven persons—ten times what an American farmer could do in 1910 and six times what a Russian farmer can do now.

What to use as a visual oasis for the long column of type in the ad? Mobil commissioned a drawing to be done by Arnie Levin, a *New Yorker* cartoonist. The drawing showed several huge vegetables,

bigger by far than two nearby farmers. One farmer says to the other, "Then I got the idea to switch from regular to premium . . . ."

Figure 8.3
F. H. Ehmcke

anthropo-morphic selling

Robert Dale engages in anthropomorphism in Figure 8.4 to produce a tough looking airplane to represent New York Air. The plane wears gloves and puts on an evil facial expression (a smile and a frown combined) to do battle with competing airlines in this newspaper ad.

Cartoon characters, usually cute and tiny, become long-lived trademarks for certain companies. "Speedy" peddles Alka Seltzer, for instance; somebody called "Snap," with a cook's hat, sells Kellogg's cereals, as do "Crackle"

and "Pop"; "Welchkin" sells Welch's grape juice; and "Doughboy" sells Pillsbury products.

Bob Poet, who works as a dealer at Harrah's in Reno while readying himself for a cartoonist's career (he's done some freelancing, mostly for advertisers), drew a mascot (Figure 8.5) for a softball team sponsored by Mac's Bail Bonds. Note the "ball" the bird is trying to pitch.

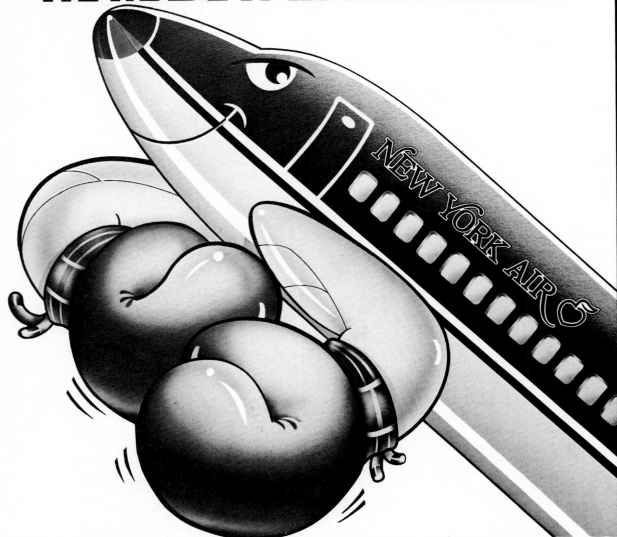

WE MADE IT IN A TOUGH TOWN. WE MADE IT IN NEW YORK.

The competition said we wouldn't last *six* months. We're celebrating our first birthday this month. Sure, we've won. But you, the traveling public, you're the big winner.

When you fly the New York-Washington shuttle route, the service is better and the fares are lower because of us.

When you go to any of the cities New York Air serves—Baltimore, Boston, Buffalo, Cincinnati, Cleveland, Detroit, Louisville, Newark, New York, Orlando, Washington—you'll find our lower air fares there too. (Compared to what fares used to be, our fares are usually more than 50% lower.)

The fact is, we've helped air travelers save over $50,000,000 in fares in this, our first, year of operation.

We did it because of the hard work and the winning attitude of the people of New York Air.

Thanks to your support, we made it in New York. And if we can make it here, we can make it anywhere.

MARKETS IN OUR FIRST YEAR	FARE BEFORE NEW YORK AIR	NEW YORK AIR FARE PLEASURE/EXECUTIVE
N.Y.–WASH.	$60	$29/49
BOSTON–WASH.	$108	$45/65
CLEVELAND–N.Y.	$135	$45/65
LOUISVILLE–N.Y.	$172	$69/89
BUFFALO–N.Y.	$69	$29/49
DETROIT–N.Y.	$128	$49/69
CINCINNATI–N.Y.	$176	$59/79
BOSTON–ORLANDO	$179	$79/99
BALTIMORE–ORLANDO	$139	$59/79
CLEVELAND–ORLANDO	$159	$89/109

NEW YORK AIR
WE'RE FIGHTING TO KEEP AIR FARES LOW.

Figure 8.4
Robert Dale
Courtesy of Ketchum Advertising, New York. Copy and concept: Steve Hunter. Art direction: Santo Cambareri.

naming names

Until recently, advertisers never mentioned competitors by name, preferring instead the "Brand X" designation. The idea was to give competitors no free advertising, even if the advertising were negative. Further, there was some question of lawsuits and even propriety. Now, in a more permissive age, advertisers—even politicians running for office—delight in being more specific. Spades are spades.

Penthouse has taken delight in twitting the longer established *Playboy*. In advertising to media buyers, *Penthouse* has played with Playboy's bunny symbol, showing it in a light designated to put *Penthouse* out front as a place to advertise. Bob Guccione himself (he runs the magazine) did the drawing in Figure 8.6.

The ad carried the headline "B.O. (Bunny Odor.)" The copy suggested that *Playboy* was engaged in cut-rate subscription drives—drives that result in readers who are not always responsive to advertising. The copy referred to "the sour smell of fumbling editorial directions, faltering newsstand sales and fading demographics." *Penthouse*'s logo at the bottom of the ad carried the slogan, "The Sweet Smell of Success."

what to show?

Some advertisers like to look for visual analogies to go with their products. Lectric Shave, for instance, shows a porcupine next to a bottle of the whisker stiffener, with the headline, "Lectric Shave Makes Your Bristles Stand Up for a Closer Shave."

"What Is the World Saying?" asks the headline for an ad for *World Press Review,* a magazine that monitors comment around the world for U.S. consumption. The cartoon art, which occupies about half of the full-page ad, consists of a globe into which are plugged some earphones. The ad could almost have been an editorial cartoon.

Often art as simile or metaphor works better as a photograph—a doctored photograph—than as a cartoon or even a realistic illustration. The United States Postal Service, to rent out its post office boxes, showed a section of them, one with the cover off. Inside was an office setup, with a man at his desk. A posted letter leaned against the wall. By box standards, the letter was normal size. By office standards, it was giant size. The art went along nicely with the ad's headline: "It's Like

Opening Your Own Little Office."

ESPN, the TV sports network, in an ad in *Advertising Age* showed a photograph of a hand reaching out from a TV screen to pull a man up from his seat. It yanked on his necktie. The ad, directed to media buyers in ad agencies, said in its headline, "It's Easier to Reach Someone Who's Sitting on the Edge of His Seat."

Whether using photographs or drawings, many advertisers like to show the real thing. In Figure 8.7, illustrator Casey Jones effectively captures the look of a traffic jam in an illustration for an ad sponsored by Government Employees Insurance Company (GEICO), Washington, D.C. The conversation in non-enclosed balloons serves as the ad's headline. The copy that went with the illustration made the point that "Unlike most companies, GEICO still offers the twelve-month auto policy . . . a full year's coverage at a low rate."

This is an illustration worth studying for its many ways of depicting frustration. For instance, one driver shakes his fist; a couple of others open up their car hoods to

Figure 8.7
Casey Jones

Figure 8.8
William Urbana

cool down their motors; another driver stands on the roof of his van to see what's tying things up.

If the copy for an ad tells a story, the illustrator approaches the assignment as though working for a magazine running fiction. William Urbana creates a heavenly scene for a *Sporting News* ad that tries to impress media buyers in advertising agencies. The copy talks about

a man in Iowa who subscribed to the magazine for fifty-seven years and asked to be buried with a copy. "Few publications inspire such loyalty," the ad concluded.

Whatever is shown, the art should illustrate what the headline is saying. Too often advertising art illustrates the opposite. For instance, a car dealer advertising its service department uses a "We'll Treat You Right" headline with a drawing showing a me-

chanic, presumably at some other shop, making a mess of things.

An agency creating advertising for a cigarette maker showed a sardine can with its lid rolled back to reveal cartons of Kents. The headline read "Uncanny taste." Get it? The trouble with the ad was that the illustration really showed "canny" taste.

fitting
the art

Who the client is, what medium the ad is to appear in, and who the readers are—all this enters into the decision about the art for an ad. Some ads are meant for multiple showings, and the art takes a middle ground. The advertiser takes something of a chance in an age of specialization. It is best to tailor ads to specific audiences. The basic theme remains the same; the approach differs from medium to medium.

MuniciCorp of California, specialists in tax-exempt municipal bonds, funds, and U.S. government securities, shows how to use advertising art appropriate to the medium; in this case, *Variety* (Figure 8.9). *Variety* is the daily bible for movie folks. The art (illustrator not named) also nicely fits the headline, which reads: "Avoid the Bite with Tax-Free Income!"

Figure 8.9
Courtesy of MuniciCorp of California.

154

advertising spreads

Often an ad spreads across two pages in a magazine or newspaper. The headline and the art may then "cross the gutter" to unite the two facing pages, as in Figure 8.10 (note the extra space between "storage" and "tank" to take care of a small part of the ad that will be lost in the binding). Illustrator Bob Larkin added a devil and an angel to the shoulders of the full-color photograph of an indecisive businessman to dramatize the fact that he was torn between building his own storage facility or leasing it. The comic-strip balloons act as sub-headlines for the ad.

This is a good example of parallel structure in advertising. One set of reasons is presented on the left-hand page, another on the right-hand page. At the end the copy relates to both the devil and angel drawings when it says,

"We've got a simply divine solution, to even the most devilish storage problems."

The comic-strip artists' device of the balloon has proved to be a useful device for advertising designers. Sometimes balloons alone do the job. Type is set inside of them, and readers sense they are coming onto conversations of people offstage. A full-page ad for Swedish vodka in the *New Yorker* has a bottle thinking. You know the bottle is thinking because the drawn balloon introduced into the full-color bleed photograph (a photograph that runs to all four edges of a page) has little bubbles instead of a stem moving toward the mouth of the bottle. Every comic-strip reader knows that bubbles stand for thinking while a stem stands for talking.

Figure 8.10
Bob Larkin
Art direction/designer: Robert Qually. Agency: Lee King & Partners, Inc. (now Bozell & Jacobs, Inc.), Chicago.

mostly-cartoon ads

Humorous art can be only incidental to an ad or, helped along by headlines or lettering, it can dominate it. A series of headlines, with drawings by Elwood H. Smith, carry the reader two-thirds of the way down and into a newspaper ad sponsored by the School of Visual Arts, New York (Figure 8.11). The ad makes the point that people in hard times should consider a career change. "Spend an evening or two a week with

When money is tight, which it is

And good jobs are scarce, which they are

This is the time to spend your evenings at Visual Arts

Where you can learn new skills, try new techniques, explore new careers

And be prepared when money loosens up, which it will

And the good jobs come around, which they will.

Figure 8.11
Elwood H. Smith
Courtesy of the School of Visual Arts.

us," says the copy. "It's a productive way to see yourself through this time. You'll learn a new skill. Or discover a new direction . . . ."

Sometimes an ad is nothing *but* a cartoon, with only a headline, as in the VW ad seen earlier, or with copy relegated to a small corner. For an ad carrying the headline, "Another Day. Another 50,833 Cases of Bronchitis"—a medical journal ad directed to physicians—Vibra-Tabs decided to go with an unusually busy cartoon spreading across two pages (Figure 8.12). Using solid black to make his figures and props stand out, illustrator Frank Marciuliano showed any number of doctors or nurses ministering to their patients. Conversation balloons appeared everywhere, some mentioning the product in boldface letters. "I'm prescribing Vibra-Tabs. I have confidence that my patients will take it," one doctor told another in one part of the cartoon. Elsewhere in the cartoon a patient told a nurse, who was supervising his chest x-ray, "I'm allergic to penicillin." "That's not a problem with Vibra-Tabs," she told him.

The physician reading the ad was likely to get the impression that all 50,833 cases of bronchitis for that day were right there in that one two-page spread. It was an illusion that only a cartoon, perhaps, could perform. But just to be sure that all the facts were covered, including precautions for physicians to take and a listing of possible adverse reactions, necessary information in any pharmaceutical advertising, Vibra-Tabs included a more conventional third page (not shown here) crowded with ordinary type, although a small section of the cartoon was included to tie that page to the previous two pages.

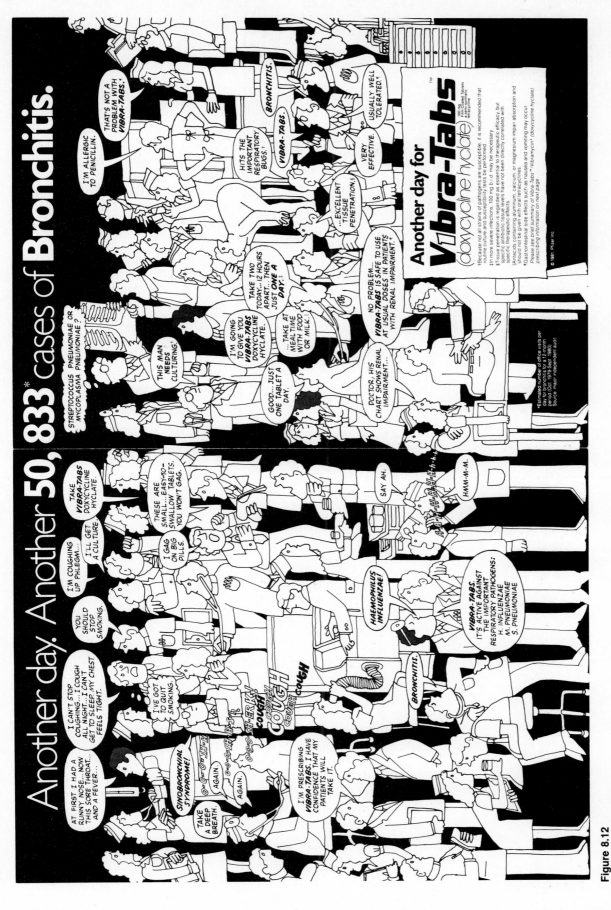

Figure 8.12
Frank Marciuliano

Figure 8.13 shows one in a series of comic-strip ads prepared by Dan Mindolovich when he was a staff artist for the *Roseburg* (Oreg.) *News-Review.* The strip, which ran a column wide and several inches deep, always featured Duffy, who ran the hotel restaurant, sponsor of the ad. Duffy was usually the victim of Mindolovich's playful pen. You get the impression in the last panel here that, wielding his gun, ol' Duffy suffered some powder burns.

This was a particularly satisfying series for Mindolovich because his relationship with the client was so solid, Duffy's sense of humor so unwavering, that the artist—creator was allowed to surprise the client each week. The client saw nothing of the ad until it appeared in print.

Figure 8.13
Dan Mindolovich
Courtesy of the *Roseburg News-Review.*

ads in color

Advertising illustrators increasingly work with color. For local ads running in newspapers and for direct-mail pieces, illustrators prepare overlays for spot-color production. For ads in major magazines, the color may be painted directly onto the original.

Ron Hansen of Kiku Advertising and Public Relations, Tacoma, demonstrates how art for a second color (spot color) is prepared in Figure 8.14. At the left is his original sketch, one of several for a folder on "Let's Learn How to Ride the Bus," published by the City of Tacoma Department of Human Development and Pierce Transit. At the right is the color overlay, made by cutting and affixing transparent red plastic sheets where color is to print. Those are "register marks" placed at the sides of the two pieces of art to help the printer fit the color.

What you see in Figure 8.14 is the folder's last drawing, illustrating the line, "After you get off the bus, watch for traffic! Travel safely as a pedestrian." Hanson, a young versatile artist and designer who works in a number of different styles, uses short, unconnected lines for all the drawings in this folder.

Figure 8.14
Ron Hansen

charts
in advertising

You don't often see charts and graphs in advertising prepared for newspapers and general-circulation magazines, but you do see them in ads for trade magazines and in direct-mail pieces, and of course they are endemic to annual reports.

The *Dallas Morning News* used picture-charts for a series of ads directed to media buyers at advertising agencies, urging them to consider the "undisputed circulation leader" in Dallas for ad placement. "While the other paper [in Dallas] scrambles, we keep our sunny side—and our numbers—up. The *Dallas Morning News. Rising and Shining.*"

Figure 8.15 shows the first in the ad series. What artist Nigel Holmes gives us here is a bar graph, the bars consisting of columns of newspaper copy. The

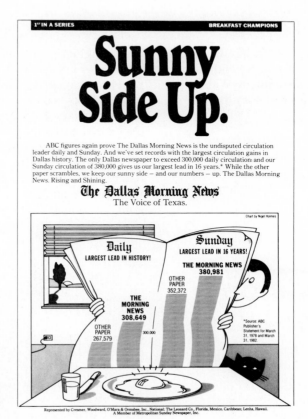

Figure 8.15
Nigel Holmes
Courtesy of the *Dallas Morning News.*

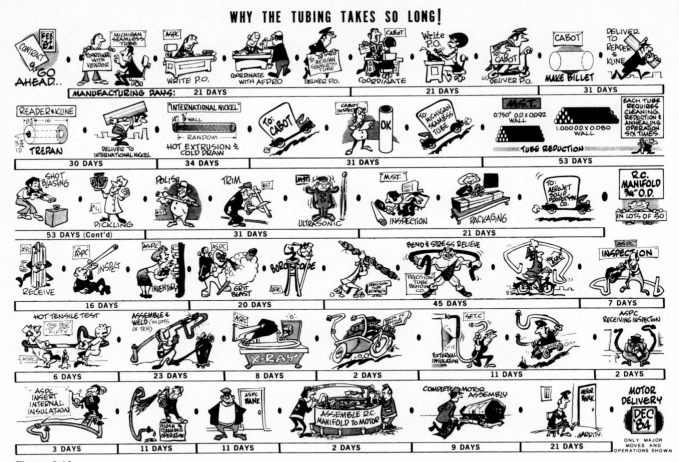

Figure 8.16
Courtesy of Martin E. Garrity and Aerojet Strategic Propulsion Company.

morning setting makes the art appropriate to the ad's headline and copy. (Cunningham & Walsh, Dallas, was the agency that prepared the ad.)

An ordinary solution to the problem of explaining to a customer why a manufacturing process takes so much time after a contract is signed would be to publish a folder or booklet with several panels or pages of sleep-inducing prose. Marty Garrity, working for Aerojet Strategic Propulsion Company, had a different idea: to produce a chart with scores of cartoons. Figure 8.16, unfortunately, reduces the chart to a point where much of what is going on is lost, but you can at least see how Garrity skillfully combines the time element—"21 days," "21 days," "31 days," "30 days," etc.—with each process or activity—to show "Why the Tubing Takes So Long!" This is a combination flow chart and bar graph.

television advertising

TV commercials that make use of animation—and all TV commercials, for that matter—start out as storyboards. A storyboard consists of a series of double boxes; the one at the top (four inches wide by three inches deep) carries a drawing and the one just below (four inches wide by two inches deep) carries information about the drawing. The drawing represents a sample frame from the commercial of what will be seen on the TV screen. The information box describes the scene and suggests camera movement, then gives the words that are being spoken.

No storyboard attempts to show all the frames in a commercial, only those that are important or that record scene changes. The storyboard for a thirty-second commercial shows anywhere from a half a dozen frames to a dozen or more.

Art stores carry special storyboard layout pads that are printed with boxes to represent the frames.

A storyboard, finished in full color, serves as a "first draft" of a commercial for client approval and also as a guide to the producer of the commercial. Artists and writers at an agency dream up the commercial and do the storyboard; outside producers take over from there. When ani-mation is called for, the producers go to houses that specialize in animation.

Freelance cartoonists often supplement their incomes by drawing the frames for storyboards used not only by makers of commercials but also by makers of feature-length films.

posters

Outdoor billboards and smaller posters use humorous art because they often rely on puns, verbal and visual, to get their points across in a hurry.

Illustrators doing poster art go in for tightly cropped closeups with bold primary colors. They also design their drawings so that they take irregular silhouettes, making them read well from a distance. A side view on a poster works better than a front view, because the side view, reduced to a silhouette, has more character.

The severely horizontal shape of an outdoor billboard gives the illustrator room to spread out. A reclining figure, for instance, can easily fit into the design; but a tall, standing figure would be a problem. A billboard usually gets by with fewer than a half dozen words, set or drawn in thick giant sans serif letters.

Poster illustrators may find that highly stylized, even abstract, art works better than more realistic art, although for some posters it is hard to beat the closeup reality of photography.

The look of art going into posters has influenced the look of art going into other media. We call the process of simplifying art—making it flat, bold and abstract—"posterizing" the art. We tend to think of posterization as belong-ing only to the present, but it goes back a long way, as the 1902 cigarette ad (Figure 8.17) from *Puck* demonstrates.

Inside posters are likely to be more finely tuned than outside posters because people have more time to study them.

AEtna Life & Casualty used a cartoon drawing by Rex Ruden of a long bank line (Figure 8.18) to illustrate the question, "Still Banking the Old-Fashioned Way?" on an inside poster urging employee participation in an automatic payroll deposit plan. A smiling if not smug fellow who walks past the line is obviously an AEtna employee who has signed up for the plan. Ruden makes him stand out with tone and color; all the other characters are in mere outline. And what a cast it is! This is a cartoon to be studied. Figure 8.19 moves in close to help you see how some of those in the line are deporting themselves. One fellow is painting a picture of the line he's standing in.

It was the first time AEtna had used a light approach to publicize a company benefit, Deena C. Williams, a communications specialist, reports; and after one month monthly participation increased 300 percent.

Figure 8.17

Figure 8.18
Rex Ruden
Courtesy of Aetna Life & Casualty.

Figure 8.19

album covers

In the old days, a record buyer could preview a record in a stall in the record store. With that service no longer offered, the album design plays an important part in convincing the browser to buy. No wonder some of the most imaginative art in advertising appears these days on album covers.

When WLS AM and FM, Chicago, put out an album of animal sto-ries, the proceeds of which were to go to the Forgotten Children's Fund, Jozef Sumichrast did the illustration (Figure 8.20). It was a full-color airbrush illustration showing animals themselves listening to the stories as broadcast over a quaint radio set, the dial set to WLS, of course.

Figure 8.20
Jozef Sumichrast
Art director/designer: Robert Qually.

direct-mail
advertising

Direct-mail is perhaps the least understood and least appreciated advertising medium in America, and yet it is everywhere. No one escapes receiving direct-mail pieces and few in advertising escape creating them. Leaflets, cards, letters, folders, booklets, broadsides, brochures, newsletters, company magazines, annual reports—these are all part of the direct-mail avalanche. From a design standpoint, direct-mail pieces range from the pathetic to the elegant. Many lean heavily on cartoon art.

Advertising people consider direct-mail (sometimes called direct advertising) the flexible medium. It can take any form and feature any fold. Part of the challenge in working with direct-mail is to figure out a fold that will work logically when the reader gets the piece.

As in other advertising, an art director is in charge of most of the design and format details, but an illustrator may well act as the art director. An advertising agency may not be involved. The illustrator is likely to work directly with the client. The design of the letterhead and of the letter itself is part of the direct-mail picture.

The *New Yorker* has a built-in art program for printed letters going out to readers reminding them that their subscriptions are running out. The letters carry gag cartoons reprinted from the magazine. The ad copy takes off from the gag. A James Stevenson cartoon, for instance, shows a surprised man and an even more surprised fortune teller with an exploding crystal ball in front of them. The gagline reads: "This is a first!" The letter, after "Dear Subscriber," opens up with, "This is the first—and we hope the last—time we will be writing to remind you that your subscription . . . is about to expire."

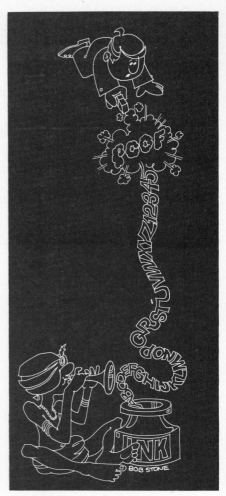

Figure 8.21
Bob Stone

Figure 8.21 shows an illustration that Bob Stone, artist and designer, did for a promotional piece for Columbia Paper Corporation, maker of illustration board and drawing paper for artists. Stone deals here with the frustration an artist feels when his work won't do what he wants it to do and he can't figure out how to correct it. You see the artist floating above his work, art-gum eraser in hand.

Sperry Corporation, a company made up of five divisions, including Sperry Univac, manufacturer of computer systems, is not "in the listening business," but, as it says in a booklet, *How Important It*

THE NINETEENTH CENTURY:
THE NINETEENTH CENTURY
CONSISTED OF THE YEARS
1801, 1802, 1803, 1804 . . . . . .

HADLEY ROBERTSON

Figure 8.22
Hadley Robertson
Courtesy of the Sperry Corporation.

Is To Listen! "In all of our businesses the ability to listen is essential. We feel that skill is so important that we designed a program to help Sperry people around the world become better listeners." The booklet resulted from an institutional advertising campaign built around the theme, "We understand how important it is to listen." It gave the company a chance to answer requests and "share some of what we've learned."

A series of charming and sensitive cartoon drawings by Hadley Robertson enliven the sixteen pages. Figure 8.22 shows one of them, a drawing illustrating the point, made in the text, that people should not be "mere collectors of facts." The drawing suggests "classroom," but without the clutter of blackboards, extra desks, or even a hint of a floor or walls. Despite the drawing's simplicity, Robertson is able to work in various patterns and textures. She

also gives us a pretty good cross section of student types. The expressions, especially, are worth studying. You feel for the teacher.

Figure 8.23 shows a later drawing, this one illustrating the point that many poor listeners are "emotional tinderboxes awaiting only the wrong word to lose track of the conversation or be distracted from the central ideas of the speech or meeting."

The University of Pennsylvania used the theme "On the Move" for a booklet announcing various University activities to members of the alumni association. Scattered throughout were photographs by Eadweard Muybridge, the "father of the motion picture" who did his "ground breaking studies in animal locomotion and instantaneous photography under the auspices of the University of Pennsylvania." While the photographic sequences had nothing to do with the contents, they had everything to do with the theme, and with Muybridge's early connection with the University, they

were much more than merely decorative.

Often a folder, especially one for a trade association, is deadly serious, and humorous illustrations—or even ordinary illustrations—would be out of place. Nothing in the copy lends itself to photographs. Dan Mindolovich faced that problem with a folder soliciting memberships, which he designed for Western Wood Products Association. Mindolovich did see a chance to show some figures of business people, which he used mostly for decorative purposes. To keep away any detail, he constructed his figures out of circles and tubes or cones, as you see in Figure 8.24. These were two-color figures, the heads (and the papers) in one color, all else in another.

In spite of their simplicity, Mindolovich was able to get a lot of character in the figures, mainly by showing arms and legs as though

YOU'RE A REAL SMART
COOKIE, SUE, AND I WAS JUST
WONDERING . . . .

COOKIE?
HE CALLED ME
A COOKIE!

HADLEY ROBERTSON

Figure 8.23
Hadley Robertson
Courtesy of the Sperry Corporation.

Figure 8.24
Dan Mindolovich
Courtesy of Western Wood Products Association.

Figure 8.25
Dan Mindolovich
Courtesy of Western Wood Products Association.

they were not fully attached. The figures look a lot like manikins.

A door's opening, as in Figure 8.25, makes a good opening for a folder. The headline for this folder welcomes appointed and elected members of a committee. The folder itself tells what will be expected of them. Mindolovich's drawing, done with a nylon-tip marker, dominates the cover and suggests that meetings to be attended will be held in swank hotels (note the room panels, the chandelier, and the tablecloth).

annual reports

Many companies issue annual reports not only to stockholders but also to employees. The annual report to employees puts a different stress on things, offering information of particular interest to employees if not to stockholders. Often a company gives over an issue of the company magazine in the spring to the annual report to employees. The Bankers Life Insurance Company has done this with its *Comment.* Tom Weinman provided a series of cartoon headings to introduce each section of one report. You see three of the headings in Figure 8.26.

In the first, Weinman interprets a heading supplied by editor Greg Boattenhamer to include a black, a woman, and an older executive type. To say "Many" he includes a number of other people in the background as one black silhouette, which helps the three main characters stand out.

A smashed piggy bank and the *Wall Street Journal* in the second heading help emphasize the idea of investing.

The third heading uses a Red Cross arm band, a tongue depressor, and crutches to put over the idea of an employee in need. The pleasant, even eager expression on the nurse's face contrasts nicely with the slightly worried look of the employee.

Boattenhamer liked how humorous art worked here because, he said, it lured readers into some serious prose they might otherwise have skipped over.

Many Heads Are Better Than One

A Penny Invested Is A Penny Earned

Employees In Need Are Answered Indeed

Figure 8.26
Tom Weinman
Courtesy of The Bankers Life.

art for public relations uses

People tend to lump public relations with advertising, but there are some differences. Advertisers pay for space and time used in the media, and what they produce is clearly advertising. Public relations people operate more subtly, and their activities are so broad as to defy listing. PR people write news releases, for instance, which publications run without charge (although perhaps with some editing) because the releases really do qualify as news. PR people hold press conferences, stage news events, arrange meetings, engage in lobbying, conduct opinion polls, create advertising, and do many other things. PR encourages management to engage in good works and then, of course, it makes sure that the good works do not go unnoticed.

We are interested here in PR's publishing activities, which are considerable. Company magazines, which have commanded a good deal of attention in this book, properly belong under the "Public Relations" heading. Many of these publications try to keep worker morale at a high level and all sell managements' points of view. These are clearly public relations activities.

Many direct-mail pieces originate in PR departments of companies, governmental agencies, institutions, and organizations. Annual reports are often produced by PR people.

Although PR people tend to take themselves a little more seriously than advertising people do, they also make wide use of humorous art in what they produce.

9
the self- contained
cartoon (part I)

The self-contained cartoon bears a close resemblance to the illustrative cartoon, and the person who draws the one is likely also to draw the other. The self-contained cartoon requires of its artist an even greater participation in the creative process. Editorial cartoons, comic strips, cartoon panels, gag cartoons, greeting cards, humorous sculptures and murals, and animated films all qualify as self-contained cartoons.

editorial cartoons

Many media observers in the 1980s recorded a resurgence of interest in editorial cartoons, those single-panel units of graphic expression appearing on editorial pages of our daily newspapers. *Newsweek* in 1980 put the number of editorial cartoonists in the United States at 170. That's not an impressive number, but it is greater by 50 than it was just a few years earlier, and there has been no increase in the number of papers being published. The newsmagazine thought that the wit of these cartoonists "has grown sharper and more personal." Looking with approval at the post-Herblock, post-Mauldin, post-Conrad younger breed, *Newsweek* concluded that "there have never been so many good [editorial] cartoonists—or more wretched excesses for them to lampoon."[1]

David Shaw, writing in the *Los Angeles Times,* felt that few of the new cartoonists come up with hard-hitting ideas. It is a case, he said, of "the bland leading the bland."[2]

Other critics have noted a monotonous style similarity. Many of the newer cartoonists are so dazzled by Jeff MacNelly, one of the profession's most admired and successful practitioners, that they have not bothered to develop their own style or approach. Shaw puts these cartoonists aside as "MacNelly clones."

Cartoonists at the turn of the century all used pen-and-ink lines and crosshatch shading for their editorial cartoons. Around World War II many of the cartoonists— especially those classified as liberals and leftists—switched to brush strokes and grease-crayon shading. The new breed of the 1970s went for the brushed-on mechanical shading made possible by Grafix paper. With Pat Oliphant leading the way, editorial cartoonists went back to pen- or brush-and-ink drawing with no mechanical shading, but the drawings were firmer than they had been in the crosshatch days. Bill Mauldin gave up his grease crayon shading for drawings with unusually heavy—but graceful—brush strokes and solid blacks.

Jeff MacNelly, Pat Oliphant, and maybe a dozen other editorial cartoonists are in the high-income brackets; the remaining editorial cartoonists perform for their hometown newspapers at modest salaries and without much national exposure. Yet it would be hard to find a single one who would trade the job for some other.

The goal of every editorial cartoonist, of course, is to be syndicated. Under such an arrangement, several of the cartoons each week not only run in the local paper but go out to newspapers

[1] "The Finer Art of Politics," *Newsweek,* Oct. 13, 1980, p. 74.
[2] David Shaw, "Cartoonists Draw Sharp Conclusions About Peers," *Los Angeles Times,* March 18, 1982, Part I, p. 14.

all over the country and even the world.

Small papers which can't afford their own editorial cartoonists rely solely on syndicate offerings. Every large paper, besides showing syndicated cartoons, features work by its own cartoonist. The *New York Times* is an exception, but it does reprint editorial cartoons from other papers. It also runs its own illustrative art on the op-ed page and throughout the paper.

Pat Oliphant leads all editorial cartoonists in number of papers reached (about 500), but Jeff MacNelly is not far behind. When Oliphant arrived in the United States in 1964 he replaced Paul Conrad as the *Denver Post*'s cartoonist (Conrad moved to the *Los Angeles Times* to replace Bruce Russell); then he went to the *Washington Star*. When the *Star* died in 1981, he moved over to the *Washington Post,* which already provided a home base for Herblock, long a fixture there. Oliphant was to appear only on the Saturday op-ed page. Of course the arrangement would not affect syndication of the two cartoonists.

Jeff MacNelly got his start on the *Richmond News Leader* in 1970, and resumed work at the *Chicago Tribune* after quitting the business for a few months in 1981–82.

An editorial cartoonist always picks a home-base newspaper with a compatible editorial philosophy, but disagreements are bound to occur. Paul Szep has frequently been at odds with his editors on the *Boston Globe*. The liberal *St. Louis Post-Dispatch* has taken a pro-abortion stand on its editorial page, but the editors do not expect Thomas Englehardt, the editorial cartoonist, to draw pro-abortion cartoons.

Editorial page editors don't mind running occasional syndicated editorial cartoons that vary from what's preached in the editorials, but the editors like the work of their own editorial cartoonists to reflect the party line. In most cases, local editorial cartoonists check rough drawings with editors before proceeding to the finish.

Tony Auth of the *Philadelphia Inquirer* says that an editorial cartoonist needs a sense of outrage. "You have to be capable of reading something and saying, 'I don't believe that!' and then translate that into a drawing." You can make plenty of enemies in the process. Once when Auth became ill, the *Philadelphia Inquirer* ran a small box announcing the fact. "The paper got all kinds of letters saying, 'We knew it. It's been obvious for years,'" Auth reports.

Editorial cartoonists are at their best while on the attack. David Low in his autobiography said that "admiration is for the poets" and a cartoonist's approval "can best be expressed by leaving its object alone."

Being *for* something doesn't make for a memorable cartoon. Editorial cartoonists don't usually reveal whom they'd vote for, but they do level their attacks mainly at the phoniest or most hateful of the candidates. In the 1980 Presidential election, however, Don Wright of the *Miami News* said that he was for John Anderson and would avoid criticizing him in his cartoons.

Editorial cartoonists show their biases in all kinds of ways. A favorite device is to make a disliked politican smaller than he is. That's what happened to Carter late in his term. The chair, for instance, was too big for him. Other people towered over him. Herblock used to make his villains—Richard Nixon, for instance—in need of a shave. Eyes get closer together on villains, too, suggesting something sinister.

Whatever the point of view in an editorial cartoon, there is no time, no room for subtlety. To an editorial cartoonist Carter was almost always toothy or thick-lipped and incompetent; Reagan was badly wrinkled and, in his campaign, often in a wheelchair; Nixon—well, Nixon was Nixon, almost too easy to pick on. There is not much fairness in all the stereotyping, but no editorial cartoonist claims to be fair.

Jeff MacNelly, as the Ruhl lecturer at the University of Oregon in the spring of 1982, said that editorial cartoonists violate all the ethics of journalism, but with all their misquoting and trifling with the truth they probably get closer to the truth than editorial writers and columnists.

Editorial cartoonists like MacNelly manage to make people laugh while also making them think. Others such as Don Wright and Paul Conrad remain consistently grim but still enormously effective. Doug Marlette of the *Charlotte Observer* gets serious one day, then retreats into jocularity the next. Bob Englehart of the Hartford, Connecticut *Courant,* holds what he calls "moderately confused" political views.

Mike Peters, editorial cartoonist for the *Dayton* (Ohio) *Daily News* (he's also syndicated), feels strongly about issues but cannot, he says, bring himself to draw hard-hitting cartoons. He prefers to make his points through humor alone. He told David Shaw that he is, by nature, a "fairly happy guy," and his colleagues report that he is something of a prankster. Peters gained attention with a cartoon in 1980 showing George Washington saying "I cannot tell a lie," Richard Nixon saying "I cannot tell the truth," and Jimmy Carter saying "I cannot tell the difference."

MacNelly stands out as an editorial cartoonist with a conservative bent, something of a novelty. Oliphant, Conrad, and Mauldin are among the many cartoonists belonging to the liberal camp, but they fool you occasionally. Oliphant comes down hard on busing. Conrad, a Roman Catholic, opposes abortion. Mauldin, from the tough, wide open Southwest, won't sit still for gun control.

Canada has its share of great editorial cartoonists, including Len Norris, Roy Peterson, a cartoonist who for a time signed his work Aislin, and, perhaps the most honored of the lot, Duncan Macpherson, who recently retired after twenty years on the *Toronto Star*. Macpherson's work is appreciated, especially by other cartoonists, both for its artistry and its design. His ideas are not only vivid but brusque. A journalist once described Macpherson as the kind of a guy who would kick in your door to deliver roses.

An editorial cartoonist with a worldwide following is Ranan Lurie, who is syndicated by both King Features and Editors Press Service. He considers himself a political analyst who happens to draw. Unique among editorial cartoonists, he travels around the world interviewing its leaders. He

stays a year or two in one location, where he usually teaches at a university, then moves on. With his diversified audience, he makes his cartoon comments only on events that everyone is aware of. He uses analogies that are universally understood.

Occasionally an editorial cartoonist makes a difference; if not that, certainly an impact. Editorial cartoonists have created enduring images, as Thomas Nast did when he created what we now recognize as Santa Claus. Cartoonists also add to the language. It was Herblock who coined the term "McCarthyism," used to describe reckless political charges of the kind made by Senator Joseph McCarthy of the 1950s.

the editorial cartoon idea

As editorial cartoonist for the *Eugene Register-Guard* I became, for a time, a one-issue artist. My target was field burning, an activity engaged in by nearby ryegrass farmers at the close of their growing season to rid the fields of stubble and disease—to "sanitize" the fields, as they put it. Their smoke often blew south into the city, choking us, making our eyes water, sending many to doctors with breathing complaints. City people pressured the state legislature for relief. At the same time, the city allowed its residents to engage in backyard burning. The hypocrisy of this provided the idea for the cartoon shown in Figure 9.1. The reader had to assume, judging from the expression of the man looking out the window, that some of that smoke was getting into the house next door.

The implication in my swimming-pool cartoon (Figure 9.2) is that voters faced a last chance to save the school budget. It got a No vote in two previous elections.

The idea for an editorial cartoon comes from a reduction of the message or thrust to a simple statement and then hunting for a scene that can be made analogous to the statement. Some examples of statements might be that the mayor is oblivious to the needs of the citizens of the south side, that an industrial complex has run out of excuses for fouling the air, that the legislature hasn't gotten the word about a national revolt against tax increases. Now: what to use to bring visual life to such statements? Not literal scenes, surely, for they can't be drawn

Figure 9.1

"IT'S TERRIBLE WHAT THOSE FIELD BURNERS ARE DOING TO THE AIR IN THIS TOWN"

Figure 9.2

"HE'S ALREADY GONE DOWN TWICE!"

Figure 9.3

and would be complex and dull if they *were* drawn. Editorial cartoonists create fantasy settings that can, with labels, stand in for what's real. They work out simple if not simplistic visual figures of speech. The mayor becomes a blind man; a figure representing the industrial complex, looking worried, reaches deep down into a barrel; a figure representing the legislature lets newspapers pile up on his front porch.

Let's say that you want to illustrate some aspect of overkill in public life. Figure 9.3 (an editorial cartoon, actually, with labels removed because the point being made was only local and not necessary to this discussion now) shows one approach. Overkill is taken quite literally here. Chains on all four limbs of the victim make him all the more pitiable; ugliness in the executioner makes him all the more hateful.

Focusing on hands in an editorial cartoon was common in the early days. No one has attempted to count the number of cartoons that showed a small, crooked politician being pressed to the ground by a

big thumb ("The Law," "Public Opinion," whatever). Sometimes it was the other way around. A big thumb was crushing a poor taxpayer, the big thumb representing, say, "The Bureaucracy." In case the reader didn't get the idea, a caption above the cartoon helped out: "Under His Thumb."

An editorial cartoonist can envision a scene or situation and then find something out there in the political world that fits. The other approach—the more likely one—is to get the political thought firmly in mind and *then* hunt for the analogy.

Sometimes cartoonists hunt for clever captions first, then work their cartoons around them. Well-known advertising slogans and song titles make excellent captions. Let's go back to one of the classics. Right after the 1960 election Bill Mauldin showed a picture of the new Vice-President, Lyndon Johnson, looking smug, playing "Dixie" on the piano. (Johnson, to the surprise of some of his critics, had helped Kennedy win the South—and the election.) The caption had him saying: "They laughed when Ah sat down at the piano." Most readers recog-

nized the line as a famous advertising slogan for a correspondence school selling piano lessons.

Art Bimrose, longtime editorial cartoonist for *The Oregonian,* Portland, uses Pac-Man, the popular computer-game figure, as a take-off point for his April 15 cartoon reacting to the 1982 income-tax deadline (Figure 9.4). Bimrose's Pac-Man becomes Tac Man, but

Tacx Man

Figure 9.4
Art Bimrose

Figure 9.5
Bill Plympton

the character exhibits the same voracious appetite. Paul Conrad also went to a Pac-Man theme that year when he showed Reagan's Secretary of Interior gobbling up the country, starting at the left—or West—end of the country. His caption was "Watt-Man."

Rubik's Cube, when it hit the market, became a favorite cartoonists' metaphor. For the various colors on the faces of the blocks, the cartoonists showed problems or whatever, with a politican manipulating the cube, trying to solve the puzzle. *Newsweek* in late 1981 used what was essentially an editorial cartoon on a cover, painted realistically by Richard Newton instead of drawn, showing Reagan's hand trying to solve world problems. Maps of Saudi Arabia, China, South Africa, etc., were on the cube.

Editorial cartoonists make use of caricature to better identify and ridicule their victims. They make use of symbols as a sort of universal language. One of Pat Oliphant's frequent symbols is a snail, which stands for the U.S. Postal Service. Animals are always useful. Bill Plympton made a turkey out of the B-1 bomber in a

cartoon (Figure 9.5) published by the *Baltimore City Paper*, an alternative newspaper.

Plympton's style is sophisticated and scratchy, and his ideas are biting. On the back cover of *Tube Strips* (New York: Smyrna Press, 1976), a collection of comic strips ridiculing TV fare, Jules Feiffer says that "Bill Plympton draws beautifully, perceives accurately and is mean to his subjects to the different degrees they deserve it." Plympton was a regular contributor to the *Sohio Weekly News* until it died. He is now syndicated by Universal Press Syndicate.

Karl Hubenthal for the *Los Angeles Herald Examiner* uses "Falconer" (without quote marks) as a title for his editorial cartoon showing President Reagan with two strange looking birds, "Tax Cuts" and "Budget Cuts." (Figure 9.6.) In dreaming up this cartoon Hubenthal saw a visual relationship between a bird's beak and both a pair of scissors and a knife.

At one time editorial cartoons carried all kinds of labels to help readers recognize people in the drawings and also to better understand the ideas. The trend now is to use fewer labels—or none at all. Bill Mauldin led the

way to fewer labels in his years with first the *St. Louis Post-Dispatch* and then the *Chicago Sun-Times*.

Captions, on the other hand, continue to serve a purpose. They come in two varieties. Those that simply describe the cartoon, as a title describes a story, go above the cartoon without quote marks. The others are like gaglines for gag cartoons. As the spoken words of someone within the cartoon, they go below and with quote marks. The latter captions are by far the most popular today, especially with the younger breed of editorial cartoonists who work in a horizontal format. The veteran Herblock, he of the grease-crayon school, perfected the gagline-like caption during his many years on the *Washington Post*. Even if you didn't always accept Herblock's liberal theology, you could laugh at the gag.

A cartoonist hand-letters the caption just outside the drawing so it won't be reproduced. It is there as a guide to the typesetter. But a few editors leave the caption as is, especially when it is lettered with a nice flair, as in an Oliphant or Mauldin cartoon. This saves any

Figure 9.6
Karl Hubenthal

errors in transferring the original to type. It also makes it less likely that the editor will tamper with the caption.

Whether set in type or hand-lettered, a caption running to more than one line should be separated, if possible, at a logical break. For instance, in the backyard-burning cartoon, it was important to keep "field burners" together rather than to put "field" at the end of one line and "burners" at the beginning of another. Phrases and word combinations should stay together as an aid to understanding.

comic strips

Nearly every cartoonist has dreamed of launching a comic strip. Comic strips started out as entertainment for the barely literate, and many strips have stayed at the barely-literate level. But many have appealed to people who don't have to move their lips when they read. A few, like the strips of Jules Feiffer, are directed to the intellectuals or at least the pseudo-intellectuals.

The first strips were comical; then, in the 1930s, strips began dealing with adventure. In the 1950s adventure gave way to comedy. Only a few adventure strips remain.

Usually—but not always—a strip is written and drawn by the same person. Many artists launching strips now come from the ranks of gag cartoonists. A typical daily strip consists of a gag stretched across three or four panels.

A strip started by a gag cartoonist usually results in watered-down work. With a contract, and with daily deadlines, the cartoonist cannot keep up with the same level of humor seen in the gag cartoons, each of which had to be marketed separately. Besides, newspaper readers taken as a whole are seen to be less demanding than magazine readers. Richard Cavalli, gag cartoonist who started *Morty Meekle* (later renamed *Winthrop*), is a case in point. *The World Encyclopedia of Cartoons* says, ". . . the innumerable gag cartoons which he contributed to *Collier's*, the *Saturday Evening Post* and other magazines often were funnier and certainly more pungent."

Most successful comic-strip artists employ assistants. In some cases, the assistant does the lettering in the balloons. Bil Keane's assistant on *The Family Circus* does the inking. Keane roughs in the drawings in pencil. And, of course, Keane dreams up the ideas. He claims to have enough ideas stored on 3 by 5 slips of paper to keep the feature going another fifty years. He spends one full day a week just answering the mail.

Being an assistant on a strip often leads to taking it over when the originator dies or retires. The job also gives the assistant confidence to break away and launch a new strip. Jim Davis, who does *Garfield*, spent nine years as an assistant to Tom K. Ryan on *Tumbleweeds* before launching *Garfield*.

Ed Sullivan got into the comic-strip field by taking over, first, a Sunday strip, J. R. Williams's *Out Our Way*, and later Al Vermeer's daily and Sunday *Priscilla's Pop*. That Sullivan was able to successfully imitate both styles shows his great versatility as a cartoonist.

With comic-strip artists like Milton Caniff in mind, the late Al Capp, who did *Li'l Abner*, said that the best art anywhere in the twentieth century could be found in the comic strips. The syndicates underwrite the arts today as the Catholic Church did in an earlier century. If some of those old masters were around today, they'd be doing comic strips, Capp said.

Its humor is only so-so, but *Tiger*, by Bud Blake, shows off some of today's best comic-strip drawing. The lines are sure and beautifully executed, and each panel is a study in composition. Hank Ketchum does a similar job with *Dennis the Menace*, a cartoon panel. Few comic-strip artists have his sure hand. Blake's work is almost solely in line and solid black; Ketchum's involves a finer line technique with a bit of pattern.

It is interesting to go back to early versions of a strip to see how it has evolved and, in many cases, how the artist's style has improved. Sometimes the change is abrupt, as when Howie Schneider changed his main characters in *Eek & Meek* in 1982 from mice to men.

The bane of most comic-strip artists is the deadline. The relentless deadline. Artists work several weeks, even several months, ahead of their dates of publication. The well-organized Russell Myers works a whole year ahead of schedule! A former Hallmark artist, Myers draws rapidly but does a lot of retouching.

Al Borelli and Steve Yoken after many encounters with syndicates finally got their *Vikings* strip (later called *Those Crazy Pirates*) launched with a somewhat reluctant Allied Features Syndicate, then decided drawing a daily strip was too much trouble (especially for only thirty-seven client pa-

pers). So they quit to do a monthly strip, *Girtha*, for *Weight-Watchers* magazine. After a while *Girtha* moved out of the American edition and into the Italian edition of the magazine, *Salvalinea*. Girtha is a fat woman facing constant frustrations in her efforts to reduce.

In an article in *Bucknell World*, an alumni magazine, Borelli, who restores old clocks when he's not drawing, asks and answers some questions about syndication, including these:

Q: How does one get syndicated?

A: I don't know.

Q: Should I submit my material personally, or mail it in?

A: Either way is fine. Neither approach is likely to work.

Q. What is so funny about some of the strips being published?

A. Beats me.

Ken Muse gave up a daily strip, *Wayout*, to devote himself to other activities but returned to comic-strip making with *Dr. Bils*, syndicated by Dickson-Bennett International Features to weekly newspapers. "I prefer doing a weekly strip, because it allows me more time to teach and freelance," he says. Figure 9.7 shows a sample of the strip. (Muse used a B6 Speedball pen for the lettering and borders, a Gillott 1290 for the other inking.)

A few comic-strip artists find deadlines no problem. In fact, they look for new deadlines to conquer. Johnny Hart is one such artist. Mort Walker is another. In 1982, Walker, who does *Beetle Bailey*, dreamed up *The Evermores*. This features characters who move back and forth from earlier eras to the present. Johnny Sajem is the artist for this one. The strip

Figure 9.7
Ken Muse

makes the point that people living in various ages are pretty much the same in their reaction to things. Walker also developed *Hi and Lois* and *Boner's Ark*.

In 1982, Art Sansom and his son Chip, who do *The Born Loser,* started a new strip: *Dusty Chaps.* The father does the art for both strips, using a less-comic style for the new strip because the syndicate didn't want a repetition of styles.

Newspapers do not pick comic strips lightly. Dropping an oldie to make room for a new one—and that's what usually has to be done—can flood a switchboard as nothing else can. Comic strips develop loyalties. Some, like *Doonesbury,* build near-cult followings.

On a newspaper the managing editor or assistant managing editor sorts through all the printed sales pitches or puts up with calls from exuberant syndicate salespeople, then takes the occasional impressive new offering to an editorial board for a final decision. The deal with the syndicate may be for a trial run; if the strip does not catch on within a few months the editor cancels it.

The larger the paper, the more it pays for the feature. Of the total amount collected by the syndicate, after expenses, the creator gets half. When only a handful of papers subscribe to a comic strip, the artist doesn't make much more than, say, a store clerk. Of course the syndicate doesn't make much money, either; and so the strip dies.

Which newspapers subscribe to a strip make a difference. Fifty big papers would be better than 200 small ones. A few strips make it over the 1,000 mark, and their creators become millionaires. But you don't exactly have to feel sorry for the cartoonists who have, say, 500 newspaper clients. Strips or panels that go to more than 1,000 different newspapers include *Peanuts, Blondie, Beetle Bailey, Hagar the Horrible, The Born Loser,* and *Frank & Ernest. Garfield* joined the select group in 1982.

An artist with a new strip to launch had better be young and in good health. John Matthews of the Tribune Company Syndicate estimates that, counting promotion and other costs, it takes $80,000 to launch a new strip. With that kind of an initial investment, a syndicate wants an artist around for a while. And it wants

an artist capable of sustained production.

In recent years the syndicates, which know the market better than cartoonists do, have sometimes dreamed up strip ideas and then gone hunting for the right artists. When it decided to launch a *Muppets* comic strip, King Features settled on a young brother team, Guy and Brad Gilchrist, suggested to the syndicate by Mort Walker, who had seen their work in *Superkernel* comic books. Of course the team had to be approved by Muppets' creator Jim Henson, who wanted an artist with a Walt Kelly-like style. The brothers provided a number of trial strips before they were hired. "I imagine one of the reasons we were considered is because we're a team, and can write gags and do the drawings, all in one house," Brad Gilchrist told Jud Hurd, editor of *Cartoonist Profiles.* "Guy and I are like one person—we both write, and I suggest things for the artwork Guy does, so that when the strip is finished, it has one 'feel' although two people have collaborated."

Figure 9.8
Alan Rose

A syndicate does everything it can to promote its strips. With twenty-four years behind him as a daily and Sunday comic-strip great dane, *Marmaduke,* Brad Anderson's creation, went on the road in 1979 as a show business attraction. United Feature Syndicate, which distributes the strip to some 300 newspapers, found a dog that greatly resembled Marmaduke and worked with the dog's trainer to develop an act. Anderson told *Editor & Publisher:* "People already think of Marmaduke as a true-to-life character so now they can look at and touch him for real."

Not satisfied with the deals they could get with syndicates, or unable to sell a strip idea to a syndicate, some artists self-syndicate their strips. Figure 9.8 is a strip from a three-week series developed and syndicated by Alan Rose as a Christmas feature for newspapers.

The story concerns two of Santa's helpers who choose to leave their toy-making jobs to act as "Santa Scouts," sizing up roof strengths and chimney sizes in one small town prior to Santa's visit. They get into trouble for not following orders. In this strip, quite late in the series, the scouts are awakened by a goat they had been chasing, a goat with a magic ring in his horn.

Rose, new to the comic-strip business, quickly mastered its techniques. For one thing, he incorporates medium, close up, and far away shots in most of the strips. The inside-the-cave panel is nicely framed, with light source closely controlled. The final frame makes use of silhouetting. The balloons make use of clear, easy-to-read capitals that have a professional feel to them. Because of his earlier work in advertising illustration, Rose knows what will reproduce well and what won't.

Early in this century the syndicates began to look for additional exposure for their strips. Comic-book publishers went into business to reprint the strips in a magazine format. The demand for these publications grew, and the publishers began originating their own strips, usually featuring super heroes. *Superman* originated as a comic-book hero to become a comic-strip hero later.

Following a public outcry in the 1950s against the violence and sex in the comic books, they turned bland and nearly died out. The underground comics (comix) of the 1960s were partly a reaction against that blandness.

Comic books have been used to tell serious stories. Fleming Revell, a religious book publisher, has brought out a series of *Archie* comic books with a Christian message. The same publisher has brought out comic-book adaptations of best-selling religious books, including *The Cross and the Switchblade.* Word Books, an evangelical book publisher, and Our Sunday Visitor, a Catholic book publisher, have collaborated to bring out a series of *Dennis the Menace* comic books with a Bible orientation.

the comic-strip idea

We look at the comic-strip idea at two levels: (1) the basic idea behind the strip and (2) the day-to-day gag. The basic idea must be something to intrigue an identifiable audience.

Universal Press Syndicate has been as successful as it has because it looks for audiences not yet served by comic strips and fills a need. For instance, Cathy Guisewite's *Cathy*, launched in 1976, was the first strip to really interest single young women. The creators of some of the newer strips apparently feel that relevance is quite enough; the drawing there causes long-established comic-strip artists to wonder what this world is coming to. Guisewite exhibits only a modest talent for drawing. Greg Howard, a lawyer who gave up a successful practice to launch *Sally Forth* with the Field Newspaper Syndicate, is in Guisewite's class. His strip, according to the syndicate, deals with "a new breed of woman—the professional wife and mother who manipulates the volatile topic of women's rights with wit that hits home."

Berke Breathed's *Bloom Country,* a *Washington Post*-circulated strip advertised as something "plunked down in the center of deepest, darkest, middlest America," is close to Garry Trudeau's *Doonesbury* in its look. *Doonesbury* itself was only indifferently drawn. But at least it was an original. What made *Doonesbury* a standout, of course, was its story line and, especially, its point of view.

Garfield is another strip drawn in a pedestrian style, but try to tell that to the strip's avid, even fanatical followers. That cat, who loves lasagna and hates joggers, has caught on everywhere. Davis launched his strip at a time when no others were devoted solely to a cat, although there were several dog strips. Davis figured that cat owners were numerous enough— some 22 million families own cats—to support a *Garfield* strip. At first the strip was to feature the cat's owner, but wisely Davis switched to the cat, who had a more powerful personality.

A few strips are both beautifully drawn and remarkable for their ideas. Take Charles Schulz's *Peanuts.* For once, an artistic triumph is also a commercial success. Although other artists have a hand in producing the many spinoffs from *Peanuts,* Schulz does everything on the strip himself, including the lettering in balloons.

Schulz over the years has used his strip to mirror, somewhat, his own family life and occasionally to work a friend into the cast of characters. Much of Schulz's deeply felt philosophy emerges in the story lines, and a couple of books, written by others, have taken off on his theology.

Schulz suggests that it takes a personality quirk or two to create and maintain a comic strip. Perhaps his most recognized traits are the loneliness and anxiety that, ironically, have accompanied his great fame and adoration. He told Robert Digitale, a reporter for the *Santa Rosa Press Democrat,* that "I'm not the first melancholy cartoonist to ever live" and that the trait is "reasonably prominent among humorists."

To be successful a strip needs memorable characters and inventive plot twists that can resurface often enough to become part of the culture. Among the many Schulz inventions, for instance, are Linus' security blanket, Snoopy's Red Baron aspirations, the Great Pumpkin, kite-eating trees, and Lucy's pulling away of the football each time Charlie Brown tries a placekick.

Reg Smythe's *Andy Capp* is about a lazy character who drinks and regularly belts his wife. The British-originated strip comes in for some criticism because of that, but Smythe argues that compared to Lucy in *Peanuts,* Andy is a sweet person.

Tom Forman and Ben Templeton picked the neglected middle class as the subject of their *Motley's*

Crew strip launched by the Tribune Company Syndicate in 1976. "We show both the joys and sorrows of middle-class life," the strip's creators say.

Russell Myers describes his main character in *Broom Hilda* as "a dirty old man in a dress." Irwin the Troll is totally innocent—the only person who has been taken advantage of by a flower. In the fall of 1978, Myers, a nonsmoker, took the cigar out of Broom Hilda's mouth because he didn't want young people to copy her. He also cut down on her drinking, explaining that ". . . as I grow older, I apparently take on a bit more of a moral flavor. . . ."[3]

Bob Johnson in *Hello Carol* deals with single people and their social problems, getting inspiration for his daily gags from reading *Psychology Today* and similar publications. He advises would-be comic-strip artists to read anything they can get their hands on, including things they disagree with.

Some comic strips deal with real people. Tom Armstrong's and Tom Batiuk's *John Darling,* run on newspapers' TV pages, shows anchor people, quiz show hosts, and similar celebrities.

Sometimes the art of cartooning itself becomes the subject of a comic strip. In a 1979 Sunday sequence, *Moon Mullins* had Lord Plushbottom at the doctor's office complaining of a lack of pep. The doctor took some tests and announced that the old gentleman was anemic. "I'm arranging for an immediate transfusion," said the doctor, and over the phone he ordered "one liter of India ink." Lord Plushbottom looked out of the last panel directly at the reader and asked: "You were expecting maybe type O?"

[3]Quoted by Jud Hurd, "Introducing Broom Hilda by Russell Myers," *The Press,* Vol. 3, No. 5, 1978, p. 5.

the cartoon panel

Closely related to the comic strip is the cartoon panel, a single-frame drawing revolving around a single theme and involving a standard cast of characters. Syndicates make available any number of cartoon panels, some of them in a convenient one-column size.

Some of the cartoon panels, appearing daily, have Sunday counterparts in comic-strip form. Some cartoon panels consist of informational excerpts or episodes supplied by readers.

A syndicated cartoon panel can be, simply, a gag cartoon with a different gag each day but roughly the same main character. Jim Unger's *Herman* is an example—a sarcastic, black-humor panel.

In reader surveys, Bil Keane's *The Family Circle* often gets a No. 1 rating among cartoon panels. In 1981, Keane, like so many energetic syndicated cartoonists, launched an additional feature: *Eggheads,* a gag comic strip given to puns. Both his features were being distributed by the Register & Tribune Syndicate. Before starting *The Family Circle* in 1960, Keane for several years did a feature called *Channel Chuckles*. He worked for fifteen years as a staff artist for the *Philadelphia Bulletin*.

One of the best of the cartoon panels is Jim Berry's *Berry World.* His well-drawn and well-reasoned feature is part editorial cartoon, part gag cartoon.

One of the most sophisticated of the recently launched cartoon panels is *The Far Side* by Gary Larson. People clip the cartoons and show them around and sometimes try to figure them out, as when Larson produces something called "cow tools." Cow tools? In defending that cartoon, Larson said he just tried to imagine what kind of tools cows would make if cows made tools. Larson's offbeat humor—and his drawing—is a little like what's found in books by B. Kliban.

One of the most fondly remembered cartoon panels is Fountain Fox's *Toonerville Folks,* a syndicated feature that lasted forty years. It featured, among others, Mickey (Himself) McGuire, the tough Irish kid so well known and admired that Joe Yule, Jr., used the name as a stage name until sued by Fox, when he changed to Mickey Rooney. There was the Powerful Katrinka, "Handlebar" Hank, "Flytrap" Finnegan, "Tomboy" Taylor, Aunt Eppie Hogg (the fattest woman in three counties), "Suitcase" Sympson, the Terrible Tempered Mr. Bangs, the Absent-Minded Professor, and, of course, the Skipper of the Toonerville Trolley that Meets All Trains. Only Chester Gould in *Dick Tracy* and Al Capp in *Li'l Abner* developed a cast of characters that were as anomalous.

10

the self- contained cartoon (part II)

So far the self-contained cartoons considered have been the preserve mostly of newspapers and their syndicates. This chapter deals first with self-contained cartoons found in magazines, then with those that are independent of any periodicals.

gag cartoons

Gag cartoons are humorous single-panel drawings with a caption or a gagline printed underneath. The gagline is a bit of conversation coming from the mouth of one of the persons in the drawing. Occasionally a gag cartoon carries no caption. The gag is in pantomime. And occasionally a gag cartoon consists of several small panels. The best gag cartoons are more than illustrated jokes. What the drawing shows and what the gagline says should be so well integrated that neither drawing nor gagline could work by itself.

Mostly magazines run gag cartoons, but several of the syndicates offer newspapers daily gag cartoons drawn by various cartoonists.

Gag cartoons are almost always created and sold by freelancers, many who work at the trade on a part-time basis. Only a few cartoonists make a full-time living doing gag cartoons.

The usual procedure is to submit a batch of a dozen or so 8½ by 11 "roughs" to cartoon editors of magazines. Most roughs are good enough to reproduce as-is, but once in a while an editor returns an okayed rough with instructions to redraw it in a more finished style and in a designated medium. Most of the time the whole batch comes back to the cartoonist with a rejection slip.

Some gag cartoonists specialize. Orlando Busino, who admits to being part of the "big nose and big foot" school of cartooning, concentrates on family gags and sells regularly—very regularly—to general-interest and women's magazines. He is one successful gag cartoonist who has stayed away from *Playboy*-type magazines. He is not interested in risqué gags.

Charles Addams concentrates on spooky subjects for the *New Yorker*. His cartoons prompted a sitcom, "The Addams Family," which ran for a couple of years on TV.

The springs of creativity sometimes run dry, so many cartoonists buy their gags from gag writers, who get 25 percent then of what the cartoon brings in—but no mention or credit line. Nor is that the concern of editors. Their checks go to the cartoonists, who do their own bookkeeping. The gag writer gets paid after the cartoonist gets paid.

In fact, bookkeeping becomes a major activity of gag cartoonists, who keep several batches of six or more roughs in the mail at all times. All roughs get numbers. Cartoonists record the numbers to prevent resubmission to editors who have already rejected the cartoons, although there are cases where editors buy cartoons they said No to earlier.

The best market—the dream market—is the *New Yorker*, which originated the form. J. B. Handelsman, the American-born gag cartoonist living in England who draws for both the *New Yorker* and *Punch*, reports that *Punch* is easier to work for. Sell *Punch* on the gag, and that's it. Sell the *New Yorker*, and the editors might send the finished drawing back several times to make minor adjustments, he says.

But selling to the *New Yorker* is worth the effort. In 1980 the magazine was paying an average of $600 per cartoon. The cartoonist working for the *New Yorker* retains the original drawing, which can bring another $500 when sold by a gallery.

While the *New Yorker, Playboy,* and a few other magazines pay handsomely for gag cartoons, smaller magazines get them for as little as $10. Editors set their own rates and keep them remarkably standard, although there is some dickering when a gag cartoonist becomes a hot property. There is also a cartoonists' guild, which watches after the interests of its members. Sadly for cartoonists, rates paid by most magazines have stayed pretty much the same in a decade when other wages have soared.

The style used for a gag cartoon is almost always simple and clean. Ben Bost (more about him in the next chapter) uses line only, with just a couple of hints of pattern in his gag cartoon on army life (Figure 10.1). The props—the truck, the garbage can, the utensils—are important to set the stage for the gag, but they do not dominate. Nor did Bost find it necessary to include buildings or other people. Gag cartooning, like most cartooning, is figure dominated, and the fewer the number of figures, the better.

An interesting thing about gag cartoons and their treatment of figures: the figures are seldom cropped. They are usually shown in their entirety and placed in some setting, however simple. The camera stays back. In comic strips, of course, it moves in close in many of the panels.

Figure 10.1
Ben Bost

"HOLD IT. THAT'S THE GARBAGE."

the gag cartoon idea

J. B. Handelsman, who dreams up all the ideas for his gag cartoons, finds the process the hardest part of his work. As he gets older, the ideas seem more elusive. But when the idea comes, "It's almost coasting downhill to do the drawing." In analyzing his own ideas—and other ideas in cartoons appearing in the *New Yorker*—Handelsman concludes that the source of humor is often "the discrepancy between what people present themselves as and what they really are. And if they have a sneaking suspicion of what they really are, all the better."[1]

A common gag approach is to take a bit of conventional wisdom or a common occurrence or observation, remove it from its expected setting, and place it somewhere else. For instance: Consider the observation that, because of high interest rates and necessarily large down payments, young people can no longer afford to buy houses. A cartoonist named Hawker, in *Punch,* showed a couple of Mexicans, their large hats covering their faces and upper bodies, taking a siesta. One said to the other: "I honestly don't know how the young people can afford their first hat these days."

Barbara Smaller in *Chicago* magazine imagined a cocktail party in an unlikely place: heaven. As usual, clusters of people stood around holding their glasses, but they were standing on clouds and wearing wings. At cocktail parties people inquire about occupations. Smaller had her people do this, too, but in past tense. Several conversation balloons over the heads carried the question: "What did you do?"

Taking things literally is often the basis of the gag idea. Leo Garel in the *Saturday Evening Post* showed a man sitting in an empty auditorium. The usher came up and said: "Pardon me, sir. That last number was Schubert's unfinished symphony."

Just plain stupidity is another basis for gags. Jim Unger provides an example with his cartoon of a TV repairman talking to a middle-aged couple at home. "Folks, the main reason you're not getting a good picture is because you bought yourself a microwave oven."

When the answer to a question is immediately apparent to the reader, it can be the basis for a gag cartoon, too. An out-of-character Santa Claus became the central figure in my pre-Christmas cartoon (Figure 10.2) drawn for a weekly newspaper in Portland. The cartoon puts up with a little more clutter than usual, but the clutter is necessary to help answer the question asked by the striped-suit store manager. The cartoon also carries more solid black areas and pattern than is usual in a gag cartoon. Three camera distances are evident: the retailers are close up, the Santa station is at middle range, and the customers are vague in the background, with columns and an escalator evident.

The purpose of a gag cartoon can be just to involve readers, making them figure out what's going on. Satisfaction comes to the reader from working out the puzzle. Figure 10.3 from *The Jumbo Entertainer* (New York: Hart Publishing Co., 1946; Harold Hart, ed.) is that kind of a gag cartoon. No wonder the rooster looks angry.

The artist proves that you can give expressions to animals as well

---

[1] J. B. Handelsman in Mark Jacobs' *Jumping Up and Down on the Roof, Throwing Bags of Water on People,* Garden City, N.Y.: Dolphin Books, Doubleday & Company, Inc., 1980, pp. 29, 31.

"How closely did you check his references?"

Figure 10.2

Figure 10.3

as people. He makes the hen look embarrassed by lowering her head, shutting her eyes, reddening her face with some pen shading on the face and some radiating lines around it.

Shawn Bird, in a gag cartoon (Figure 10.4) drawn for the Caricature and Graphic Humor course, forces the reader to look around a bit to figure out what is going on. It is soon evident that someone in

the building has a sensitive sense of smell. Bird made the hand and spray can as large as he could, considering the size contrast he had to maintain between the Empire State Building and the beast and the screaming woman.

Some cartoons make use of several kinds of humor. Arnie Levin used three in one of his *New Yorker* cartoons. Judge, lawyer, and witness were almost buried in the punched tape coming from a court reporter's machine. The lawyer said: "Your Honor, I believe that the court has heard quite enough." The amount of tape, indicating the amount of talk coming from the witness, was *exaggeration*. The lawyer's response was *understatement*. And the line, "has heard quite enough," could be considered a *cliché*. Many gag cartoons are combinations of gag types.

To come up with their ideas, some cartoonists make use of the switch: a takeoff on an already published cartoon. One gag leads to another. This they would regard as creative copying.

A few scenes have been used over and over again and probably should now be shelved: the guy and gal on a tiny tropical isle, the guy crawling in the desert, the missionary in the cannibal's pot, the rich businessman in a posh restaurant with a young—and dumb—woman, the person on the psychologist's couch, the fellow carrying an end-of-the-world sign, the fakir. Some gags seem to get reinvented every few months. Charles Schulz's nominee for the hoariest gag is the one showing the Devil operating an elevator. As the door opens he asks, "Down?"

Perhaps the most famous gag cartoon ever drawn belongs to Charles Addams. It showed ski tracks that spread around a tree and then head downhill. It has been borrowed by any number of editorial cartoonists to show slick maneuvering by politicians.

Gag cartoon ideas tend to boil down to just a few categories,

Figure 10.4
Shawn C. Bird

including exaggeration, understatement, clichés, inventiveness, getting out of character, staying painfully in character, ridiculous or impossible situations, the grotesque, taking things literally, and visual puns. They can start with the cartoonist or gag writer imagining a scene with characters and props and then coming up with a funny line. Or they can start with the line, with the cartoonist coming up with an illustration afterward to make the line funny.

The wording of the gagline is terribly important, possibly more important than the idea itself, certainly more important than the drawing. The gagline needs a cadence, but it cannot be very long.

It should read as though someone really said it, using words appropriate to the setting. Word choice must be precise. No word should be included that does not contribute to the gag. There should be no asides and no preoccupation with cute names.

greeting cards

The industry dominated by Hallmark likes to call them "social expressions." Most people call them greeting cards, although some of them seem more insulting than friendly. The zaniest of them—the ones involving cartoons—are "studio cards."

Hallmark occupies a nine-story building in Kansas City, Mo. It keeps 600 artists and writers busy producing cards and related products in twenty languages for distribution in 100 countries. Hallmark got in on the studio-card craze rather late, it being a conservative organization. But seeing the success of the smaller,

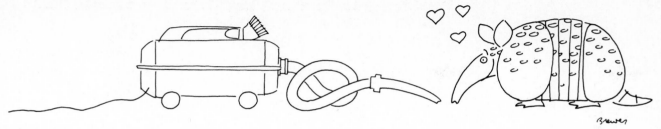

Figure 10.5
Bill Brewer
© 1980 Hallmark Cards, Inc.

sick-humor companies, it expanded its line to get at the younger buyers. One of its most successful cartoon cards was a Bill Brewer creation (the creators of greeting cards do not become well known, although a few, like Charles Schulz, are already famous before they do cards) that carried the line: "Happy Birthday! May the seat of your jeans hold out for another year!"

Brewer, who studied art at Chouinard Art Institute and whose works have won prizes in many art shows, directs and creates cards at Hallmark. One of his lines is "Funny Expressions."

Figure 10.5 shows one of Brewer's creations. This reprinting can't show the embossing and the full but quiet colors, but evidence of Brewer's fine craftmanship is still there. The inside of the card reads: "You take my breath away! Happy Valentine's Day!" A variation shows an ugly hippopotamus on the cover. This time it's a cute bird who's making the observation.

Another Brewer-conceived card shows a cat with a lovesick mouse who, on the cover, says, "You are the answer to my prayers." On the inside the message continues: "You're not what I prayed for, exactly, but apparently you're the answer."

Brewer says that for his line at Hallmark the words come first;

then the drawing. He often brings in freelancers for the art. That way he gets a "varied, a more noncorporate look."

Studio cards formerly came only in a narrow, deep size, but today they come in a near-square size as well. Typically a studio card utilizes a thick paper stock, folded once, with the teaser and art on the cover and the final message or gag inside on page 3. Page 2 is usually blank, and page 4 carries, in small type, the card maker's name and other information. Some studio cards take on more elaborate folds and go to several panels or pages. For instance, they may fold out in what is known as an accordion fold, and carry art and words in both sides of the sheet. Full color may be used. Of course cards like this sell for higher prices than less elaborate cards.

Dale Cards ("They're funny!" is the slogan on the back) published by RPR, Inc. of Chicago, gets by with printing in black only, but large areas of coarse Zipatone give the cartoons the impact color might give, saving the publisher the cost of color.

Writer's Market and *Artist's Market,* annuals published by *Writer's Digest,* Cincinnati, carry lists of greeting card publishers and tell something about them. A freelancer wishing to sell to one of the companies sends in a comprehensive rough, with art and lettering in place on a card cut to size. The company may buy the idea and

assign the finished art to a staff illustrator.

Perhaps no business is easier for the creative artist to set up than a greeting card business, and hundreds of new firms start up each year. Often the artist-owner does it all, including calling on nearby stores to stock the cards.

Kate Gawf puts out a series of postcards with a cartoon on one side, an explanation and a place for a message and an address and stamp on the other. Figure 10.6 shows one of them.

Several of Gawf's cards feature Mrs. Bomblatt, a character many women can identify with. Although no ideologue, Gawf wants senders and receivers of this card to feel the isolation and loneliness of all the Mrs. Bomblatts of the world.

Syndicated artists often branch out into greeting cards. Sometimes it works the other way around. Vivian Greene started a greeting card business with her "Kisses" characters before launching her *Kisses* comic strip, which she self-syndicates. Ashleigh Brilliant's *Pot Shots* became a syndicated feature, and his card ideas have appeared in several book collections. In 1982 Steve Carpenter, who developed a curly-haired dog for Hallmark cards, got together with Hallmark writer Ed Wallerstein to launch a comic

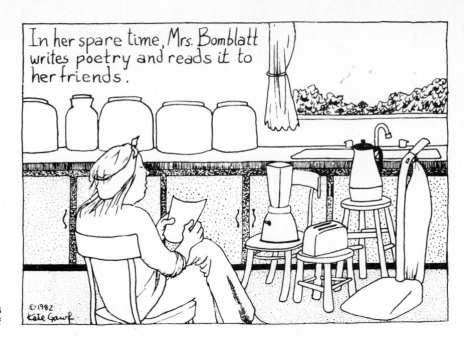

Figure 10.6
Kate Gawf

strip, *Ribbons,* featuring the dog, for King Features. The dog is sophisticated, sensitive, and trendy.

The *New Yorker* cartoonist George Booth draws greeting cards for a company in Texas.

Even editorial cartoonists have drawn greeting cards. In 1982 Recycled Paper Products, Chicago, offered a line of thirty greeting cards featuring Punk the Penguin, the little character at the bottom of Pat Oliphant's editorial cartoons who makes an additional statement or who offers an additional jab. The greeting cards were described by the company as "wry, not pointed or acidic." The cards were apolitical.

Cartoonists not otherwise identified with the greeting-card industry can be counted on each Christmas to create and print cards to be sent out to friends or to be used by clients. Figure 10.7 shows a sardonic Christmas card, reflecting the times, drawn by England's John Geipel. Santa Claus himself stands in a job line. This reproduction doesn't show it, but to make Santa stand out, Geipel, using a felt-tip marker, applied a quick layer of red to his suit, card after card.

Cards drawn for personal use often feature caricatures of the originators. Byron Ferris, a de-

Figure 10.7
John Geipel

Figure 10.8
Byron Ferris

signer who also draws, caricatures himself and his wife in one of his cards (Figure 10.8). He deftly captures her good looks and build

while exaggerating the swept-up hairdo, the widely spaced slanted eyes, the tiny nose (it disappears altogether here). He acknowledges his own firm chin and his thinning hair that curls at the ends. The gaiety of the greeting is enhanced by the spritely stride and by the seemingly hurried placement of the blacks, which do not follow the figures' outlines. The drawing has a relaxed look, but the original shows that Ferris retouched the lines with white paint in several places to get precisely the look he wanted.

Steven Heller, art director for the *New York Times Book Review,* provided some real inspiration when he put out his *Artists' Christmas Cards* (New York: A & W Publishers, 1979). He shows only privately printed cards drawn by cartoonists and other artists to be distributed to their friends and relatives. The cards "range from the beautiful to the grotesque; from the loving to the cynical." Among cartoonists represented are Edward Koren, Tony Auth, R. O. Blechman, Tomi Ungerer, Edward Sorel, Robert Osborn, Ralph Steadman, Edward Gorey, Gahan Wilson, Ronald Searle, Walt Kelly, Charles Addams, and Johnny Hart.

The Zigrosser Collection at the Philadelphia Museum of Art contains one of the largest and most varied selections of greeting cards in the nation.

sculptures, murals, and other works of art

Sculpture provides yet another way of creating a humorous piece of art that stands by itself. Lou Rankin creates funny animals out of cement, molding them into their pathetic states, apparently, as the cement begins to harden, and selling the results to stores catering to the carriage trade. They have a flattened look, making them ideal for placement on tables to add character to a room (Figure 10.9).

The metal nude in Figure 10.10 has the look of one of the ample ladies drawn by Eldon Dedini for *Playboy,* the *New Yorker,* and other magazines. She created quite a stir when she was given permanent display in downtown Portland. She has been stolen, mutilated, and subjected to other abuse, but she stands there today, adding a bit of culture to the Rose City. One enterprising poster maker put a man—a live man—dressed only in a long coat, the coat open, in front of her, added the line

"Expose Yourself to Art," and sold copies through stores all over the country.

Soft sculpture, wall hangings, and other home accessories and artifacts provide another outlet for cartoonists. Alan Rose provided the basic drawing and Kathy Rose made the colorful baby quilt seen in Figure 10.11. What you see is a detail: about a third of the quilt.

The cartoonist may also be called upon to paint a mural or to create cartoons to be projected as backdrops. *No End of Blame,* an off-Broadway play in early 1982, dealt with a radical political cartoonist moving from his home country to Russia to England, looking for complete freedom but never finding it. Gerald Scarfe drew the cartoons in a kind of David Low style for large backdrop projection.

Figure 10.9
From the collection of Roy Paul Nelson.

Figure 10.10
Photo by Roy Paul Nelson.

Figure 10.11
Courtesy of Alan Rose.

Figure 10.12
Peanuts character © 1958 United Features Syndicate, Inc.

While Charles Schulz was recovering from heart surgery at Santa Rosa Memorial Hospital in 1981, he drew a wall mural showing Snoopy blowing into a device used to exercise the lungs (Figure 10.12). The mural—and the fact that Schulz had gone through the operation—would bring encouragement to heart surgery patients who followed.

animated films

All of us try our hand at animation at an early age when we draw stick figures at the edges of pages in books and then flip the pages to make the figures move. Students at college, where film studies are popular, draw frames and then photograph them with a stop-action camera, one frame at a time, to produce actual animated films. Some work with traditional cartoon figures, some in more abstract forms. Some redraw each scene completely, one for each frame; others work with overlays, called "cels" (for Cellophane).

Figure 10.13 shows two successive frames executed by Tom Ettel for his short film contrasting the joy children feel for the snow with the hardship snow can bring to a tree that is old and ready to fall. Ettel also uses his film to deal with death and regeneration. A small tree sprout springs up alongside this tree in a later sequence.

Winsor McCay, a comic-strip artist, was among the first of the animators. His *Gertie the Dinosaur* played to enthusiastic and even incredulous theater audiences in 1914 and afterward.

A milestone in animation came in 1928 when *Steamboat Willie*, a Walt Disney production, appeared with a sound track. Sound, including music, greatly improved the effects of animation that people were used to seeing.

In 1930 Walter Lantz produced the first Technicolor cartoon, a five-minute opener for the film, *The King of Jazz*. The film featured Paul Whiteman's orchestra. Walter Lantz Productions went on to produce some 600 animated films, including many featuring Woody Woodpecker.

The idea for Woody came to Lantz when a pesky woodpecker

Figure 10.13a
Tom Ettel

Figure 10.13b
Tom Ettel

193

pecked at the roof of his honeymoon cabin in 1950. Mel Blanc did the Woody voice at first, but in a few months Lantz's wife Grace took over because Warner Bros. signed Blanc to an exclusive contract. She's been the voice for Woody ever since.

Even more popular have been Mickey Mouse and the other endearing creatures coming out of the Walt Disney Studios in Burbank. Many of our most successful comic-strip artists and gag cartoonists got their start there. A number of animators trained at Disney moved on to form their own studios, in some cases to produce work less slick and more experimental.

The animation part of the business dwindled following the death of Disney in 1966. The organization failed to adjust to changing tastes; it put more emphasis on its amusement parks and regular films. But the great animated films produced earlier continue to be re-released to intrigue audiences.

Many of the popular comic strips have moved into animation for TV and theater showings, and occasionally editorial cartoons evolve as animated films on network news. Animated films became an important part of television following that medium's coming of age after World War II. Saturday morning's lineup became cluttered with low-budget shows for youngsters. Prime-time saw programs like *The Flintstones* created for adults. Advertisers to all audiences found that animation could sell products. Animated characters who have helped sell products over the years include Speedy (for Alka-Seltzer), Mr. Magoo (for General Electric), Charley the Tuna (for Star-Kist), and the Hamm's Beer bear.

Animation can be used for causes as well. The Lutheran Church of America, with Charles Brackbill handling the concept, called in Kim & Gifford Productions, Inc., New York (you met this firm in chapter 4), to do a thirty-second TV commercial that proved humor and religion could, in the words of Lew Gifford, "hit it off together." Figure 10.14, a frame from that commercial, depicts a man showing off his church to a reluctant friend.

Figure 10.15 shows a frame from another Kim & Gifford production for a Ketchum/Philadelphia commercial put together for its client, Green Tree, an insurance company. A bemused crowd of neighbors watches a man gathering in a harvest from his money tree. Charles Tyson, president of the agency, came up with the concept.

Big companies like animated art, provided it is done at an adult level, because they feel that it warms their images and makes the companies appear more human. Sophisticated advertisers like Xerox and IBM call in cartoonists such as Ed Koren and R. O. Blechman to do the work. The drawing of these cartoonists is experimental, even vacillating, the color subtle and subdued. The humor is droll, not slapstick.

Figure 10.14
Courtesy of Kim & Gifford Productions, Inc.

Figure 10.15
Courtesy of Kim & Gifford Productions, Inc.

Koren and Blechman films do not have the slickness of, say, the Disney films.

Blechman's talking-stomach commercials for Alka-Seltzer were greatly admired at the time for their humor and charm. In 1978 he drew *No Room at the Inn,* a telling of the Nativity story, for showing on public television.

Ralph Bakshi, who got his start at Terrytoons, New York, is a different kind of animator. He enjoyed a few years of popularity in the 1970s as the creator of X-rated feature-length animated films. At one time his studio employed 100 animators. Believing that animated films should work like editorial cartoons, Bakshi produced *Fritz the Cat* to satirize radical college students and *Coonskin* to satirize people who used the social revolution to further their careers. Some critics labeled *Coonskin* as "racist." Bakshi's *Hey, Good Lookin',* released in 1983, deals with dehumanized life in the 1950s in Brooklyn, where he grew up.

In *Lord of the Rings* and *American Pop* Bakshi used a technique called rotoscoping in which he first shot film with real actors, then painted over each frame.

Talking with a reporter for *USA Today* in 1983, Bakshi, who had just closed his studio, said that the difficulties he had with his films were due partly to the fact that he was ahead of his time. He admitted that some of his material was outrageous, even scatalogical. ". . . there were scenes in those early movies that I blush at now." He said that he had not been mature enough to hold back.[2]

[2]Jack Mathews, "Maker of Frisky 'Fritz the Cat' Retires from Adult Animation," *USA Today,* January 25, 1983, p. 1-D.

11
the role of the editor

My own move from art into journalism came after the editor of my high school newspaper on several occasions cropped the sense out of my cartoons and tampered with their carefully crafted captions. It became clear to me that if my work was to remain inviolate it was going to have to go through hands more sympathetic and receptive. Mine. I took the journalism course, worked hard, and the next year, largely by default, became the paper's editor.

It was a paper only modestly objective and not overly appreciated by its readers, but it was generously illustrated. Colleagues who fancied themselves as budding Roy Cranes, Cliff Sterretts, or George Herrimans flocked to the paper, happy in their new freedom, but probably no cartoonist got as much space as I did.

I look back on that year with some embarrassment, because having worked both as a real-life artist and an editor in the interval, I think I can better appreciate now the real place of art in a publication and a dispassionate editor's role in shaping it.

the editorial process

Here's how the editorial process works for one humorous illustrator.

Lee Sokol, a Pittsburgh cartoonist who does gag cartoons and illustrations mostly for industrial publications, gets a Xerox copy of a manuscript from his editor, reads it to find illustration possibilities, and sketches out half a dozen roughs. The editor chooses three or four for finishing, and Sokol goes to work with his stop-and-start, carefully controlled pen lines.

Captions set in sans serif type (to set them apart from the text type) accompany his *Plant Engineering* illustrations, two of which you see here (Figure 11.1). The captions are set by the magazine. Sokol picks the sentences from the articles he illustrates and letters or types them at the bottom of the sheets carrying his art.

It is the editor (or art director) of a publication who makes decisions about when to use art and who

When an employee files an OSHA safety complaint, he often quickly falls from management's favor. Section 11(c) is his only protection from repercussion.

Action in an OSHA discrimination suit must be brought by the Secretary on behalf of an employee against an employer in a U.S. district court. Employees may not bring the action themselves.

Figure 11.1

Reprinted with permission from the Oct. 11, 1980 issue of *Plant Engineering* magazine.

should get the assignment to do it. It is the editor (or art director) who looks for lapses in the final drawing and who suggests ways to make it more effective.

Even humorous art needs consistency and a thread of logic. It needs to relate easily to the text-matter that it illustrates. An editor checks these things. In addition, an editor watches over all the wording in the illustration, for cartoonists are not noted for their ability to spell. An editor learns to live with the fact that a possessive "its" in a cartoon balloon is likely to carry an apostrophe, "a lot" will show up as "alot," and "all right" will appear as "alright." Alerted to the mistake, a cartoonist, under an editor's prodding, can easily white out the offending unit and reletter it correctly.

It is the editor who makes decisions about captions. Some illustrations need them; others don't. Captions don't always have to be of the left-to-right variety. When an illustration features a number of people or items informally arranged and they have to be identified, the editor can have a tracing made, key numbers to it, and reproduce it next to the art itself, but in a smaller size. In the accompanying caption, the names would be included with the numbers.

the editor's choices

A character in a Peter DeVries novel (*The Tunnel of Love,* 1954) somewhat irreverently refers to the editor as "a kind of pimp" who brings the artist and his public together.

It is a good idea for the editor to offer readers a variety of art approaches over a span of several issues. Working with freelance illustrators, the editor keeps a file of available people and notes their specialties. Chapter 3 showed some of the variety of styles and techniques that can be used. The computer adds to the possibilities.

These days some paintings, musical compositions, movies, and certainly animation are being produced through manipulation of a remote-control cursor. Computer-generated imagery (CGI) has become a reality. Most of the backgrounds for *TRON,* the Walt Disney science-fiction movie of 1982, were drawn by a computer.

Computers allow film makers to put real people into surreal settings. They also allow artists for the print media to quickly and skillfully produce charts, graphs, and maps, as well as more photographic pieces of art. Computers can now produce curves and texture to modify the earlier harsh geometric shapes.

In producing computer art under one of the 1980s systems, an artist uses an electronic stylus to draw on a tablet, watching the drawing appear on a larger screen. A second screen displays various colors. The artist touches the stylus to colors as needed, transferring them to the main screen.

Some critics question this as art, just as critics long ago questioned the product of the camera. Computer art will not take the place of more traditional art forms, but it will in time no doubt come to be regarded as one more perfectly acceptable and even commonplace medium. As with any medium, the skill of the user will determine the computer's usefulness.

uncovering the humorous illustrator

Where do editors find humorous illustrators? Editors of company magazines find them, sometimes, right out there in the front row among employees. Barbara Ellis, editor of *Life at Standard,* an insurance company publication for employees and sales representatives, found hers in Ben Bost, an employee in the supply department. It turned out that Bost had studied under Burne Hogarth, illustrator of the *Tarzan* strips, at New York's School of Visual Arts. Before going to work for Standard, he did some cartoons for *Stars and Stripes* and for trade journals. Bost found that making a living as a full-time cartoonist "wasn't very funny" so he took a full-time job in business.

The monthly assignment he gets from editor Ellis keeps his drawing arm warm, and like most hobby cartoonists he dreams about serious freelancing to national magazines, but "the ever increasing postal rates" keep him pessimistic.

Editor Ellis writes a monthly two-page essay exploring life's challenges in business and personal relationships. "On Celebrating the Virtues of Leading a Dull Life" is a typical title, and Bost's head-on view (Figure 11.2) of an ordinary couple at home is a typical illustration. Ellis, who once worked for *Life* magazine, writes with a light touch, but there is always the danger that in dealing with the subjects she chooses, she could become pedantic. The humorous illustrations are a guarantee that nobody will feel preached to upon leaving the two-page spread.

Using a simple, clean style, Bost rightly depends upon exaggeration to put over his ideas. Figure 11.3 went with an article urging readers to avoid being dominated by others, even by bosses. Ellis quoted Haim Ginott: "Take your sails out of their wind." She ends on this note: "Liberate yourself from others' moods. There'll be no weeping with delight when someone gives you a smile nor trembles of fear at the frown."

This drawing represents Bost at his exaggerated best. The boss at the right doesn't merely frown and talk; he frowns and shouts and puts a finger into the air to better dramatize his point. He is angry enough to double his right hand into a fist. The reader makes no mistake about the mental state of the two cowering, trembling employees. Hair stands on end, eyes pop out, one set of hands fold in supplication, another covers a mouth. Sweat marks and shake lines complete the picture.

Another Bost drawing (Figure 11.4) went with an essay, "On the Very Human Need to Belong." It illustrated the line, "Deny it or not, there's pain in isolation." Look at that poor bespeckled, striped woman, the turned-in toes, the pathetic self hugging! There is meanness in the trio ignoring her, seen especially in the

Figure 11.2
Ben Bost

200

'They wept with delight when he gave them a smile, and trembled with fear at his frown...'

Figure 11.3
Ben Bost

Figure 11.4
Ben Bost

combination frown and open-mouth smile on that pot-bellied gentleman.

Ellis usually sprinkles her two-page essays with a couple of one-column drawings—"drop ins," they're called—and one big one. What you've seen here are the big ones, not necessarily shown in their published sizes.

Ken Tokarz, editor of *Emhart News,* a company newspaper published by the Emhart Corporation, Hartford, Conn., turns to Dave Granlund, an editorial cartoonist for a daily newspaper in nearby Middlesex (you met Granlund in an earlier chapter), for feature-story illustrations. "Essentially, when I have a story for the *Emhart News* that lends itself to a cartoon (usually humorous, off-beat or not lending itself to photography), I call Dave on the telephone and we chat about illustration possibilities," Tokarz says. "Sometimes I have a general cartoon concept in mind; other times I just ask Dave what ideas he may have. Usually, he has two

or three to suggest almost spontaneously."

Tokarz adds: "I never call Dave absolutely committed to a cartoon idea. Cartoonists, I feel, should not have their imaginations shackled by an editor. Their minds are a creative resource that should be tapped and not truncated by editors."

The "Let me rephrase that!" drawing (Figure 11.5), used to illustrate a feature on international business and the problem of speaking the language, shows a fellow who has said the wrong thing in a Middle East country.

In Figure 11.6, Granlund illustrates a feature about the recording of various plant sounds, including those from a rivet-producing factory, a tire plant, a shoe machinery plant, and others. The resultant score, "The Rhythmic Sounds of Productivity," was available on a floppy disc and in cassette form. In his drawing Granlund sees a relationship between an orchestra conductor and the person arranging for the sounds in this recording, putting

the new conductor in an appropriate uniform and giving him the right kind of a baton.

In an illustration for a feature on the correct use of English, Granlund shows an Englishman who lives by the book attacking word use in the *Emhart News.* The letters of the words bounce off the page, as though they were press-on letters put on a pasteup. The paper had conducted a survey among the employee/readers in thirty countries and found a number of them, particularly in Great Britain, unhappy with "American journalese" and colloquialisms used.

To illustrate one of her articles in *Pause,* Coca-Cola's magazine for employees in the Dallas, Texas area, editor Shelley Cleary went to a freelancer who is attached to Hallmark cards: Stephanie McFetridge Britt. Cleary's article dealt with caffeine and its effects, a subject Coca-Cola was more than casually interested in. The national press and advertisers had been giving the subject much at-

Figure 11.5
Dave Granlund
Courtesy of Emhart News.

Figure 11.6
Dave Granlund

Figure 11.7
Dave Granlund

Figure 11.8
Stephanie McFetridge Britt
Courtesy of *Pause*, published by the Dallas Coca-Cola Bottling Company.

tention. The article was detailed and rather heavy going, compared to other articles and stories the magazine runs, so Cleary decided a cartoon illustration was needed. It was the first time she had used a humorous illustration,

and she was, she reported later, "thrilled with it."

The article mentioned tests of the effects of caffeine on pregnant rats, hence the setting: a woman, possibly the article's writer, visiting with a pregnant rat who, from the looks of things, has been consuming a lot of Coke. One touch has a lamp made from a Coke

container. Britt used a wash technique for her black-and-white drawing, which, in reproducing, spanned the gutter to unite the two pages and nicely dominate the spread. It was the article's only illustration, so it didn't need a caption.

turning the illustrator loose

Some illustrators need a lot of direction; others work better on their own. What they offer, unencumbered by inflexible guidelines, can be substantial. When the cartoonist is as important a figure as

Ronald Searle, the greatly admired and much imitated British cartoonist, an editor can sit back and prepare to be pleased by what's submitted.

The Participative Manager
"We, the President's Office...."

The Marketing VP
"We can sell anything...."

The Personnel VP
"We love you.... You're fired...."

Figure 11.9
Ronald Searle
Courtesy of Price Waterhouse & Company.

Today's Executive, a quarterly published by Price Waterhouse & Co., asked Searle to offer his versions of "contemporary executive personalities, as they seem to appear in modern folklore." Figure 11.9 shows three of them.

The drawings appear to have been done in ink with at least two instruments, one for the fine lines, another for the thick lines. The style is highly inventive. Note especially Searle's depiction of the personnel officer, whose condition goes somewhat beyond being merely two-faced.

An editor should be willing to let an illustrator take a few liberties with the text. Susan Dundon in a *Redbook* article entitled, "The White Lie Test, or How Honest Can You Be with Your Friends?" suggested tongue-in-cheek that a couple, invited to dinner at a house where a mean dog roams, should respond with a Yes, provided they can have the dinner "to go." Lady McCrady, in one of her full-color, loose-style illustrations for the piece, showed a couple already there, being attacked by a vicious dog. The wife is saying: "We'd *love* to stay for dinner . . . but could we have it 'to go?'" It made for more action than showing someone writing that in a note.

rejecting the art

Sometimes an illustration, even when it's adjusted, just doesn't work. The editor has no recourse but to pay off the artist with either a "kill" fee or the full fee and run the article without an illustration or hold it up for art from some other freelancer. Of course, some hard feelings may result from the action. A soft-hearted art director at the old *Saturday Evening Post* was known to accept an inferior illustration occasionally and run it smaller than the original page layout called for.

The editor's or art director's dealings with an illustrator are always more personal than the dealings, say, with a gag cartoonist. Gag cartoons are submitted on speculation, usually by mail. Most are rejected, and they are rejected by printed rejection slips.

Gluyas Williams once rejected a rejection slip from Harold Ross of the *New Yorker.* He sent it back with a little essay on humor that is said to have changed Ross's mind on aspects of running his magazine. Williams went on to be a regular contributor to the magazine.

credit where it's due

Roy Doty. Doug Anderson. Leo Hershfield. Seymour Chwast. Roy Carruthers. John Huehnergarth. R. O. Blechman. Ray Cruz. Robert Grossman. Brad Holland. Jack Barrett. David Seavey. Arnold Roth.

Not exactly household names. Yet each is the name of a highly successful humorous illustrator. Many other names could go on this list.

People pay little attention to the names of those who provide the illustrations for the stories, features, articles, and books they read. Nor do they notice the names of people who draw the gag cartoons we laugh at. Even the names of editorial cartoonists get lost in the rush of things. Of the people who draw funny pictures, only comic-strip artists get much attention, and that is because their work appears on a consistent and daily basis and their strips develop avid followings.

Editors themselves contribute to the anonymity of comic artists when they or their writers in published articles describe or quote from cartoons without naming the cartoonists. Editors and writers are far more careful to credit sources when they quote other writers or politicians. Yet, in those cases, they quote only a small portion of what has been said. When editors quote gag cartoonists, they quote *everything:* the entire gag line, or 100 percent of what was written; and they describe 100 percent of what was drawn. All without credit to the creator. It is true that the gag line may have been written by someone other than the cartoonist, but so, probably, was the politician's speech or the book by the movie actor that gets all the headlines. Nobody holds up the credit there.

Some of the fault for the anonymity belongs to the cartoonist, who may have failed to sign the work or who signed it with the attention to clarity that a physician uses to scribble out a prescription.

There is an opposite problem: the oversize signature. I once knew a cartoonist who, first thing when he sat down at his drawing board with a piece of Bristol board, carefully penned his generous signature in the lower right-hand corner; then he began his drawing. (I won't mention his name, as he is likely to recognize it if he sees it in print.) Of course, an editor dealing with a cartoonist too eager for a quick reputation can delete an oversize signature and substitute a small-type credit line next to the drawing. The credit line can run up the side of the drawing to keep from interfering with the caption.

If the art is prominent enough in the layout, the artist may get a *byline,* along with the writer's. The artist's byline ordinarily would be in smaller type than the author's byline, for the art, after all, merely decorates or illustrates what the author has written and occupies considerably less space.

Because so many publications run only reprints of cartoons, an editor running an original may want to label it as such. *Time,* which reprints editorial cartoons from various newspapers, nevertheless uses original drawings for departments like "Americana" with credit lines such as: "Illustration for *Time* by Michael C. Witte."

Local editorial cartoonists often include the names of their papers with their signatures in order to show that the work has not come from a syndicate. Even syndicated editorial cartoonists put the names of their home-base papers with their signatures. Comic-strip artists paste down tiny credit lines identifying their syndicates.

arranging
art on a page

Comic strips in a newspaper belong together on a page or a section set aside for them. When a strip becomes too political or controversial, an editor may move it off the comics page and onto the editorial or op-ed page or somewhere else. *Doonesbury* faced such moves, and no wonder. It did win a Pulitzer Prize for editorial cartooning.

Elsewhere in the paper, or in magazines and books, editors make a mistake when they put two same-size self-contained cartoons together. This sets up a relationship between them not intended by the artists. It also pits one against the other.

A clustering of cartoons is necessary when it is the purpose of the cluster to cause readers to compare, as when an editor shows how various editorial cartoonists react to a single event or idea. Such a cluster merits an umbrella headline and maybe an editor's note explaining the connection.

The editor faces fewer restrictions in the display of humorous illustrations than in the display of self-contained cartoons. Any size, any shape can work. The idea is to vary the display of art from article to article and issue to issue.

Illustrations can float out away from the text or they can fit into the text rather tightly. Some editors like to wrap copy around illustrations, letting a column of copy go narrow for a time, then widen out again. A wraparound can take other than a narrow flush-left, flush-right form. It can fit the contours of the art. Often it is simpler and maybe even more effective to insert the art between lines or paragraphs, letting it take the same width as the text or centering it, leaving white space on either side.

One way to exhibit a cartoon illustration is to divide it into two parts and let columns of type intervene. The art then stirs the grayness of the type at more than one place. Its appearing in two parts may make it more expressive. For instance, the *New York Times* for a feature on airline deregulation showed a Jurek Wajdowicz drawing of an opened bird cage at the bottom left and a flying airplane at the top right of the six-column feature. Two men stood at the birdcage site (it was a giant bird cage to accommodate the plane), one looking into the empty cage, its door open, the other looking up at the departing plane.

An illustration like that can come into the editor in one piece; the editor then decides to cut it apart. Or it can be planned as a two-unit drawing in the first place.
To tie later pages to the first page or spread of an article, the editor can reuse a portion of the opening art. A little redundancy can't hurt. Many editors use a portion of opening-spread art on the Contents page, a page that has been dressed up considerably in recent years on most magazines. The small piece of art there, along with an oversize page number, helps the reader quickly locate an article or story.

playing
with type

The selection of a typeface and the placement of type can become part of an illustration's effectiveness. Typefaces come in a great variety of styles. Often it is possible to match a type style with a drawing style. The type and drawing then work as a visual unit.

A roman typeface—a typeface with thick and thin strokes—may

Figure 11.10

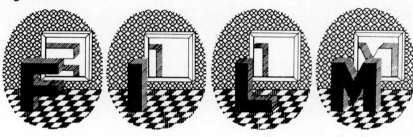

go well with a line drawing made with a combination of thick and thin lines. A bold sans-serif typeface—a typeface with singularly thick strokes—would go well with a drawing made with singular strong lines and areas of solid black. Some typefaces have distinct personalities. Some seem to fit certain periods in our history. There are art-deco typefaces, for instances, that complement art-deco drawings. A study of a type-specimen book suggests the many possibilities.

The editor or art director usually picks the typefaces for the headlines or titles that go with an illustration, but if type and illustration are intertwined, the illustrator may do the job, using press-on letters, available from any art store, or hand-lettering the type.

Good typography asks for standard typefaces, but occasionally an editor turns to an oddball or decorative face for a word or two in a headline or an initial letter at the beginning of an article and at intervals later.

For a title of an article that deals with mirrors or reflections, the type could be run backward, in

mirror reverse. Or the editor can turn to Miroir, one of two-dozen faces offered by designer Jean Larcher in *Fantastic Alphabets* (New York: Dover Publications, 1976). Figure 11.10 shows a word set in Miroir.

Encouraged by *U & lc.*, a typography magazine, many artists and cartoonists in the 1970s and 1980s designed alphabets of letters made from people, animals, and props. The magazine reproduced the best of them. One of the popular cat foods adopted a package logo made of letters (designed by Milton Glaser) that were really cats in playful contortions. Editors find such letters useful as initials to begin articles or chapters.

Alphabets of letters like these are easy enough to create. The idea is to keep them simple so that the letters in combination read first as words, then as individual pictures. An anonymous artist for *Werbezeichen: An Album* (Munich) demonstrates with an animal turned into an "O" (Figure 11.11). Another anonymous artist for *Harper's* makes a "J" of an animal.

Mark Gorman, a student in an Advertising Layout course, designed a cat alphabet for one of his assignments. I've spelled out a

Figure 11.11

word using his letter-characters (Figure 11.12).

The *placement* of the type can be inventive, too, provided it doesn't interfere with readability. Type trickery works best where only a word or two are involved. The cover designer for the paperback version of Robert Benchley's *Inside Benchley* (New York: Grosset & Dunlap, n.d.) featured a Gluyas Williams drawing of Benchley and put the words "INSIDE BENCHLEY" *inside* the drawing. The letters were big and bold enough to be read from a distance.

Sometimes an editor can remove a single letter from an ordinary typeset title—especially the title of a book on a cover or jacket—and substitute a piece of art. A capital "I" especially lends itself to this treatment. Scribner's, the book publisher, for its "Scribner Crime" imprint, uses a dagger for the "i" in crime, and the "i" is in lower case.

Figure 11.12
Alphabet by Mark Gorman.

living with advertising

The editors of company magazines enjoy an advantage over the editors of other magazines in that they are not bothered by pages and columns of advertising interfering with the design flow. Illustrations for articles do not have to compete for attention with illustrations for advertisements.

The *New Yorker* represents the ultimate triumph of advertising display over editorial display. There is virtually no art in the magazine except for the gag cartoons. This makes the color and flair of the advertising all the more dazzling.

In any magazine or newspaper supported by advertising, the editor or designer has to work around the ads. What the ads say is of little interest to the editor. This results sometimes in some interesting coincidences.

Bang & Olufsen in a full-page ad in the *New Yorker* showed its Beo-center 7000 "music system," with a closeup of a hand holding the separate control module. "There's Nothing Remotely Like It," the headline punned. Turn the page and there was a Jack Ziegler cartoon of a man sitting in front of a yo-yo hanging from the ceiling. The yo-yo was hooked up to a plugged-in electric cord. The caption read: "Late additions to the home entertainment center: the electric yo-yo with auto-control." My guess is that the ad, as a result, lost a little of its effectiveness. A final check of any page proofs ought to involve the editor's moving through the editorial and advertising portions of the publication looking for uncomfortable juxtapositions. The ad must stay in place, but it is easy enough to move a piece of editorial art to another page.

the principles of design

On a newspaper, the editor works one page at a time and gives most attention to the front page and the first pages of special editions. On a magazine or for a book, the editor thinks in terms of spreads, because the reader takes in two pages at a time. The pages are small enough for that.

Either way, editors (or their art directors) utilize the design approaches that were treated briefly in the "Composition" section of Chapter 4.

Basic design principles are followed, mostly unconsciously, by everyone who brings order to a chaos not only of pictures and type but also of paint and canvas, bricks and redwood, flowers and ferns, and even (at the table) dishes and silverware. Whatever the design or arrangement problem, the principles apply.

The first involves balance. It suggests that you should be able to draw a line down the center of your page or spread and end up with elements on either side that, in total, "weigh" the same. The easiest way to achieve this balance, of course, is to center everything; although everything-centered pages or spreads can have a classic beauty and simplicity, they can also turn out to be rather dull. So most editors go for *informal* balance. As a heavy person moves into the center of a teeter-totter to allow a lighter person to balance him, a big illustration in an editor's hands moves closer to the center of a spread while a smaller illustration on the opposite side moves out to the edge. Figures 11.13 and 11.14, rough sketches, illustrate formal and informal balance.

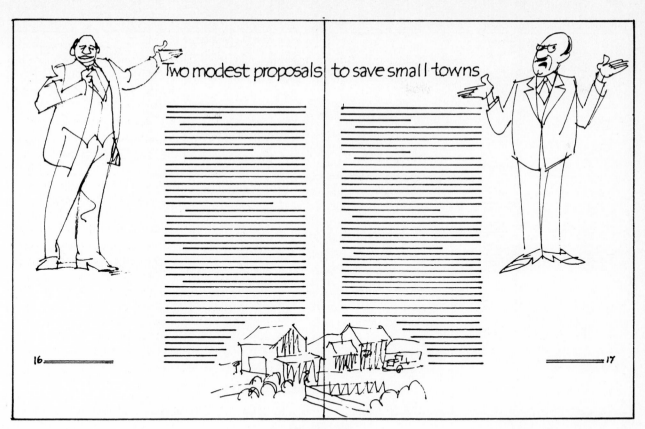

Figure 11.13

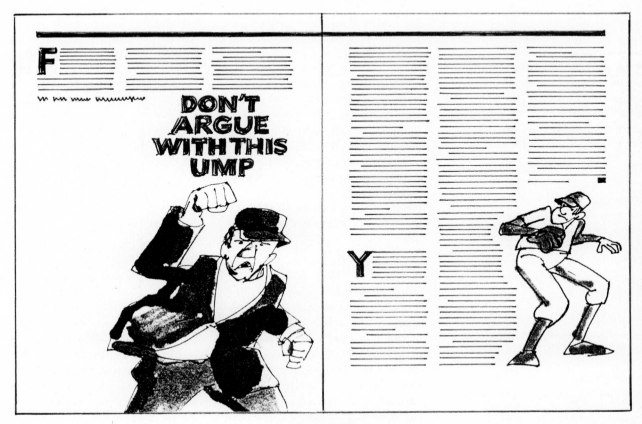

Figure 11.14

Figure 11.15

Balance comes easily enough to even the amateur editor; but it helps to remember that big elements "weigh" more than usual-shape elements, dark or black elements "weigh" more than gray elements, and color "weighs" more than black-and-white.

The second principle involves proportion (Figure 11.15). It holds that unequal space divisions are more interesting than equal divisions. A square, with its equal dimensions, is not quite so interesting as a rectangle. Hence the typical magazine page is deeper than it is wide.

Of course, for the sake of parallel structure, you would be consistent in the amount of space you put between headlines and story-beginnings in a news section, but in many other instances you would vary your spacing. The space between the title and article-beginning would be different from the space between picture caption and body copy, for instance. You take your inspiration for pleasing proportion from nature, which, to cite one example, makes the diameter of a tree trunk different from the diameter of one of the tree's branches. At least that seems to be the order of things in the Pacific Northwest, where I live.

The third principle (Figure 11.16) asks that you help your readers along by setting up some kind of a path for them to follow. Call it eye travel or sequence, it capitalizes on the fact that readers—readers of many languages at any rate—read from left to right and then down the page. To take full advantage of this, you could arrange the elements—photos, titles, copy blocks, etc.—in a sort of a "Z" pattern. But this would result in wasted space and sheer monotony. There are other possibilities. Readers also go from big to little, unusual shape to usual shape, darkness to grayness, color to black. This means that you can get readers started almost anywhere on the page or spread and move them up, to the left, or any other way. When there is a question of sequence, you can number the elements: 1, 2, 3. Often the order in which elements are taken in by readers is not important. Sequence becomes a design principle needing only minimal attention.

A fourth design principle has to do with unity (Figure 11.17). Under this principle, every item on the page or spread appears to be

210

Figure 11.16

Figure 11.17

related. If art is used, it is all produced by the same person. Instead of using a wide range of type, you use just one face, getting variety in the sizes and weights of that type.

Unity's big job is to make left and right pages appear related. The gutter stands there daring you to span it. Many editors run photographs or titles across the gutter to unite the pages. Or they set up imaginary axes (more than one axis) from which they "hang" or

"fly" several photographs or titles or copy blocks. That these elements share the same axis unites them.

Small illustrations can tie a series of pages together by appearing in

211

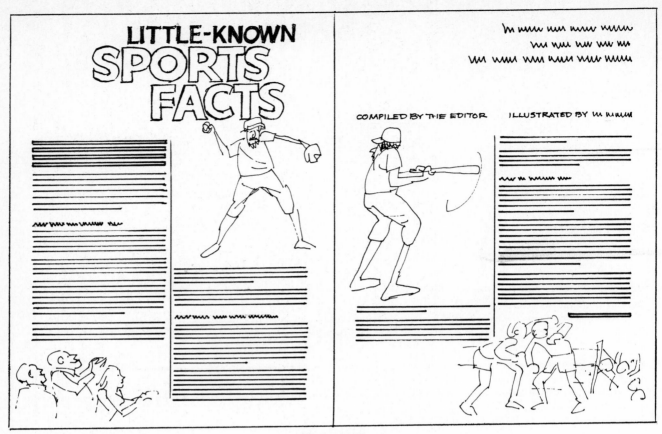

Figure 11.18

a continuous flow at the bottoms of the pages, telling a story to supplement the main story. *The Atlantic,* for its 125th Anniversary Issue (November 1982), got illustrator Guy Billout to produce a marvelous example for a James Fallows article on "Entitlements." Fallows speculated on the problem: "If all Americans are 'entitled' to help, who will pay for it?" The first page showed a red-white-and-blue Uncle Sam sitting at a desk handing out a check to a man standing at the head of a line. As your eye traveled along the line you noticed an old gentleman with a cane, a middle-aged woman, and various other types. As you turned the page you saw many other types: a black woman,

a woman with a baby, a man with a beard, etc. The line continued spread after spread until you got to the last page of the article, where the line ended with Uncle Sam, in color again to make him stand out, looking a bit dejected, waiting for *his* handout. The long string of art was but two inches high, but high enough to provide visual movement to unite the pages and to make a dramatic point. The nation faces a real problem. ". . . all causes are in jeopardy as long as more and more of us are 'entitled' to support from everyone else."

Finally, editors follow the principle of contrast or emphasis (Figure 11.18). This principle says that one item on the page or spread should stand out from all

the others. When you allow two or more elements to vie for first attention, they cancel each other out.

There they are: five basic principles of design. Obviously, you would not follow them blindly, and you would remember that they carry with them many exceptions. Furthermore, they tend to contradict each other. How can you have perfect unity, for instance, when you have one item standing out from all the others?

But they are principles worth considering if you are just entering the world of design. If you have been out there a while, they are principles worth reconsidering.

making reproduction decisions

Originals give the editor the best reproduction, of course, but certain kinds of prints—like Veloxes and PMTs—are almost as good. In fact, some syndicated artists no longer put their originals in the mail to their syndicates. They send photocopies.

Editors can sometimes get perfectly good reproduction from already printed cartoons, provided the image is sharp and the printing is on a smooth or coated stock. Where the image is poor, as in a newspaper clipping, the art can be reduced to minimize the imperfections. If a screen or pattern is involved, it must be strong enough and coarse enough to take reduction. Fine-screen halftones can be reprinted, too, by ordering a rescreening from the printer. Of course, any reprinting involves dickering with the copyright holder for permission, and a fee may be involved.

It is not a good idea to reduce one illustration in a series to a different degree from the others. Different-size illustrations bring welcome variety to related pages, but line quality should be consistent. You don't want the lines of one of the drawings to be thicker than the other lines. Editors should settle on sizes before the art is assigned, or, with the artwork in, they should design the pages around it. All the art for a single article should take the same degree of reduction or enlarging.

Cartoonists rightly complain when their work is run too small. Comic-strip artists have been particularly vocal about size reductions in recent years. The reductions have virtually killed off the adventure strips, which needed large panels to show off the detail necessary to tell the stories. In 1978, to keep the situation from getting any worse, the Newspaper Comics Council and the syndicates set a standard 43-pica width for comic strips and a 21-pica width for panels (there are 6 picas to an inch). Since then the Council has resisted newspapers' pressure to further reduce these widths. If papers want these features to take up even less space, they have to reduce them themselves.

the art of cropping

Editors feel more comfortable cropping photographs than cropping drawings or paintings. Presumably a drawing or a painting is carefully composed to begin with, and any chopping at the edges could destroy the balance and the proportions the artist has worked out. Many photographs—especially those taken for newspapers—are taken in a hurry, one after the other, with the realization that later an editor, to fit things together, will do some adjusting.

This is not to say that photographers, any more than illustrators, like to be cropped. A photographer who is also an artist puts as much thought into composing a photograph as in picking the subject matter and setting the dials.

Cropping, like composing itself, can greatly change what a piece of art says. Peter Masters, director of graphics for the General Services Administration in Washington, D.C., told editors attending an American Press Institute meeting that "The picture will say different things depending on what you do with it." Say the picture is of a man walking down a road. Show him walking into the picture, and you say he has a way to go. Show him walking out, and you say he's come a distance. Show him in the middle, and you say he's come a distance; still, he has a way to go. There is an additional consideration: if you show the subject walking out of the picture you may encourage the reader to leave with him. The eye goes where the action is. Most editors try to choose pictures that lead readers into a layout, not out of it.

To show the platemaker where an illustration is to be cropped, the editor draws two short lines at the bottom to show left and right edges wanted and two short lines at the right of the drawing to show the top and bottom edges. Between the two lines at the bottom the editor writes the width desired in the printing. The depth will take care of itself.

the shape of the art

Some illustrations work well as silhouettes; others seem better suited to rectangular shapes. The rectangle doesn't need outlining. The illustrator, using a pencil with light blue lead (the lines won't reproduce then), can surround the drawing with a box, then work pen, brush, or marker up to those lines but not past them. Or the illustrator can establish hard edges after the inking by touching up with opaque white or by pasting strips of white paper on all four sides. The editor can get the same effect by using crop marks.

Sometimes an illustrator draws a box around a drawing so that the box will print. Boxing a drawing gives it a bit more formality, unifies it, separates it from other art nearby, and keeps it from tipping. Without the box, an editor may straighten up a figure the artist meant to lean, for instance.

The box can take on a thick and thin or slightly wavy character, or it can be carefully ruled with a ruling pen, ball-point pen, or thin-tip marker. In the box in Figure 11.19, a wisp of smoke breaks the box at one point, adding a little variety. Boxes can also be drawn smaller than the figures or scenes, allowing parts of bodies or parts of props to jut out from them, a technique used these days for silhouetted photographs as well. The editor can

Figure 11.19

arrange with the printer for a box after a drawing is turned in. Such a box is made with a role of thin black tape.

When newspapers used to carry eight rather than six columns to the page, the feeling among editors was that a piece of art only a column wide had to run as a vertical. Art two columns or wider could go either as a vertical or as a horizontal. Because space was at a premium, most large drawings and photographs ran as horizontals. With wider columns now, newspapers are more willing to use one-column horizontals. For instance, cartoons that are used to illustrate one or two of the letters to the editor might run as horizontals. That way, not a lot of space is sacrificed to the art, and the letters columns are suitably decorated.

giving color
to art

A humorous illustration takes on another dimension when an artist can paint it in full colors. This kind of art calls for process-color reproduction. Not many editors or advertisers can afford it, so color, when it is used in a drawing, usually involves one color other than black. The artist supplies a separate piece of art to represent the color, usually in the form of a frosted acetate overlay. The artist paints in the areas that are to appear in color. Two plates are made: one for the art itself, the other for the color.

An artist can also produce what is known as a "keyline drawing," a single drawing carrying the to-be-printed-in-color areas as well as the to-be-printed-in-black areas. A tissue-paper overlay roughly marks the areas to be in color and carries instructions to the printer.

If no second-color art is available, the editor can run the entire drawing in color, provided the color available in the press run is dark enough to hold onto all the detail in the drawing. Another last-minute use of color involves printing the drawing in the usual black ink over a tint block of color. Still another way to introduce color is to surround the drawing with a box printed in the second color.

Color works best when an editor allows the artist to plan for it ahead of time and produce a drawing that takes full advantage of the color. For instance, an artist may want to do more than simply fill in an area with a solid color. Some of the drawing outlines themselves could be in color.

settling
on numbers

The question arises: What in an article or story deserves illustrating with humorous art? The occasional *bon mot,* isolated from the theme? Or the article's general thrust? Obviously, you can make a case for either approach. Following the first course, you probably would end up with a number of illustrations. Following the second, you could get by with a single drawing.

The art, however used, should not upstage the prose or over-

power it. Occasionally, though, a feature can be half prose and half art. Or the feature can be all art except for captions or running commentary.

Every issue of a publication can carry humorous illustrations, but only a few stories and articles will really benefit from them. Too many humorous illustrations scattered throughout a publication destroy their novelty.

12
humorous illustration as a career

Cartoonists often look for new ways to exercise their creativity. Gag cartoonists like Charles Schulz, Mort Walker, and Johnny Hart create comic strips. Even editorial cartoonists do it: people like Jeff MacNelly, Doug Marlette, Bill Schorr, Tony Auth, Don Addis, and Paul Szep. Editorial cartoonist Dick Locher took on *Dick Tracy* in 1983. Successful comic-strip artists launch additional strips. All cartoonists—editorial cartoonists, gag cartoonists, comic-strip artists—draw occasional humorous illustrations. Some end up on magazine covers.

Cartoonists like the late Al Capp turn to painting as a diversion. Paul Conrad, the editorial cartoonist, became a sculptor. Edward Koren, the *New Yorker* gag cartoonist, has created "The Beast" and "The Fish" wood sculptures that, in a limited edition, were going for $295 in 1981. Ferd Johnson, who, with his son Tom, produces *Moon Mullins* (the strip originated by Frank Willard), paints about thirty canvases a year and sells them through a gallery in Corona del Mar. His paintings have an impressionist feel. Tom Johnson, when not working on the strip, draws editorial cartoons and produces art for filmstrips and advertisements, including commercials.

Late in life Rube Goldberg moved from creating comic strips and crazy cartoon inventions to creating editorial cartoons, for which he won a Pulitzer Prize, and then highly praised sculptures. Robert Minor gave up a brilliant career as an editorial cartoonist to work full-time for the Communist Party as an editor and propagandist.

Jules Feiffer is as much recognized as a playwright as a satirical comic-strip artist. James Stevenson has written as well as drawn for the *New Yorker*. Lou Myers, a cartoonist with a unique broadline style, writes short stories for the *New Yorker* about his mother's life in a nursing home. James Thurber was more a writer than a cartoonist, although more people probably saw and laughed at his improbable drawings than read him. Clarence Day, Jr., author of *Life with Father* and other works, was also a humorous illustrator. The late *New Yorker* cartoonist Carl Rose wrote for and illustrated the "Accent on Living" column in *The Atlantic*. He also worked as an editorial cartoonist for two newspapers, and he illustrated some fifty books.

Dividing one's time between drawing and writing is not unique. Max Beerbohm earned enough of a reputation as both a critic and caricaturist to be knighted in 1939. Edward Lear, the nineteenth century British author and illustrator of a whole series of *Nonsense* books, including books of limericks, was originally a serious science and medical illustrator.

A number of classic writers have dabbled in cartooning and caricature, if only for diversion. Victor Hugo, the nineteenth century French novelist and poet who wrote *The Hunchback of Notre Dame* and *Les Miserables,* was not only a landscape painter but also a caricaturist. While in exile he produced a series of drawings attacking the government, its system of justice, and the clergy. "For Hugo the Romantic, painting and drawing were not the preserve of academies," wrote Werner Hoffman in his *Caricature: From Leonardo to Picasso* (New York: Crown Publishers Inc., 1957), "but a spontaneous means of self-expression." In caricature Hugo found "an important safety valve . . . ." It was Hugo who, on vacation, dashed off a note to his publisher inquiring about how one of his books was selling. It was one of the shortest letters on record. Just this: "?" His publisher's reassuring letter was just as short: "!"

William Makepeace Thackeray, the British novelist of Victorian manners and morals, illustrated many of his writings, including his masterpiece, *Vanity Fair* (1847–48). George du Maurier, a regular contributor of cartoons to *Punch,* also wrote novels. His novel *Trilby* (1894) carried his own illustrations. O. Henry, the American writer with the surprise endings, sometimes illustrated his own stories. He liked to make drawings first, then weave stories around them.

For many, drawing funny pictures must be a sideline, not a way of making a living. Enrico Caruso, one of the world's great opera singers, used drawing as a form of relaxation, scribbling on scraps of paper caricatures like those seen in Chapter 2. For a time he sold a weekly cartoon to an Italian newspaper. Music and acting, like writing, have a relationship to drawing. Bandleader Xavier Cugat was a caricaturist. Actor John Barrymore drew cartoons and serious illustrations for the Hearst newspapers around the turn of the century. Jerry Marcus, who does *Trudy* and sells gag cartoons regularly to magazines, is a member of the Screen Actors Guild.

G. K. Chesterton, the British writer known as "the prince of paradox," first studied art, and he produced humorous drawings throughout his career as a short-story writer, novelist, biographer, and critic. His friend, novelist Hilaire Belloc, used to send him scenarios with the request that Chesterton sketch the characters.

"I always write much better when you have already done the pictures," he wrote to Chesterton.[1] The sketches would often end up as printed illustrations in the books.

In our own time, Tom Wolfe, whom we associate with the "new journalism," produces caricatures as well as articles and book-length manuscripts for publication.

the cartoonist as character

Mike Peters, syndicated editorial cartoonist for the *Dayton* (Ohio) *Daily News,* has been known to step into an editorial conference in a Superman suit after having waited on an outside ledge for the meeting to begin.

Ray Collins as a staff artist for the *Seattle Post-Intelligencer* used to wear a Conoco service station shirt with "Leonard" embroidered above the right pocket. He picked it up at a St. Vincent de Paul outlet. Guest lecturing to students in grade schools in the area—he did a lot of that—he would say, "My name is Ray and my shirt's name is Leonard."

Cartoonists do like to pose as unlikely characters, but compared to other creative people they lead rather subdued lives. Reg Smythe, who does *Andy Capp,* told Jud Hurd in *The Press* that "Most cartoonists are very rational because you have to be rational to appreciate the irrational. That's why cartoonists are so flipping normal." Doug Marlette of the *Charlotte* (N.C.) *Observer* thinks cartoonists—at least editorial cartoonists—are on the dull side. He says that at their conventions cartoonists are mistaken for Rotarians.

Normal and dull, and like other clowns cartoonists do a lot of crying on the inside.

"Maybe you have to be misera-ble," muses B. Kliban, looking back on his own life. He adds: "It's a cliché that all the great comics are close to tragedy. I think it's true."

"Sometimes just by the fact that you are down or feeling depressed or something like that you can do your best work," says gag cartoonist Brian Savage. "Sometimes I do my best work when I'm angry." He adds: "I think you have more to work with if you're a pessimist."

Gahan Wilson, the master of ghoulish drawings, says: "One humorist was asked what was the prime requisite for being a humorist and he said an unhappy childhood. I think he's got a point."[2]

Enrico Caruso, admittedly better known as a singer than a cartoonist, was given to bouts of melancholy in spite of his worldwide acclaim. He made no important move without consulting an astrologer. A slave to cleanliness, he bathed and changed clothes several times a day. When he died in 1921 at forty-eight, someone came out with one of those songs that often follow the death of a star. "They Needed a Songbird in Heaven So God Took Caruso Away" was the kind of song a cartoonist with a feel for the absurd could appreciate.

[1]Dudley Barker, *G. K. Chesterton,* New York: Stein and Day, Publishers, 1973, p. 13.

[2]Mark Jacobs, *Jumping Up and Down on the Roof, Throwing Bags of Water on People,* Garden City, N.Y.: Dolphin Books, Doubleday & Company, Inc., 1980, pp. 58, 109, 125.

with age as no barrier

The charm and simplicity of what children produce so naturally is what older cartoonists often strive for. Really working on kids to get them drawing while they're uninhibited is probably worth the effort. Early in life, everybody is a cartoonist. When young, people see magic in everything around them. No rules intrude to force them into hard-edge realism. Most people grow up and move away from the cartoon world. A few never leave it. They stay on to do the editorial and gag cartoons that need doing, the comic strips, and the humorous drawings for stories, articles, books, and advertisements.

Bill Mauldin won his first Pulitzer Prize at twenty-three, Jeff MacNelly at twenty-four. When MacNelly, only a few years later in 1981, decided to abandon editorial cartooning (temporarily, it turned out) to concentrate on his comic strip *Shoe,* the distributor of his strip tapped Jack Ohman to succeed him. Jack Who? Ohman, at twenty-one, had just graduated from the University of Minnesota where he did cartoons for the school paper, and was at work on the *Columbus Dispatch.* MacNelly had been his idol; he had patterned his style after MacNelly, and he had MacNelly's more-conservative-than-liberal outlook. Everyone—not just right wingers—became his victims. ". . . I would guess Ted Kennedy and Ronald Reagan and Jimmy Carter are about the same," he told *Newsweek,* which devoted a page to "Cartooning's Newest Star." And: "I don't sit down at the drawing table with some grand mission to indoctrinate the American people with to my philosophy." Because he was going to 370 newspapers, Ohman was earning a six-figure salary, according to *Newsweek* (September 14, 1981, p. 80).

It is never too early to start. A number of the comic strips we see today originated with young men still in college. Kevin Fagan was twenty-three in 1979 when United Feature Syndicate launched his *Drabble,* which, by the end of the year, appeared in 150 papers. He got his start as a comic-strip maker at college and on a local daily. He was still in college when his strip took off.

Nor does cartooning end for people reaching sixty-five, seventy-five, or even eighty-five. William Steig, celebrating fifty years of drawing cartoons for the *New Yorker,* brought out *William Steig/Drawings* (New York: Farrar, Straus & Giroux) in 1979. He was seventy-two, still drawing regularly for the *New Yorker,* always experimenting. Lillian Ross, in the book's introduction, says that his most recent work "indicates that he has finally arrived at an authentic youth, for it is joyful, spontaneous, playful, innocent, and wise." Steig used to draw conventional gag cartoons: strong and tight. His work is much looser now, even fragile. He says it has taken him a lifetime to learn to draw like a child.

George Price, born in 1901, was still doing gag cartoons, and frequently, for the *New Yorker* as this book was written. He had started with that magazine in 1926. If anything, his beautifully controlled lines were better than ever.

At age seventy-six, in 1980, Maw Maw Booth, mother of George Booth, was drawing a weekly cartoon in the *Princeton* (Mo.) *Post-Telegraph.*

Probably the most durable of the editorial cartoonists was Cy Hungerford who, at eighty-nine, retired from the *Pittsburgh Post-Gazette* in 1977 after sixty-five years on that paper and its prede- cessor, the *Sun.* His first cartoons had to be scratched through chalk that had been hardened on steel plates. Plates were then cast from these masters. His later cartoons were done in bold brush and pen strokes for regular letterpress reproduction. His cartoons were less cluttered than those of many of his fresh-faced contemporaries.

the morale factor

Possibly no other profession can boast of such high morale. It is the rare cartoonist who doesn't enjoy the work. George Booth, who specializes in seedy interiors, unshielded light bulbs and stretched extension cords, uncomprehending cats and dogs, and assorted eccentric characters for the *New Yorker,* quotes I. F. Stone and speaks for most cartoonists when he says: "I feel so happy doing what I do that I should be arrested."

A cartoonist in a staff position— say as editorial cartoonist for a newspaper—rarely leaves. Occasionally a cartoonist goes through the files to count published cartoons and is surprised at the volume. Jay N. "Ding" Darling, editorial cartoonist for the *Des Moines Register,* produced some 17,000 cartoons before his death in 1962.

Outsiders look at how a cartoonist makes a living and rightly conclude that it is a good life. Clarkson N. Potter, the publisher of *Pigs in Love,* a 1982 cartoon collection, says of cartoonist Revilo that

he earns his living "by marking up clean pieces of paper with ink and then selling the used paper . . . ."

"I used to get thrown out of high school for drawing cartoons about my principal in the school paper; now I do vicious cartoons about the President and they give me awards!" said Mike Peters in 1981 on the occasion of his winning a Pulitzer Prize.

Still there are disappointments.

The artist specializing in humorous illustration experiences difficulties in keeping company with more serious illustrators. Nobody quite trusts a clown nor takes the clown seriously. The witty Adlai Stevenson discovered that in his two unsuccessful runs for the Presidency in the 1950s. John Kennedy didn't get funny until after he won the 1960 election.

As Woody Allen observes: "When you do comedy, you're not sitting at the grownup's table."

the cartoonist's background

Some people become cartoonists after a career in another field. Other people are cartoonists from the start. Many pursue cartooning and another career simultaneously. A likely combination involves journalism and cartooning or graphic design and cartooning.

A number of the early comic-strip artists started work as reporters. Fontaine Fox, for instance, who produced *Toonerville Folks* for so long, began as a reporter for the *Louisville* (Ky.) *Herald,* and did his cartooning at first only as a part-timer. Late in his career as a syndicated artist he visited the war zone in Europe (1939) and wrote a series of humorous features for the *New York Sun.*

Jay N. "Ding" Darling, the editorial cartoonist, started out as a reporter. A sketch he did of a trial lawyer who refused to be photographed started him on his drawing career.

Cathy Guisewite, creator of *Cathy,* started out as a copywriter for advertising agencies in Detroit. One of the agencies encouraged her to bring humor into her copy. She says that advertising copywriting also taught her to condense what she created, a practice useful to anyone drawing a comic strip. Her strip evolved from illustrated letters she sent home to her parents.

M. C. Stevens, a *New Yorker* cartoonist, spent some time as an underground cartoonist in San Francisco, "but my stuff just kept coming out too straight." His flirtation with the counterculture and his unwillingness to take an ordinary, steady job made freelancing for Establishment magazines an attractive possibility. He had turned to cartooning at an early age in Portland, Oregon because the serious things he drew caused people to laugh. He sold his first drawings to Navy magazines.

In the early 1980s Stevens, whose work has been described as "wacky," was hitting the *New Yorker* an average of every other issue. He also was doing some advertising illustrations. In 1982 he illustrated Charles A. Monaghan's *The Neurotic's Handbook* (New York: Atheneum).

George Booth, another *New Yorker* cartoonist, worked for a number of years as a magazine art director before becoming a full-time freelance gag cartoonist. As a trade-magazine art director, he did many of the drawings needed in his magazine.

Jean-Claud Suares, who does weekly drawings for the op-ed page of the *New York Times* and who provided the illustrations for a recent edition of *The Devil's Dictionary* by Ambrose Bierce, is the design director for *New York* magazine. He was once a *Times* art director. He turns to drawing, a first love, from time to time because, he says, "art directing is working with other people's ornaments, and drawing is more yourself."

Becoming an art director or graphic designer for a publication or an advertising agency is an especially appropriate preliminary activity for a cartoonist. The design thinking needed for a magazine spread or an advertisement is the same as for a cartoon. In a cartoon, the figures and props take the place of the headlines, photographs or drawings, and blocks of body copy.

One way to break into the graphic design field is to be a pasteup artist. Pasteup work is also invaluable to the cartoonist, who learns at the job the rudiments of printing and reproduction.

Some cartoonists do it the other way around. They draw first and then design. Martin Garrity started out as a freelance gag cartoonist (he sold to all the major magazines except the *New Yorker,* and even there he sold some gag ideas). He then taught cartooning for ten years, ending up as an art director and graphic artist for major corporations and a state university. But he continued to freelance. He has also done illustrations for magazines, including *Popular Mechanics,* and has written, illustrated, and designed greeting cards. Most of his later cartoons have been for advertisers. Like most cartoonists, he prefers editorial to advertising work. "In advertising there are too many people to please." But, of course, in advertising the pay is better.

"I personally think cartooning is one of the best occupations (actually professions) a person could pick," Garrity says. "It makes you think, learn . . . ." He admits that it also causes frustrations. "You look for work. It doesn't come to you—at least in the beginning." Cartooning becomes easier as you grow older, he thinks, "but ideas fight you a lot."

a cartoonist's schooling

How much schooling a cartoonist needs, and what kind, depends upon the cartoonist's innate abilities. Some cartoonists make it without formal training. But "I learned that you have to know the basics," says gag cartoonist Charlie Rodrigues. "Whether you learn them in art school or on your own doesn't matter, but you have to know the basics."

Peter Arno, the jazz musician who became one of the *New Yorker*'s most celebrated gag cartoonists, had no formal art training but on his own studied the works of Daumier, Picasso, and others. His beautifully composed, powerful wash drawings had a fine-arts feel. Arno held many cartoonists in contempt for their settling for drawing clichés and shortcuts.

Some cartoonists go to art schools not to study cartooning but a broader subject: the fine arts. Don Martin, a long-time favorite at *Mad* magazine, studied for three years at the Newark School of Fine and Industrial Art and one year at the Pennsylvania Academy of Fine Arts before becoming a cartoonist. Frank Modell, *New Yorker* cartoonist, studied at the Philadelphia College of Art. Etta Hulme, editorial cartoonist for the *Fort Worth Star-Telegram,* earned a degree in art at the University of Texas. Calvin Grondahl, editorial cartoonist for the *Deseret News,* Salt Lake City, earned a degree in art from Brigham Young University.

Chicago had one of the few great schools for cartoonists in its Chicago Academy of Fine Arts. One of its best-known teachers was Marty Garrity, who taught there full time in the late 1940s and early 1950s. Among his many stu-

dents were George Booth, Gahan Wilson, Shel Silverstein, Frank and Phil Interlandi, Dick Locher, and Shaw McCutcheon. Bob Zschiesche, who also studied under Garrity, said in *Cartoonist Profiles,* "To me, Martin Garrity *was* the Academy."

Because having a broad background and being able to reason is so important to cartoonists, some feel that a liberal arts background is more important than an art background. A cartoonist needs to know a little about almost everything. For instance: history. It puts things in perspective. "You can see the latest dumbness as just the end of a long line of dumbnesses that have been taking place for thousands of years," says J. B. Handelsman.[3]

Earlier in this century many young people studied cartooning through correspondence courses. The most famous of the courses was the one run by C. N. Landon of Cleveland. Gil Fox, who does *Side Glances,* subscribed to the Landon course. Fox is admired by other cartoonists for his versatility. He has worked as an animator, a comic-book artist, and a

[3]*Ibid.,* p. 31.

comic-strip artist for major advertisers. He took over *Side Glances* in 1962, after it had been well established, and he readily adjusted to its sketchy style.

Landon supervised comic-strip buying at Newspaper Enterprise Association, and many of his best students in the 1920s, including Roy Crane, ended up with NEA contracts.

Figure 12.1 shows one of the many Landon "plates" published on slick paper and included in the backs of the lessons, which always ended with the line: "Dictated by C. N. Landon." The lessons had the look of typewritten copy.

W. L. Evans ran another popular correspondence course. R. A. Herschberger started one in 1924 that ran until 1970.

Correspondence courses served a need in the days when would-be cartoonists found themselves isolated in rural areas. Although a few courses still operate, most areas now are served by community colleges and other institutions where in-person training in art and even cartooning is readily available.

Figure 12.1

the cartoonist as inventor

People who draw or paint pictures find often that they have an ability to invent things as well. Visualization plays a part in invention just as it plays a part in art. Leonardo Da Vinci, who painted "The Last Supper" and "Mona Lisa," is perhaps the most accomplished artist-scientist of all time, developing among other things, a canal system, a fortification system, a cannon, an armored vehicle, flying machines, and buildings in the Vatican. Robert Fulton, who invented the steamboat, made a living at an early age as an artist. Samuel F. B. Morse, who developed the first electric telegraph and who invented the Morse code, was a successful portrait painter. He also helped found the National Academy of Design.

Carl Anderson, before he created *Henry* (first a *Saturday Evening Post* panel and later a syndicated comic strip), was a cabinetmaker who invented and patented a folding desk that was still being manufactured in the 1970s (Anderson died in 1948).

Rube Goldberg, a comic-strip artist and editorial cartoonist, is best remembered for his comic inventions (on paper only). So impressive were these diversions that Rube Goldberg can be found in most dictionaries, under "R." When people talk about a Rube Goldberg machine now they mean a complicated set of wheels and belts and gears and gimmicks put together to accomplish a rather simple if not useless job. The old Linotypes that were used to set type when newspapers were printed letterpress could serve as examples of Rube Goldberg-like machines.

a cartoonist's specialty

A cartoonist can become so firmly associated with a subject that when the subject is covered in a newspaper feature or a magazine article the editor feels almost compelled to turn to that cartoonist. When *The Oregonian* of Portland ran a feature on war games (played on boards with miniature figures) it got permission to run a couple of Willy and Joe drawings with the feature. Willy and Joe were characters, still remembered and recognized, that Bill Mauldin made famous in World War II. (You can see them in *Up Front,* New York: Henry Holt & Co., 1945.)

To illustrate its feature, *The Oregonian* also could have turned to works by at least two other World War II cartoonists: the late David Breger and the late George Baker. Breger developed *Private Breger* for King Features (renamed *Mr. Breger* when the war was over) and introduced "G.I. Joe" into the language. Baker developed Sad Sack for *Yank.* It was syndicated later.

serving the needs of editors and clients

The art world makes room, even commercially, for people who worry a lot about integrity, who refuse to let the marketplace dictate the direction of their art. Some of this is good, but when it blinds artists to the needs and sensibilities of their clients, it becomes a bore. While preliminary discussions and even rough sketches can reduce the chance of misunderstanding between artist and editor, it's always possible that what's turned in at the end will be an embarrassment.

City officials in San Francisco found this out when they commissioned sculptor Robert Arneson to do a bust of Mayor George Moscone, who had been shot and killed not long before. The $37,000 unit was to be installed at a new convention center. When it was unveiled, its pedestal carried Arneson-supplied graffiti that showed red spots resembling blood, a number of "Bangs," and even a Twinkie replica (the person who killed the mayor had claimed that his consumption of sugary junk foods was partly to blame for his mental state). Officials and the late mayor's wife were outraged, but the sculptor refused to change the pedestal, reminding his critics that he was a "realist" who "doesn't deal in illusion." The bust and pedestal were removed to a museum.

Every few months you read in the papers of another case where some government agency commissions a piece of art only to endure a public outcry when the piece is put on display. In the state of Washington in 1982 the House of Representatives voted to take down two "Twelve Labors of Hercules" murals, huge abstractions created by an art professor, Michael Spafford. That they were abstract instead of realistic was one problem; they also, for many legislators and visitors, appeared to be vaguely pornographic. Close to $83,000 had been spent acquiring the works. Another estimated $25,000 was involved in removing them.

slanting the work

Except for their cartoons that run afoul of trendy movements promoted by the media, cartoonists can get away with more now than in the past. But they must tailor what they do to the biases and sacred cows of each editor they work for. The *New York Times* will accept things the *New Yorker* won't, and vice versa. Gahan Wilson varies the grotesque content of his cartoons as he moves from one publication to another. ". . . when I do something for *National Lampoon* [for instance], I make sure it's in bad taste."

Dick Guindon, whose work is syndicated, worked first as a free-lancer to *Esquire, New York, Playboy,* and an underground satirical magazine called the *Realist.* As a cartoonist working now for newspapers, Guindon has had to make an adjustment. The offbeat humor is still there, but it is more family oriented than before. ". . . I came to newspaper cartooning very much under the impression that without a target, you can't do good humor. It was a case of 'us against them,'" he told Tom Daly in an interview in the *Duluth* (Minn.) *News-Tribune and Herald.* "Then I discovered the secret. It is really 'us against us.' From then on, the cartoons worked."

Guindon says that Charles Schulz's *Peanuts* showed him how to introduce affection in his work without it becoming maudlin. Daly observes that Guindon in his newspaper cartoons moved from "the polemical to the placid, from the tempestuous to the temperate."

public service aspects

People are always asking cartoonists to do quick sketches ("It'll just take a few minutes of your time") for worthy causes. No fees are involved, of course. A certain amount of this work is inevitable. It is hard to say No to some of the requests.

Some causes or activities are close enough to home to prompt the cartoonist to volunteer some art.

Figure 12.2 shows one piece of art—a montage—Dan Mindolovich contributed to Marylhurst College, Oregon for its printed program for Young Musicians & Artists, an annual cultural summer camp (Mindolovich's daugh-

Figure 12.2
Courtesy of Dan Mindolovich.

ter was in attendance). The bearded man in the center was one of the camp's well-established leaders.

A good thing about volunteer work is that you can't put a lot of time into it, so it has to flow easily. There is no overkill. A piece like this often carries the same flair a rough drawing carries for a pay-

ing client. The rough is often better than the tight, finished rendering that would follow client approval.

business aspects

To be published, a cartoonist either joins the staff of a publication or turns to freelancing. To be a freelancer requires more discipline than many cartoonists have, and not many make the grade. Those who do freelancing find it necessary to go out looking for assignments. The first order of business is to get some cards printed.

Kate Gawf, who does greeting cards and other cartoons, turns

her business card on end, and includes a tiny reproduction of one of her greeting cards (Figure 12.3).

Pick up Alan Rose's business card and at first you think you're reading a tiny comic strip. You are, except that it's a strip with not much of a plot, it turns out, and the transitions between panels are abrupt. Then you realize it is a business card you're reading, an

226

Figure 12.3
Courtesy of Kate Gawf.

effective one for its surprise. It turns out to be a showcase of Rose's clean, clear, reproducible style.

Rose prepared a booklet to send to editors to interest them in his work. The cover (Figure 12.4) reproduced his card, putting it into a cartoon hand about to deliver it to a harried editor. Inside were examples of his work and an invitation. "I'm a freelance cartoonist looking for assignments. If you think I can be of service to you, please contact me."

Tom Chalkley, a Baltimore cartoonist and activist, announces his availability in a folder reproducing some of his work. "Art for the movement is what I produce . . . . Because organizations working for *people, not profit,* need all the help they can get," his folder says.

A sketch showing an excavation (Figure 12.5) carries the caption: "We see the continuing, insane overconsumption, waste, and abuse of our own resources."

Figure 12.5
Courtesy of Tom Chalkley.

Figure 12.4
Courtesy of Alan Rose.

227

Figure 12.6
Courtesy of Tom Chalkley.

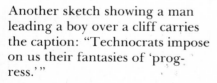

AND NOW A WORD FROM OUR SPONSOR...

CONSUME!

Figure 12.7
Courtesy of Tom Chalkley.

Another sketch showing a man leading a boy over a cliff carries the caption: "Technocrats impose on us their fantasies of 'progress.'"

Figure 12.7 (not from his folder) shows, in better detail, Chalkley's feeling about consumption urged on by advertising. The crosshatch technique here is reminiscent of some of the work found in underground comics, where Chalkley has appeared in the past.

What to charge for freelance work is always a problem. What use the drawing is to be put to makes a difference. So does the financial standing of the client. A cartoonist can work at an hourly rate ($10 and up) or on a per-piece basis. Sometimes a client will make an offer like this: "I have $150 for this job. What can you give me?"

A beginning cartoonist keeps rates down to break into the market but does not charge so little as to make the work unappreciated.

reprint rights

Though not as businesslike, perhaps, as some entrepreneurs, freelance cartoonists find that with their success they must direct increasing attention to costs and prices. Where once they gave their originals away, they now sell them. They also dicker more in assigning reprint rights.

The question of who owns cartoons after publication and who profits from further use—the publication or the cartoonist or both—needs to be settled at the time of sale. Most editors don't really care what happens to cartoons once they appear in their publications, so a cartoonist's asking for the return of the original and for second and subsequent

228

publishing rights is easy enough to arrange. Of course, the history of a cartoon's appearances must be made clear to whoever buys reprint rights. Publications that ran the cartoons originally expect to get credit lines.

The big magazines hire permissions editors who take care of the matter of granting reprint rights and arranging payment, if any, to their cartoonists. To reprint a *New Yorker* cartoon, for instance, the editor of a lesser magazine or a book publisher or author signs a contract, agrees to run a specified credit line (which designates the cartoon as a "drawing," by the way—not as a "cartoon"), and pays a fee that is substantial but not unrealistic.

A successful cartoonist gets a surprising number of reprint requests, many from editors with inadequate budgets. Cartoonists who hold second (and subse-

quent) publication rights make their own decisions as to who gets to re-run the cartoons and at what payment rate, if any. Jack Corbett, freelance gag cartoonist, holds to a firm policy: "Freelancers shouldn't give their work away. Period." His only exceptions involve friends or charities. He notes that some requests for freebies come on embossed stationery, some even from banks that publish magazines. Corbett doesn't even *answer* requests for free cartoons if he finds no self-addressed, stamped envelope. "If an SASE is enclosed, I write back, first to thank them for their interest. I then attempt to explain the economics of full-time freelancing . . . ."

Feature syndicates seem especially insistent on fees to reprint any of their cartoonists (or writers), for whatever purpose.

As one who has both asked for reprint rights (as for this book) and granted them, I think requests should be separated into

two distinct categories. The first, which would not involve reprint fees, would cover cartoons examined by a critic whose purpose would be to either praise or damn them. The second category, which *would* involve fees, would cover cartoons used by an author to illustrate points on subjects other than the art itself or to brighten the dull pages of, say, an economics or sociology textbook. The fee could be expected to be less than what a magazine paid for the cartoon originally. The cartoon is, after all, merely recycled.

Some freelance gag cartoonists have formed a guild that has set rates for first publication and reprinting of cartoons. Occasionally you hear the argument that a cartoonist who gives away a reprint right cheats some other more businesslike cartoonist from making a few bucks in substitution.

dealing with censorship and censure

In the past, comic strips like *Little Orphan Annie, Li'l Abner, Pogo,* and *Doonesbury* ran into problems with editors because they wandered into politics. Recent confrontations have involved cartoon treatment of women.

You wouldn't think that an innocent looking young woman like Miss Buxley (Figure 12.8) would cause controversy, but in the early 1980s her role at Camp Swampy in *Beetle Bailey* came under fire from some feminists and a few editors. Mary Kay Blakely, a writer in *Vogue* who reported being pawed at a picnic by someone she calls Mike Swift, saw a connection between an unpleasant afternoon (". . . I couldn't shake him, couldn't regain control of my

space and my time . . . .") and Mort Walker's strip: "How could I show [Walker] the intricate connection between General Halftrack and Miss Buxley and Mike Smith and me?" She charged that Walker, by showing the general's foolish and unrelenting infatuation with a dumb secretary with "tennis-ball breasts," stereotypes women and trivializes the problem of sexual harassment. Although Blakely did not identify Smith as a *Beetle Bailey* reader, she felt that the strip set the stage for episodes like the one she experienced.

Earlier a *Minnesota Tribune* editor had killed a *Beetle Bailey* episode

Figure 12.8
Courtesy of Mort Walker. © King Features Syndicate.

and published this note in its place: "Beetle Bailey does not appear on today's comic page because the subject matter was considered by the editors to be sexist." The strip, published later in the paper's ombudsman's column in response to reader outcry, showed the general dictating to Miss Buxley, who had forgotten to bring in her steno pad. She apologizes to the general: "I'm just not all here today." As she leaves in her well-filled mini skirt in the following panel, the general says to his aide: "If there was any more of her here, I don't think I could take it."

The *Tallahassee Democrat* and the *Concord* (N.H.) *Monitor* announced they were going to watch the strip more closely, clamping down on it when necessary. Several papers decided to run polls to see if readers wanted offending strips eliminated. An overwhelming percentage of readers responding in each case said No. One editor

following the survey reluctantly announced: "We'll run the strips, sexism and all."

A number of readers raised the issue of censorship, but of course editors have the right to decide what goes into the paper and what stays out, and their decisions can be purely arbitrary. It is a question not of censorship—censorship comes from outside authority—but of judgment. Dan Cohen, a Minneapolis public relations man, was one of those questioning the *Tribune*'s judgment. "A better policy would be to leave comic strips alone," he said "and save editorializing for the editorial page."[4]

Figure 12.9 shows a typical *Beetle Bailey* strip when Miss Buxley makes an appearance. Walker builds an episode around her about once a week, usually on Wednesdays.

[4]From a feature included in Mort Walker's *Miss Buxley: Sexism in Beetle Bailey?* Bedford, N.Y.: Comicana Books, 1982.

He seems genuinely surprised that charges of sexism would be leveled at the strip. In 1982 he brought out a book, *Miss Buxley: Sexism in Beetle Bailey?* (Bedford, N.Y.: Comicana Books) reprinting many of the strips featuring Miss Buxley, along with news accounts, features, and letter excerpts dealing with the controversy. He included roughs of some strips that he didn't finish because they *did* go too far.

Alleged sexism isn't *Beetle Bailey*'s only problem. Early in its life, in 1954, *Stars and Stripes* dropped the strip because of "lack of interest." Translation: the strip made fun of army officers. Walker's introduction of the black Lt. Flap caused something of a stir in 1970.

Comics scholars point out that women, pretty or otherwise, aren't the only group ridiculed and stereotyped by comic-strip

Figure 12.9
Courtesy of Mort Walker. © King Features Syndicate.

artists. Many, if not most, of the men turn out to be weak and pitiful. Dagwood is almost always outwitted by Blondie, and so is Charlie Brown by Lucy. In *Beetle Bailey* General Halftrack comes out often looking more stupid than Miss Buxley. Walker says he has a soft spot in his heart for the general. "I feel that he's a rather tragic figure, too old to have a chance but still possessing the same urges he had in his youth." When he shows the general doing his girl-watching, Walker feels that he is "making fun of the situation, not recommending it."[5]

the message in humorous art

Wilhelm Busch, the German cartoonist and writer whose *Max and Moritz* (1865) and *Pater Filucius* (1872) are said to be the precursors of the comic strip as we know it, was out for more than laughs. In some of his work he satirized the Catholic clergy and the military.

Like other creative people, cartoonists harbor deep feelings about matters that are important and often use their drawings to try to bring people around to their points of view. Vaughn Shoemaker, a two-times Pulitzer Prize winning editorial cartoonist for the now defunct *Chicago Daily News,* was a born-again Christian who lectured in churches and even preached on street corners. Whenever he could he worked in a Christian message in his syndicated cartoons, even though they went to secular papers. One of his most famous editorial cartoons—a Christmas cartoon carrying the verse John 3:16 from the Bible—

almost didn't make it in the *Daily News.* It wasn't Christmasy enough, his editors insisted. But Shoemaker was adamant, and the editors took it to publisher Col. Frank Knox, who decided in Shoemaker's favor. "If it weren't for John 3:16 there wouldn't be any Christmas," Knox said.

Betty Swords exercised her feminism with a series of getting-back-at-them cartoons drawn for the *Male Chauvinist Calendar '74.* Figure 12.10 shows the cartoon used on the calendar cover.

Dr. Nick Dallis lectures readers about health in his comic strip, *Rex Morgan, M.D.* He does it so effectively that the Federal Bureau of Alcohol, Tobacco, and Firearms hired him to do a booklet, "Rex Morgan Talks About Your Unborn Child!" The booklet points to the danger of alcohol to the fetus. (Dallis also created

[5]Mort Walker, *ibid.*

231

Figure 12.10
Courtesy of Betty Swords. © RIM Hurley.

"MARTHA!"

Apartment 3-G and *Judge Parker,* two other popular strips. It was while researching a sequence for *Judge Parker* that he became especially interested in "fetal alcohol syndrome.")

No message is more blatant than the message in an editorial cartoon or a caricature. A caricaturist can be especially devastating. When England's Mark Boxer (he signs his work "Marc") depicted an anti-pornographer there, Lord Longford, he made an erect phallus of the man's head and neck. Christopher Terry Mosher, the Canadian caricaturist, in the days when he signed his cartoons "Aislin," showed a recognizable politician, naked and contorted so that his head was partially inserted into his rear end.

Ralph Steadman is another caricaturist whose work reeks of anger. In *Man Bites Man* (New York: A & W Publishers, 1981) Steven Heller calls English-born Steadman "savagely critical . . . an adept satirical journalist who creates visual essays that report on the absurdity of political life . . . . The screaming, scaping, and scratching of his drawings call out for attention."

"I'm not the kind that would go out in the street and commit violence, so I do it in drawings," Steadman told Heller. His full-color "Save the Seals" cartoon, for instance, drawn in 1978, showed a classy woman in a fur coat, standing on ice, being sprayed by blood squirting up from what is apparently a battered baby seal.

Steadman's early drawings appeared in *Private Eye,* a radical

humor magazine published in England. His later work has appeared in several adventurous American magazines and in book collections.

Edward Sorel is another caricaturist whose work is often savage. Sorel, with Seymour Chwast and Milton Glaser, founded Push Pin Studios, an influential New York firm which has set many trends in both publication and advertising design. He was especially hard on those who promoted the Viet Nam War or who were involved in the Watergate scandal. His work has appeared in *Monocle* and *Ramparts* (both defunct), *Esquire,* and the *Village Voice.*

Sorel told Heller that he felt no drive to "comment on the starving masses. What concerns me are the liars that rule us." He centers his attacks more on liberals than conservatives because, he thinks, liberals are more hypocritical.

Ben Shahn, who accepted illustration assignments from advertisers as well as book publishers, used his paintings and drawings also to make strong political points. To protest the 1927 executions of anarchists Sacco and Vanzetti, who had been convicted of murder in Massachusetts, Shahn did a series of twenty-three paintings.

These people work in the tradition of the "social realists" of the nineteenth century: people like William Hogarth, who in Great Britain used his engravings to attack what we today would call the "lifestyles" of both the rich and the poor; Francisco de Goya, who in Spain used his etchings to point out the horrors of war; and Honore Daumier, who in France used his lithographs to ridicule the political leaders and to express his social concerns.

As the Ruhl lecturer at the University of Oregon in 1982, Jeff MacNelly told his audience that he enjoys being provocative especially when he deals with people who take themselves too seriously. "It's really a great joy to come up with a cartoon every once in a while that unites the country in one angry palpitating spasm." There is a feeling of accomplishment when a cartoonist finds a villain not generally recognized as a villain. In the words of Tony Auth, editorial cartoonist for the *Philadelphia Inquirer,* "Sacred cows make the best hamburger."

Going out after an occasional villain is one thing. Devoting yourself fully to a cause is something else.

B. Kliban, who in his forties has grown somewhat mellow, says, "I don't think I could ever give my life for a cause, now that I know how these causes [that capture the fancy of activists] eventually diminish and grow rancid in the tides of history." In a 1980 cartoon Kliban nicely summarizes our condition. A man stands before an audience giving a talk, his lectern a drawing table. He says: "Gentlemen, I regret to inform you that we're all drawings!"

**annotated
bibliography**

The following bibliography covers books published since 1978. For books published between 1975 and 1978 see the listing in my *Comic Art & Caricature* (Chicago: Contemporary Books, 1978). For books published before 1975, see the listing in my *Cartooning* (Chicago: Contemporary Books, 1975).

ABRAMS, ROBERT E. AND JOHN CANE-MAKER. *Treasures of Disney Animation Art.* New York: Abbeville Press, 1982. (More than 500 preparatory drawings from the Disney Archives, reproduced in full color. Impressive but expensive.)

ADDAMS, CHARLES. *Creature Comforts.* New York: Simon and Schuster, 1981. (A collection of Addams' remarkable gag cartoons published during the preceding six years. Not all of them are morbid.)

APPIGNANESI, RICHARD AND OSCAR ZARATE. *Marx for Beginners.* New York: Pantheon Books, 1979. (Cartoon treatment of a man and his ideas.)

———. *Freud for Beginners.* New York: Pantheon Books, 1979. (Cartoon treatment of another man and his ideas.)

ARNDT, WALTER (editor and translator). *The Genius of Wilhelm Busch: Comedy of Frustration.* Berkeley: University of California Press, 1982. (Picture stories, comic poems, and illustrations by a great cartoonist of an earlier era, with a solid introduction.)

ARNO, PETER. *Peter Arno.* New York: Dodd, Mead & Company, 1979. (More than 250 great Arno cartoons—his largest collection. Some are published for the first time.)

BAGINSKI, FRANK AND REYNOLDS DODSON. *Splitsville.* New York: E. P. Dutton, 1980. (Reprints of a comic strip devoted to a family hit by a marital breakup.)

BARKS, CARL. *Uncle Scrooge McDuck: His Life and Times.* Millbrae, Calif.: Celestial Arts, 1982. (A lavish and expensive collection of comic strips starring a duck character who is a rich tycoon with a real-life cult following. Barks, who worked for Disney for twenty-three years, is a highly respected artist and storyteller.)

BARRIER, MICHAEL AND MARTIN WILLIAMS (editors). *A Smithsonian Book of Comic-Book Comics.* New York: Smithsonian/Abrams, 1982. (A study of the earliest and best comic books,

with many reproductions. Basil Wolverton, Will Eisner, and Harvey Kurtzman are there, along with many others.)

BARSOTTI, CHARLES. *Kings Don't Carry Money.* New York: Dodd, Mead & Company, 1981. (A collection of cartoons by a *New Yorker* cartoonist who has been called a cross between James Thurber and Otto Soglow.)

BAXENDALE, LEO. *A Very Funny Business.* London: Gerald Duckworth & Co. Ltd., 1978. (An examination of "the closed and secretive world of British comics.")

BAXTER, GLEN. *The Impending Gleam.* New York: Alfred A. Knopf, 1982. (A collection of single-panel cartoon non sequiturs, with captions, drawn in a 1930s comic-book style by an English artist.)

BERQUIST, MAURICE. *The Doctor Is In.* Anderson, Ind.: Warner Press, 1982. (Theology presented as conversation with Charlie Brown, with illustrations from *Peanuts.*)

BLACKBEARD, BILL AND MALCOLM WHYTE. *Great Comic Cats.* San Francisco: Troubador Press, 1981. (A comprehensive history of the cat in caricature, with 300 illustrations. Foreword by Jim Davis, creator of *Garfield.*)

BLECKMAN, R. O. *Behind the Lines.* New York: Hudson Hills Press, 1980. (Autobiographical material, plus sketches by a much-admired nervous-line artist. The book includes his earlier *Juggler of Our Lady.*)

BLITZ, MARCIA. *Donald Duck.* New York: Harmony Books, Crown Publishers, 1979. (500 cartoons and photos, covering Donald's career, with instructions on how to draw him.)

BLOCK, HERBERT. *Herblock on All Fronts.* New York: New American Library, 1980. (One of several collections of cartoons by the *Washington Post's* three-time Pulitzer Prize winner—with plenty of his prose.)

BOND, SIMON. *Bizarre Sights & Odd Visions.* New York: Clarkson N. Potter, Inc., 1983. ("Truly tasteless Bond is back!" says the publisher in an advertisement. This Bond book has 90 weird cartoons.)

———. *101 Uses for a Dead Cat.* New York: Clarkson N. Potter, 1981. (Cartoons that brought to the publisher a cat-lover's suggestion for a new book: *101 Uses for Dead Simon Bond.* Bond brought out a sequel in 1982: *101 More Uses for a Dead Cat.*)

———. *Unspeakable Acts.* New York: Clarkson N. Potter, Inc., 1981. (A

collection of cartoons "so outrageous, so perverse, they . . . [are] guaranteed to offend everyone," says the publisher.)

BOOTH, GEORGE. *Pussycats Need Love, Too.* New York: Dodd, Mead & Company, 1980. (Gag cartoons by the son of Maw Maw Booth.)

BOOTH, GEORGE; GAHAN WILSON AND RON WOLIN (editors). *Animals, Animals, Animals.* New York: Harper & Row, 1979. (Cartoons about animals.)

BOSKER, GIDEON AND JIM BLASHFIELD. *Brainstorm.* Portland, Oreg.: Marble Press, 1983. (A doctor and a cartoonist get together to do a humorous set of gags with the brain as the chief character.)

BRILLIANT, ASHLEIGH. *I May Not Be Perfect, But Parts of Me Are Excellent.* Santa Barbara, Calif.: Woodbridge Press, 1979. (Drawings and observations by a syndicated philosopher/cartoonist, creator of a line of greeting cards. One of several book collections.)

BROOKS, CHARLES (editor). *Best Editorial Cartoons of the Year.* Gretna, La.: Pelican Publishing Co., Inc. (Annual compilation that gives a good cross section of what's being done in this field.)

BURROUGHS, EDGAR RICE. *The Golden Age of Tarzan, 1939–42.* New York: Chelsea House Books, 1978. (Edited by Maurice Horn.)

CALDWELL, JOHN. *Running A Muck: A Bunch of Zany Cartoons.* Cincinnati: Writer's Digest Books, 1978. (Gag cartoons by a cartoonist who appears regularly in *Writer's Digest* and other magazines.)

CAPP, AL. *The Best of Li'l Abner.* New York: Holt, Rinehart & Winston, 1978. (Capp was one of America's most brilliant and outspoken artists.)

CARLINSKY, DAN (editor). *College Humor.* New York: Harper & Row, 1982. (Cartoons and stories from nearly 100 campus humor magazines published since the 1870s.)

CHAST, ROZ. *Unscientific Americans.* New York: The Dial Press, 1982. (Chast, who appears frequently in the *New Yorker*, has an original cartoon approach. The book reprints 126 pieces.)

CHRISTENSEN, DON (compiler). *Tips from the Top Cartoonists.* Woodland Hills, Calif.: Donnar Publications,

1982. (Advice from thirty-two cartoonists, including Mort Walker, Mort Drucker, and Bil Keane.)

CRANE, ROY. *Buz Sawyer: Book One.* Buffalo, N.Y.: Quality Comic Art Productions, 1980. (A collection of Crane's second comic strip, launched years after *Wash Tubbs.* Brilliant.)

_____. *Buz Sawyer: Book Two.* Buffalo, N.Y.: Quality Comic Art Productions, 1980.

CRAWFORD, H. H. *Crawford's Encyclopedia of Comic Books.* New York: Jonathan David, 1978. (Thirteen chapters of history, with an emphasis on the major comic-book publishers.)

CRAWFORD, TAD. *The Visual Artist's Guide to the New Copyright Law.* New York: Graphic Artists Guild, 1978. (Sixty-three-page booklet covering various aspects of copyright law that would interest cartoonists and other visual artists.)

CROALL, STEPHEN. *The Anti-Nuclear Handbook.* New York: Pantheon Books, 1979. (Cartoon treatment of a serious subject.)

DAVIDSON, MARION AND MARTHA BLUE. *Making It Legal: A Law Primer for the Craftmaker, Visual Artist and Writer.* New York: McGraw-Hill, 1979. (Necessary information.)

DEYRIES, BERNARD AND DENNYS LEMERY. *The History of Music in Cartoon.* New York: Arco, 1983. (English edition of a European bestseller.)

DISNEY, WALT. *Best Comics.* New York: Abbeville Press, Inc., 1978—. (A projected ten-volume collection of Disney comics.)

DOUGHERTY, DON. *Croakers.* New York: Warner Books, 1982. (Frog cartoons, including one showing a frog in a restaurant complaining that there's no fly in his soup.)

DUFFY, J. C. *Moot Points.* Reading, Mass.: Addison-Wesley, 1981. (Cartoons that for their weirdness resemble somewhat the work of B. Kliban.)

ENGLEHART, ROBERT. *Never Let Facts Get in the Way of a Good Cartoon.* Dayton, Ohio: *Dayton Journal Herald,* 1979. (Englehart is now editorial cartoonist for the Hartford, Conn., *Courant* and is syndicated by the Los Angeles Times Syndicate.)

FEARING, JERRY. *Fearing Revisited.* St. Paul: *St. Paul Dispatch and Pioneer,* 1981. (A collection of all kinds of cartoons, including about 180 editorial cartoons.)

FEAVER, WILLIAM. *Masters of Caricature: From Hogarth and Gilray to Scarf and Levine.* New York: Alfred A. Knopf, 1981. (A handsome volume showing the work of many caricaturists.)

FEIFFER, JULES. *Tantrum.* New York: Alfred A. Knopf, 1979. (A novel in cartoons about a man who doesn't want to be responsible anymore.)

FINCH, CHRISTOPHER. *Walt Disney's America.* New York: Abbeville Press, Inc., 1978. (Informative and anecdotal biography with more than 360 illustrations, most of them in color.)

FRADEN, DANA. *Insincerely Yours.* New York: Charles Scribner's Sons, 1978. (Gag cartoons by a *New Yorker* regular.)

FRANK, PHIL. *Travels with Farley.* San Francisco: Troubador Press, 1980. (Reprints of a campus comic-strip favorite, with an introduction by Russell Myers, creator of *Broom Hilda.*)

FRASCINO, ED. *Avocado Is Not Your Color.* New York: Harper & Row, 1983. (A collection of gag cartoons about middle-age couples that will make middle-age people squirm. Frascino is a long-time *New Yorker* cartoonist.)

FREEMAN, RICHARD B. AND RICHARD SAMUEL WEST (editors). *The Best Political Cartoons of 1978.* Lansdale, Pa.: The Puck Press, 1979. (*Some* of the best, anyway.)

GOREY, EDWARD. *The Gashlycrumb Tinies.* New York: Dodd, Mead & Company, 1981. (Reissue of 1962 "appalling alphabet" of "dreadful demises" of children. For instance: "G" is for George smothered under a rug. There are twenty-six same-size careful line drawings in a small-format book.)

GOULD, ANN (editor). *Masters of Caricature.* New York: Alfred A. Knopf, 1982. (A solid, illustrated reference book, with an introduction and commentary by art critic William Feaver.)

GOULD, CHESTER. *Dick Tracy: The Thirties: Tommy Guns and Hard Times.* New York: Chelsea House Books, 1978. (Reprints edited by Herb Galewitz.)

GRAY, HAROLD. *Little Orphan Annie in the Great Depression.* New York: Dover Books, 1979. (231 consecutive comic strips from Jan. 1 to Sept. 26, 1931.)

GREEN, CHARLES AND MORT WALKER (compilers). *The National Cartoonists Society Album.* New York: National Cartoonists Society, 1980. (344 biographies of cartoonists, with photographs and samples of work.)

GRONDAHL, CALVIN. *Freeway to Perfection.* Salt Lake City: The Sunstone Foundation, 1978. (A collection of well-drawn gag cartoons, many about Mormon Church members and missionaries.)

_____. *Faith Promoting Rumors.* Salt Lake City: The Sunstone Foundation, 1980. (More gag cartoons involving Mormons by the editorial cartoonist of the *Deseret News.*)

GROSS, S. *"I am Blind and My Dog is Dead."* New York: Avon Books, 1978. (Macabre cartoons by a *New Yorker* cartoonist.)

_____. *An Elephant Is Soft and Mushy.* New York: Avon Books, 1982. (118 more Gross cartoons.)

GRUSH, BYRON. *The Shoestring Animator: Making Animated Films with Super 8.* Chicago: Contemporary Books, 1981. (Enough to get you started.)

GUISEWITE, CATHY. *The Cathy Chronicles.* Mission, Kansas: Sheed Andrews and McMeel, 1978. (Reprints of a comic strip that deals with a single woman and her conflicts.)

_____. *"What Do You Mean, I Still Don't Have Equal Rights?"* Fairway, Kansas: Andrews and McMeel, Inc., 1980. (More reprints of the *Cathy* comic strip.)

HARRIS, SIDNEY. *Chicken Soup and Other Medical Matters.* Los Altos, Calif.: William Kaufmann, Inc., 1979. (Collection of Harris' gag cartoons from the *Wall Street Journal, Saturday Review,* etc.)

HARRISON, RANDALL P. *The Cartoon: Communication to the Quick.* Beverly Hills, Calif.: Sage Publications, Inc., 1981. (A skillful merging of shop talk and scholarly research by a professor at the University of California at San Francisco.)

HELLER, STEVEN (editor). *Man Bites Man: Two Decades of Satiric Art.* New York: A & W Publishers, Inc., 1981. (200 drawings, 31 of them in full color, by some twenty artists. Tom Wolfe wrote the foreword.)

_____ (editor). *Jules Feiffer's America from Eisenhower to Reagan.* New York: Alfred A. Knopf, 1982. (A collection of cartoons and strips by the widely admired artist/writer who deals tellingly with neurotics and politicians. Kenneth Tynan once called him "the best writer now cartooning.")

HEWISON, WILLIAM (editor). *Cartoons from Punch.* New York: St. Martin's Press, 1980. (Any collection from *Punch* is worth looking at.)

HIRSCHFELD, AL. *Hirschfeld by Hirschfeld*. New York: Dodd, Mead & Company, 1979. (More than 200 caricatures of people in the arts and entertainment business.)

_____. *Hirschfeld's World*. New York: Harry N. Abrams, 1981. (A reprinting of 143 caricatures drawn over a fifty-year period, with an essay by Hirschfeld on the art of caricature.)

HOCKNEY, DAVID. *72 Drawings by David Hockney*. Salem, N.H.: Chatto, Bodley Head & Jonathan Cape, 1979. (Witty drawings by a British artist.)

HOLLANDER, NICOLE. *I'm in Training to be Tall and Blonde*. New York: St. Martin's Press, 1979. (Cartoons mostly dealing with women by a Chicago-based illustrator.)

HOLLANDER, NICOLE AND OTHERS (EDITORS). *Drawn Together*. New York: Crown Publishers Inc., 1983. (More than 300 gag cartoons by various artists on male-female relationships.)

HOLYOAK, CRAIG. *It's a Dirty Job . . . But Somebody Has to Do It*. Cedar City, Utah: Public Works, Golden West Printing, 1981. (Editorial cartoons with stories from the *Iron County Record* to put some of the cartoons, mostly local, into perspective. Holyoak, a policeman who did his cartoons on the side and who now draws for the *Deseret News*, has a Gahan Wilson-like style.)

HORN, MAURICE (editor). *The World Encyclopedia of Cartoons*. Detroit: Gale Research Company, 1981. (More than 1,200 signed articles about American and foreign cartoonists, with hundreds of illustrations, some in color. In two volumes. Expensive.)

JACOBS, MARK. *Jumping Up and Down on the Roof, Throwing Bags of Water on People*. Garden City, N.Y.: Dolphin Books, Doubleday & Company, Inc., 1980. (Cartoons and commentary by Sam Gross, J. B. Handelsman, B. Kliban, Charlie Rodrigues, Brian Savage, and Gahan Wilson, with an introduction by Mark Jacobs, who conducted the interviews.)

JOHNSON, FRIDOLF (editor). *Treasury of American Pen-and-Ink Illustrations*. New York: Dover Publications, 1982. (More than 200 illustrations by about 100 artists, covering the period from 1890 to 1930.)

JOHNSTON, JOHN J. *Latin America in Caricature*. Austin: University of Texas Press, 1980. (Collection of U.S. cartoons dealing with Latin America from the 1860s to the present.)

JOHNSTON, LYNN. *Do They Ever Grow Up?* Wayzata, Minn.: Meadowbrook Press, 1978. (Cartoons about children by a syndicated cartoonist with two earlier collections to her credit.)

KARLIN, NURIT. *No Comment*. New York: Charles Scribner's Sons, 1978. (Gag cartoons by a *New Yorker* cartoonist.)

KEANE, BIL. *That Family Circus Feeling*. Fairway, Kansas: Andrews and McMeel, Inc., 1982. (A collection.)

KELLER, CHARLES (compiler). *The Best of Rube Goldberg*. Englewood Cliffs, N.J.: Prentice-Hall, Inc., 1980. (More than 100 of his inventive cartoons, dating from 1915.)

KLEMIN, DIANA. *The Art of Art for Children's Books*. Greenwich, Conn.: Murton Press, 1982. (Paperback reprint of 1966 book featuring work of sixty-four illustrators, including Maurice Sendak and André Francois.)

KLIBAN, B. *Tiny Footprints*. New York: Workman Publishing Company, 1978. (Outrageous material by one of the geniuses in the profession.)

_____. *Playboy's Kliban*. New York: Wideview Books, 1979. (Kliban's *Playboy* gag cartoons.)

_____. *Two Guys Fooling Around with the Moon and Other Drawings*. New York: Workman Publishing Company, 1982. (More work by an off-the-wall cartoonist. Some of it is crude, some weird, some hilarious.)

_____. *Luminous Animals*. New York: Penguin, 1983. (Oversize book of wild cartoons.)

KOREN, EDWARD. *Are You Happy? And Other Questions Lovers Ask*. New York: Pantheon Books, 1978. (Hairy troglodytes act out the clichés of love.)

_____. *"Well, There's Your Problem."* New York: Pantheon Books, 1980. (More cartoons by the squiggly-line *New Yorker* cartoonist.)

LANES, SELMA G. *The Art of Maurice Sendak*. New York: Harry N. Abrams, 1980. (A tribute to the author and illustrator of children's books, with 280 reprinted illustrations.)

LARDNER, RING. *Ring Lardner's You Know Me Al: The Comic Strip Adventures of Jack Keefe*. New York: Harcourt Brace Jovanovich, 1979. (293 comic strips drawn by Will B. Johnstone and Dick Dorgan featuring a Ring Lardner baseball player.)

LARSON, GARY. *The Far Side*. Mission Springs, Kansas: Andrews and McMeel, 1982. (Reprints of the popular and strange new syndicated panel.)

LAYBOURNE, KIT. *The Animation Book*. New York: Crown Publishers, 1978.

LENBURG, JEFF. *The Encyclopedia of Animated Cartoon Series*. Westport, Conn.: Arlington House Publishers, 1981. (Documents the history of animation.)

LENDT, DAVID L. *Ding: The Life of Jay Norwood Darling*. Ames, Iowa: Iowa State University Press, 1979. (A biography, with examples of "Ding's" editorial cartoons, which stretched over many years. "Ding" was an ardent conservationist before being one was popular.)

LEVIN, ARNIE. *I'll Skip the Appetizer—I Ate the Flowers*. New York: Plume Paperback, 1980. (Gag cartoons by a *New Yorker* cartoonist.)

LEVINE, DAVID. *The Arts of David Levine*. New York: Alfred A. Knopf, 1978. (Shows 170 caricatures plus 64 paintings.)

LORD, M. G. *Mean Sheets*. Boston: Little Brown, 1982. (Reprints of *Newsday* editorial cartoons by one of the few women editorial cartoonists.)

LORENZ, LEE. *Real Dogs Don't Eat Leftovers*. New York: Long Shadow Books, Pocket Books, 1983. (A take-off from *Real Men Don't Eat Quiche*, this book is written and illustrated by the *New Yorker*'s cartoon editor.)

LUCIE-SMITH, EDWARD. *The Art of Caricature*. Ithaca, New York: Cornell University Press, 1981. (A history, with 200 illustrations.)

LURIE, RANAN R. *Lurie's Worlds, 1970–1980*. Honolulu: University Press of Hawaii, 1980. (Lurie is one of the world's most respected editorial cartoonists.)

MACK, STAN. *Stan Mack's Real Life Funnies*. New York: G. P. Putnam's Sons, 1979. (More than 150 comic strips from the *Village Voice*.)

MACNELLY, JEFF. *The Very First Shoe Book*. New York: Avon Books, 1978. (Collection of strips by the Pulitzer-Prize winning editorial cartoonist. Sixty-four pages are in full color.)

_____. *The Other Shoe*. New York: Avon Books, 1980. (The second collection of *Shoe* comic strips, many of them in full color.)

_____. *The New Shoe*. New York: Avon Books, 1981. (MacNelly's third collection of *Shoe* comic strips, starring P. Martin Shoemaker, editor of the *Treetop Tattler-Tribune*.)

MALTON, LEONARD. *Of Mice and Magic: A History of American Animated Car-*

toons. New York: McGraw-Hill Book Co., 1980. (An excellent illustrated history, with attention paid to Walt Disney, Max Fleischer, Paul Terry, Walter Lanz, Ralph Bakshi, and others.)

MANKOFF, ROBERT. *Elementary: The Cartoonist Did It.* New York: Avon Books, 1980. (Collection by an unconventional *New Yorker* cartoonist who uses dots—"raisins," George Booth calls them—to get some of his effects.)

MCCALL, BRUCE. *Zany Afternoons.* New York: Alfred A. Knopf, 1981. (Cartoon parodies, fully captioned and beautifully designed.)

MEGLIN, NICK. *The Art of Humorous Illustration.* New York: Watson-Guptill Publications, 1981. (Paperback republication of the 1973 hardcover, with its survey of the work of twelve artists, including Jack Davis, Mort Walker, and Maurice Sendak.)

MENDELSON, LEE. *Happy Birthday, Charlie Brown.* New York: Random House, 1979. (*Peanuts* creator Charles Schulz collaborates with Mendelson to produce this book based on a TV special. Schulz's favorite strips are included.)

MILLAR, JEFF, AND BILL HINDS. *The Tank McNamara Chronicles.* Mission, Kansas: Sheed Andrews and McMeel, 1978. (Reprints of a comic strip, appearing in 200 newspapers, that spoofs sports and sports heroes.)

MODELL, FRANK. *Stop Trying to Cheer Me Up!* New York: Dodd, Mead & Company, 1978. (Gag cartoons by a *New Yorker* cartoonist.)

MORICE, DAVE. *Poetry Comics.* New York: Simon & Schuster, 1982. (Using a variety of cartoon styles, Morice puts some well-known poems into comic-strip form and hence "tweaks the nose of the poetry world," as one reviewer put it.)

MORROW, SKIP. *The Official I Hate Cats Book.* New York: Holt, Rinehart & Winston, 1980. (A collection of cartoons the publisher says "will catapult you into gales of laughter.")

MUSE, KEN. *The Secrets of Professional Cartooning.* Englewood Cliffs, N.J.: Prentice-Hall, Inc., 1981. (Solid advice by a pro, with examples of his own work and the work of other cartoonists. The whole book is handlettered in Muse's readable all caps.)

MYERS, LOU. *Absent & Accounted For.* New York: Workman Publishing Company, 1980. (About 150 drawings.)

OLIPHANT, PAT. *Oliphant!* Mission, Kansas: Andrews and McMeel, Inc., 1980. (Paperback collection.)

_____. *But Seriously, Folks!* Fairway, Kansas: Andrews and McMeel, Inc., 1983.

OSBORN, ROBERT. *Osborn on Osborn.* New Haven, Conn.: Ticknor & Fields, 1982. (An illustrated autobiography by one of America's most important cartoon illustrators and satirists. Garry Trudeau wrote the foreword.)

PEARY, GERALD AND DANNY PEARY. *The American Animated Cartoon.* New York: E. P. Dutton, 1980. (A critical anthology.)

PETERS, MIKE. *"Clones. You Idiot . . . I Said Clones."* Dayton, Ohio: *Dayton Daily News,* 1979. (Reprints of the work of the syndicated editorial cartoonist for the *Dayton Daily News.*)

_____. *Win One for the Geezer.* New York: Bantam Books, 1982.

PHILIPPE, ROBERT. *Political Graphics: Art as a Weapon.* New York: Abbeville Press, Inc., 1982. (The *New Yorker* calls it "quite wonderful": some 400 images since the fifteenth century, including cartoons used to propagandize. The author is a history professor.)

POWELL, DWANE. *"Surely Someone Can Still Sing Bass."* Raleigh, N.C.: The *Raleigh News & Observer,* 1981. (A collection of 196 editorial cartoons by a cartoonist syndicated by the Los Angeles Times Syndicate.)

PRESTON, CHARLES (editor). *The Wall Street Journal Cartoon Portfolio.* Chicopee, Mass.: Dow Jones Books, 1980. (Reprints from that estimable national daily.)

_____ (editor). *Can Board Chairmen Get Measles?* New York: Crown Publishers, Inc., 1982. (Gag cartoons reprinted from the *Wall Street Journal,* some going back thirty years.)

RAY, GORDON N. *The Art of the French Illustrated Book, 1700 to 1914.* Ithaca, N.Y.: Cornell University Press, 1982. (Expensive two-volume set with lots of beautiful illustrations by important artists, including Grandville, Doré, and Picasso.)

REED, WALT. *Great American Illustrators.* New York: Crown Publishers, Inc., 1979. (Works by some fifty illustrators are shown in a big-format book, with biographical material about each. Most are serious artists, but comic artists like Harry Beckhoff, Albert Dorne, A. B. Frost, Charles Dana Gibson, John Held, Jr., and E. W. Kemble are represented, too.)

RIEWALD, J. G. *Beerbohm's Literary Caricatures.* Hambden, Conn.: Archon Books, 1977. (Drawings and explanations by Sir Max Beerbohm, British artist and writer.)

ROBINSON, JERRY. *Skippy and Percy Crosby.* New York: Holt Rinehart & Winston, 1978. (A biography, with reprints of cartoons from the 1920s and 1930s.)

_____ (editor). *The 1970s: Best Political Cartoons of the Decade.* New York: McGraw Hill, 1981. (Cartoons by more than 263 artists, including some from abroad.)

SAGENDORF, BUD. *Popeye: The First 50 Years.* New York: Workman Publishing Company, 1979. (Celebration of a durable strip that still appears in 250 newspapers.)

SALZMAN, ED AND ANN LEIGH BROWN. *The Cartoon History of California Politics.* Sacramento, Calif.: California Journal Press, 1978. (Contains 119 cartoons spanning California history, starting from the Gold Rush. Covers the attempt by the Legislature in 1899 to ban political cartooning.)

SANDERS, BILL. *The Sanders Book.* Milwaukee, Wis.: *Milwaukee Journal,* 1979. (Contains 202 reprints of editorial cartoons called by *Newsweek* "ornery and unorthodox.")

SCARFE, GERALD. *Gerald Scarfe.* London: Thames and Hudson, 1982. (Caricatures and satirical drawings by a widely admired British artist, along with autobiographical information about his career as an animator and illustrator.)

SCHULZ, CHARLES M. *Snoopy's Tennis Book.* New York: Holt, Rinehart & Winston, 1979. (More than 100 *Peanuts* strips, with some cartoons published for the first time.)

_____. *Classroom Peanuts.* New York: Holt, Rinehart & Winston, 1982. (Close to 200 different Schulz collections are in print. Some appeal to the young, some to older readers. Many narrow in on a single subject, as this one does. It reprints many of the *Peanuts* strips dealing with the characters at school. The several Sunday strips are in color—color much more dazzling than the color used in newspapers. Reading these helps to remind us of the important contribution Schulz has made to our understanding of human nature.)

SCHWARTZ, JOSEPH AND MICHAEL MCGUINNESS. *Einstein for Beginners.* New York: Pantheon Books, 1979.

(Cartoon treatment of a man and his ideas.)

SCOTT, HUGH (compiler). *The Best of Quincy Scott.* Portland: Oregon Historical Society, 1980. (Reprints of work by the editorial cartoonist for *The Oregonian,* Portland, in the 1930s and 1940s.)

SEARLE, RONALD. *Ronald Searle.* New York: Mayflower Books, 1979. (200 full-page cartoons by the influential British artist with a feel for irony. With essays on Searle by Henning Bock and Pierre Dehaye.)

_____. *Big Fat Cat Book.* Boston: Little, Brown, 1982. (Cat drawings by the celebrated English cartoonist, who has been recording his reactions to the cunning animals for many years. *Time* calls the book "futuristic comedy.")

_____. *The Situation is Hopeless.* New York: Viking Press, 1981. (The admired humorous illustrator looks at various animals, including an agnostic serpent and a hypochondriac cow.)

SEMPE, JEAN-JAQUES. *The Musicians by Sempe.* New York: Workman Publishing Company, 1980. (Quietly humorous drawings, in various media, of musicians, prompted by the French artist's long fascination with music and the "charming madmen" who produce it. Large format.)

_____. *Displays of Affection.* New York: Workman Publishing Company, 1981. (An album of cartoons about love by the French satirist. Translated by *New Yorker* cartoonist Edward Koren.)

SILVERSTEIN, SHEL. *Different Dances.* New York: Harper & Row, 1979. (Cartoons dealing with male-female relationships.)

SMITH, BRUCE. *The History of Little Orphan Annie.* New York: Ballantine Books, 1982. (This book takes advantage of the renewed interest in Harold Gray's creation.)

STEINBERG, SAUL. *The Passport.* New York: Random House, 1979. (Reprint of a 1954 book of drawings that parody passport officials and travel.)

STEVENSON, JAMES. *Let's Boogie!* New York: Dodd, Mead & Company, 1978. (Cartoons by a *New Yorker* regular.)

SZEP, PAUL. *To a Different Drummer.* Brattleboro, Vt.: The Stephen Green Press, 1983. (The first collection by this hard hitting editorial cartoonist since 1980.)

_____. *Warts and All.* Mission, Kansas: Andrews and McMeel, Inc., 1980. (Collection by the *Boston Globe*'s two-time Pulitzer-Prize winning editorial cartoonist.)

THELWELL, NORMAN. *Brat Race.* New York: Charles Scribner's Sons, 1978. (Droll cartoons about kids by an English artist.)

THOMAS, FRANK AND OLLIE JOHNSTON. *Disney Animation: The Illusion of Life.* New York: Abbeville Press, 1982. (More than 2700 illustrations, many in color, from the Disney archives, with extensive information on animation by two artists who worked at the studios.)

TRUDEAU, G. B. *Doonesbury's Greatest Hits.* New York: Holt, Rinehart & Winston, 1978. (With an "overture" by William F. Buckley, Jr.)

_____. *The People's Doonesbury.* New York: Holt, Rinehart & Winston, 1981. (Another of many collections, this one substantial. In reviewing it *The Atlantic* spoke of "the subtleties of his seemingly coarse drawing and the skill of his verbal parody.")

UBINAS, DAVE AND ESTHER LANGHOLTZ. *Pick-up Book of Cartoon-Style Illustrations.* New York: Arco, 1979.

UNGER, JIM. *The 1st Treasury of Herman.* Mission, Kansas: Andrews and McMeel, Inc., 1979. (800 panels of a feature that is syndicated to 250 newspapers.)

VAN DER MEER, RON AND ATIE VAN DER MEER. *Oh Lord!* New York: Crown Publishers, Inc., 1980. (Comic-strip telling, very unconventional, of the story of creation.)

WAGNER, PETE. *Buy This Book.* Minneapolis: Me Publications, 1980. ("The Great UnAmerican Novel!" illustrated with several hundred drawings, defending "The Slandered Seventies." Wagner left a job with *TV Guide* after "accidentally" listing "Oral Roberts" as "Anal Roberts.")

WALKER, MORT. *The Lexicon of Comicana.* Greenwich, Conn.: Comicana Books, 1981. (Advice and satire on comic-stripping by one of the country's most successful cartoonists.)

_____. *Miss Buxley: Sexism in Beetle Bailey?* Bedford, New York: Comicana Books, 1982. (The cartoonist's defense of his use of the well-built camp secretary, with sample strips and news stories, columns, and letters dealing with the controversy.)

WARDROPER, JOHN. *The Caricatures of George Cruikshank.* Boston: David R. Godine, 1979. (120 drawings by a nineteenth century British caricaturist, including savage attacks on King George IV.)

WATSON, ERNEST, W. *How to Use Creative Perspective.* New York: Van Nostrand, Reinhold Company, 1955. (Necessary information.)

WESTIN, ALAN F. (editor). *Getting Angry Six Times a Week.* Boston: Beacon Press, 1980. (A collection of editorial cartoons, with an essay, all with a left-liberal slant.)

WILSON, GAHAN. *Is Nothing Sacred?* New York: St. Martin's/Marek, 1982. (160 cartoons from the *New Yorker, Playboy,* etc.)

WOLFE, TOM. *In Our Time.* New York: Farrar, Straus & Giroux, 1980. (About 100 drawings making fun of the "Me Decade" of the 1970s. By a writer best known as a "new journalist.")

WRIGHT, DON. *Wright Side Up.* New York: Simon and Schuster, 1981. (Wright's second collection of editorial cartoons, run large so you can appreciate them. John Keasler, *Miami News* columnist, writes an essay about the cartoonist.)

YOUNG, DEAN AND RICK MARSCHALL. *Blondie & Dagwood's America,* New York: Harper & Row, 1981. (A memoir upon the fiftieth anniversary of the strip, which appears in 1800 papers. More than 100 representative strips are shown, many in color.)

ZIEGLER, JACK. *Filthy Little Things.* Garden City, N.Y.: Doubleday, 1981. (A collection by a *New Yorker* cartoonist whose sense of humor can be compared to B. Kliban's.)

The Best Cartoons from New Woman. Fort Worth, Texas: New Woman, 1978. (Cartoons from a women's magazine.)

Humor, Wit, & Fantasy. New York: Hart Publishing Company, Inc., 1976. (2100 public-domain pictures.)

The Illustrator's Handbook. New York: A & W Visual Library, 1978. (3000 public-domain drawings, mostly in line, many of them humorous, all of them dated.)

Walt Disney Silly Symphonies and Animated Features. New York: Abbeville Press, 1980. (Large, full-color format.)

index
to authors' names

*Numbers in italics indicate pages with drawings or cartoons.